EVALUATION IN THE FACE OF UNCERTAINTY

MRC Social & Public Health Sciences Unit
4 Lilybank Gardens
Glasgow G12 8RZ

Evaluation in the Face of Uncertainty

ANTICIPATING SURPRISE AND
RESPONDING TO THE INEVITABLE

JONATHAN A. MORELL

THE GUILFORD PRESS
New York   London

© 2010 The Guilford Press
A Division of Guilford Publications, Inc.
72 Spring Street, New York, NY 10012
www.guilford.com

Printed in the United States of America

This book is printed on acid-free paper.

Last digit is print number: 9   8   7   6   5   4   3   2   1

Library of Congress Cataloging-in-Publication Data

Evaluation in the face of uncertainty : anticipating surprise and responding to the
inevitable / [edited by] Jonathan A. Morell.
     p. cm.
  Includes bibliographical references and index.
   ISBN 978-1-60623-857-8 (pbk. : alk. paper) — ISBN 978-1-60623-858-5 (hbk. : alk.
paper)
  1. Evaluation research (Social action programs)   2. Social service—Evaluation.
I. Morell, Jonathan A., 1946–
  H62.E84755 2010
  001.4—dc22

                                                                          2010021055

For Marge, my woman of valor—
for the inspiration, wisdom, support, and love

Preface

Throughout my professional life I have drawn pleasure from two very different activities. As a working, hands-on evaluator, the fun came from doing immediately practical work. Sometimes I felt like a dog on a bone. Someone would point to an innovative program and ask: What happened? No hesitation. I would jump. I would grab whatever collection of techniques I could and try to come up with answers that people could use. Figuring out how to start grabbed my imagination. What methodologies could be used? What data could be obtained? What comparisons were possible? How could the team be assembled? Who were the stakeholders? How could they be reached? What knowledge use strategies could be invoked? What could be done within the limitations of time line and budget? All of these questions, and the relationships among them, dominated my attention.

I stayed engaged as the process unfolded. I was continually scouting for the small changes in plan that presaged major challenges to the evaluation. Did my sponsor seem a little hesitant about getting me the data he promised? Are a few minor deadlines beginning to slip? Are preliminary data providing tidbits of information we did not expect to see? Are respondents postponing interviews? Is the program acting a bit differently from what stakeholders told us would happen?

Any of these occurrences can be trivial, and indeed they usually are. But sometimes they are not. Sometimes any of them, or some combination of them, can signal major changes with attendant consequences for executing the evaluation. The trick is to know the difference. There is no formula. The fun is in interpreting the auguries. Throughout my career I have had a lot of this kind of fun. I have also had lots of trouble. I have often gotten it wrong, much to the detriment of my evaluation work and my self-esteem. Thinking about why I got it wrong so frequently led to a bridge to my other favorite professional activity, and to this book.

At the opposite end of the practicality scale, I have drawn a good deal of pleasure from abstract thought. I have never been good at detail. As far back as I can remember, I would listen, pull principles from what I heard, put the principles in categories, identify relationships among the categories, and then promptly forget the details. Over and over, I would repeat this process, evolve my thinking, and use what I thought I understood to develop new ways of organizing the world. The more abstract, the better. The greater the connections among diverse intellectual boundaries, the better. I have always had a penchant for boundary spanning.

I see this book as an exercise in two kinds of boundary spanning. One is the distance between my practical interests and my theoretical interests. The second constitutes the various topics that have interested me during my professional career—complex systems, organizational innovation, life cycle change, and the nature of practical action. I was drawn to writing this book because it gave me a chance for a Grand Integration that combined my practical and theoretical work with my substantive interests.

The seed for this book was thinking about the practical problems I ran into as I conducted my evaluations. Why did I have trouble anticipating what happened? Why was it difficult to adjust to those changes? As I spoke to my colleagues I realized that they had the same problems. It was not just me. The problem was endemic. It was impossible for me to answer those questions without mapping my practical problems into abstract categories, and without incorporating a diverse set of intellectual traditions. This book constitutes the second round of my efforts to span these boundaries.

The first round started with a question posed to Evaltalk (the Listserv of the American Evaluation Association), asking why programs had unintended outcomes, and culminated with an article in the *American Journal of Evaluation* (Morell, 2005). My interest was not in unintended outcomes per se, but in what evaluators could do to improve their ability to evaluate programs that exhibited such behavior. A problem with that article was that it did not sufficiently span the abstract–practical divide. It did not sufficiently project my theoretical thinking about unintended consequences into the practicalities of everyday evaluation work. The article was not sufficiently data-based. (Later I shift from a focus on "unintended consequences" to the broader notion of "surprise," in acknowledgment of my realization that the dynamics that cause uncertainty in programs and evaluations are the same. But more on that later. Right now I am talking about beginnings, and the beginning was a focus on the evaluation of unintended consequences of program action.)

I wrote this book to correct that deficiency. This time, in addition to developing my theoretical ideas, I was determined to base my thinking on the situations that real evaluators encountered. I needed cases. One need for cases was that my own work did not cover enough evaluations. A bigger problem was sampling and representation. I do a particular kind of evaluation work for a particular set of clients. What happens to me might not happen to others, hence the use of cases from as wide a variety of evaluation settings as I could tap. Again I reached out to the evaluation community through Evaltalk, through my personal contacts, and through the authors and reviewers I came to know as the editor of *Evaluation and Program Planning*. Thanks to these evaluators, I was able to draw extensively on actual evaluation cases that represent a wide range of evaluation topics and geographical areas. All of these cases describe instances in which either the program does not work as planned, or the evaluation does not work as planned, or both. Usually we treat these situations as "fires" (i.e., we exercise our skills to meet the crisis). This book steps back from crisis mode and presents a systematic treatment of why these situations pop up, the continuum from "unforeseen" to "unforeseeable," tactics that can be used along the continuum, and why caution is needed because anything we do to minimize surprise may cause yet other difficulties. The intent is to provide readers with skills and knowledge to better serve stakeholders' needs for information, in light of the uncertainties that always attend evaluation exercises.

Acknowledgments

Many people challenged my thinking and my writing. All of their efforts improved this book. Heartfelt thanks go to Dennis Affholter, Deborah Bonnet, Huey Chen, Mike Coplen, Chris Coryn, Lois-ellin Datta, Molly Engle, Peter Hancock, Glenda Haskell, C. Deborah Laughton, Laura Leviton, Lena Lundgren, Steve Magura, Marge Pacer, Ralph Renger, Daniela Schroeter, Deborah Wasserman, and Brian Yates.

An Invitation to Build
a Community of Interest

Engagement with community has been an important theme throughout my writing on unintended consequences. My original article required input from the evaluation community by means of Evaltalk. This book required contributions in the form of cases. As I wrote, I came to realize that if this book ends up making any contribution at all, that contribution will involve community building. My long-range goal is embodied in the title of Chapter 1: "From Firefighting to Systematic Action." I want to help the field of evaluation develop a community of interest that is dedicated to understanding why surprises occur in evaluation, how to anticipate them, and how to deal with those that cannot be anticipated. I see this book as the second round of what I hope will be an ongoing process. To that end, I have established a Web presence to further discussion. Please visit *evaluationuncertainty.com*.

Contents

CASES

Contents

Chapter 1

From Firefighting to Systematic Action

This book is about surprises that challenge evaluation. But surprise does not mean random. There is rhyme and reason to unanticipated occurrences. There is pattern. There is sense. The purpose of this book is to help evaluators appreciate the rhyme, understand the reason, see the pattern, and apply the sense. I hope to provide a theoretical understanding of surprise that affects evaluation, a social understanding of how unanticipated changes appear, and practical advice on how to act. My hope is to start a movement in our discipline toward collective thinking about how to incorporate consideration of surprise into our routine of planning and conducting evaluation.

ADDING "SURPRISE" TO THE MIX

When we think about how to conduct an evaluation we ponder topics such as evaluation models, evaluation theory, stakeholder relationships, information use, evaluators' roles, research design, data quality, funding, deadlines, and the logistics of evaluation implementation. We may place more or less emphasis on any of these. Sometimes our reliance on these intellectual tools is explicit and carefully planned. Sometimes the potential of these tools exerts an implicit pull on our consciousness and inclinations. But always, in one way or another, these concepts shape our view of how an evaluation should be done.

I believe that the science, technology, and craft of evaluation would be strengthened if another set of considerations were added to the mix, that is, a systematic understanding of how to contend with surprise,

1

with situations in which programs and evaluations do not behave as expected. Those surprises may be welcome or unwelcome, but either way, we need to be able to evaluate them.

Until recently, evaluators have not stepped back to look at surprise in a systematic manner, as a field of inquiry in its own right. This is beginning to change. The framework for this change is the rapidly growing influence of the "systems perspective" in evaluation, as evidenced by the enthusiastic acceptance of a Systems Topical Interest Group in the American Evaluation Association, discussions about simulation as an evaluation tool, and a growing awareness that evaluation must look not just at single programs in isolation, but at the context in which those programs are embedded. The systems view is important because much surprise comes from relationships, fluctuations, and uncertainties in how parts of a whole affect each other. The next step is to focus specifically on methods and procedures that evaluators can use to anticipate surprise, to ameliorate its impact on the integrity of evaluation designs, and to provide stakeholders with an enhanced understanding of the consequences of their actions.

HISTORICAL ROOTS:
EVALUATION, PLANNING, AND SYSTEM BEHAVIOR

The notion of unintended effects in evaluation has a long history. The notion of an unintended effect is critical in Scriven's advocacy of goal-free evaluation, an approach that focuses attention on what a program actually does rather than its stated goals (Scriven, 1991). Goal-free evaluation considers a wide range of change, but does not delve into why so many different program impacts occur, whether there are different categories of impacts, or what evaluators can do to improve their methods of detection and assessment. The theme of unintended effects is also echoed in the literature on how the act of evaluating a program may change the program that is being evaluated (Ginsberg, 1984; Glenwick, Stephens, & Maher, 1984). While the literature on evaluation–program reactivity does treat the question of how and why unintended effects occur, it is limited to a focus on the relationship between measurement and program action, rather than on the more general question of unintended consequences. The one article I could find that dealt with how evaluators might treat unintended consequences was titled "Identifying and Measuring Unintended Outcomes" (Sherrill, 1984). Had the ideas in that article become mainstream in our field, I would probably not have felt a need to write this book. Sherrill touched on many of the ideas I elaborate on these pages—the difference between foreseeable and unforeseeable consequences, the value of theory and past experience, system-related reasons for surprise, and using diverse points of view to discern a program's consequences.

The notion of surprise is prominent in the planning literature of a wide variety of fields. Examples from a brief literature review include: industry sponsorship of university research (Behrens & Gray, 2001), marketing (Fry & Polonsky, 2004), tobacco restrictions (Hoek, 2004), drinking age regulation (DiNardo & Lemieux, 2001), speed and quality relationships in new product development (Lukas & Menon, 2004), welfare (Courtney, Needell, & Wulczyn, 2004), national fiscal reform (Kildegaard, 2001), teacher empowerment (Pugh & Zhao, 2003), nongovernmental organization (NGO) activity in developing countries (Stiles, 2002), and workplace safety (Kaminski, 2001).

Stepping outside discussions of unexpected change in particular fields, we find more general explanations that cut across specific domains of policy and planning. These explanations are typified by the works of Meyers (1981), Tenner (1996), and Dorner (1996). Their explanations focus on the principle that complex systems by their nature can yield unpredictable behavior because of the interplay of factors such as uncertain environments, cross-linkages, self-organized behavior, ecological adaptation, and feedback loops of different lengths. I do not want to leave the impression that systems exist in a perpetual state of flux. Under the right conditions they can be exceedingly stable over protracted periods of time. Stability, instability, and the boundary between them is one of the major concerns in the field of complex adaptive systems (CAS) (Kauffman, 1995; Marion, 1999). For our purposes, though, we must accept the fact that the potential for unpredictable behavior is inherent in the settings where we work.

In addition to the principles of complex systems, three behavioral/ organizational dynamics are at play. First, our decision making is always based on less information than we are able to collect. But to say that we can get "more relevant information" is to say that we know what information is relevant and how much information is enough. We can only know this in retrospect. Second, we are not as vigilant as we could be in scouting for developing changes in the system we are working with. But here, too, only a backward-looking view will tell us whether we were vigilant enough and whether we were looking in the right places. Third, the nature of the planning process is such that opportunity for major intervention occurs only infrequently along a program's life cycle. It is only so often that budgets are set, requests for proposals are published, contracts are modified, staff are hired, or strategic plans made. Thus it is almost certain that knowing that action is needed will not synchronize with the ability to act.

In sum, our efforts to change systems take place during intermittent windows of opportunity, at which time we scramble to organize relationships among a finite (and often small) number of components (e.g., staff, money, time, client characteristics, material, procedure, information, and treatments). Because we are inescapably enmeshed in this process of systems change, we are destined to build models that are incomplete in their own right, and even more so when embedded in the larger system that we call the real world. To say that there will be no unexpected occurrences is akin to saying that a finite model can fully specify a complex system. That is impossible. It is akin to violating the First Law of Thermodynamics, and as we know, there cannot be a perpetual motion machine.

The difficulty with all these explanations for surprise is that while they help understand why unexpected events occur, they do not say anything about what evaluators should do about them. They do not inform our methodology. They do not help us resolve two competing design requirements—the requirement to plan as carefully as possible in advance, and the need to be flexible enough to provide useful information as circumstances change.

FROM EXPLAINING SURPRISE TO DEALING WITH IT

As evaluators our problem is not that the unexpected occurs. Our problem is that we react only when surprise falls upon us, when we need to put out a fire. At those times we exercise our craft. What we need is a framework for anticipation and for systematic action. We need to move beyond crisis management. For that, we need an answer to three questions.

1. When is the likelihood of surprise high?
2. Under what circumstances will surprise disrupt evaluation?

3. When the probability of surprise and disruption is high, what can we do about it?

A word of caution is in order. No matter how well we answer these questions we will always find ourselves in trouble. One problem we cannot escape is that any solution we conjure will entail overhead. Any commitment of resources will incur opportunity costs, and any tactic we deploy to deal with surprise will have its own drawbacks (much more on this topic to come in Chapter 7). Moreover, our evaluations are often themselves composed of many tightly linked elements. As we tinker with them, other surprises will occur. Our situation is like the problem faced by safety managers who must confront what Perrow calls a "normal accident" (Perrow, 1999). These kinds of accidents occur as a result of interactions among many tightly linked elements of complicated systems. Error in system design is not the problem. Rather, the very existence of those elements and their dependencies creates conditions where small changes in parts of the system can cause major disruptions. No matter what redesign is tried there will inevitably be many elements and many dependencies to consider, combining in unpredictable ways to bring about more mishaps.

We may not be able to escape surprise but we can appreciate how it works, and by so doing, we can develop strategies that will leave us better off. Unfortunately, no matter how much better off we become, there is no magic elixir that will turn the invisible visible, or that will make known all that cannot be predicted, or that will always allow us to react to change in a timely fashion. The best we can do is to increase the range of what we can see. We can give ourselves longer lead times to react. We can find ways to glimpse the hazy outlines of what was previously invisible.

So far I have used the term "surprise" as if it was simple and unitary; that is, either something happened that was expected, or something happened that was not expected. Either we are surprised, or we are not. In fact, surprise comes in different flavors. "Unexpected" can be divided into events that might have been foreseen had proper mechanisms been in place, and events that can never be foreseen. Different procedures are needed to buffer against each of these two types of surprise.

Respect for the difficulty of prognostication is needed when talking about surprise that might have been anticipated. Our problem is that we are looking into a future in which multiple causal chains can lead to the same outcome, and in which chance events can change what seemed like a sure thing. In the discussion that follows I try to walk a fine line between claiming that sometimes eventualities might reasonably be anticipated in some way, shape, or form, and respecting the unknowability of how processes combine and interact.

DEVELOPMENT PATH OF THIS BOOK

This book began as an exercise in putting a foundation under a castle in the air. In 2005 I published a theoretical article on why unintended consequences exist, why some are truly unforeseeable while others might have been dimly foreseen, and what tactics evaluators might use to deal with each (Morell, 2005). While everything I said in that article made sense (to me and a few reviewers, at least), I was left with a discomfort over my lack of knowledge about what kind of unintended consequences evaluators actually face, and what they really do when faced with those circumstances. I set out on a quest to find real-world examples, to map them into my thinking about the evaluation of unintended consequences, and to use the synthesis to extend my understanding. From this effort came an expanded framework to categorize unintended consequences, and the rest of this book's content.

My data collection plan employed a 2-year-long snowball sampling methodology that worked through different avenues of outreach to the evaluation community. I reached out to members of the American Evaluation Association by distributing notices at their annual meetings and posting on their Listserv. I also used my connections as editor of *Evaluation and Program Planning* to query authors, reviewers, and advisors. I included my search request in any conversations or e-mail exchanges I had with friends and colleagues. Throughout, my message was always the same: Do you have cases? Do you have colleagues who have cases? Do you know people who may know others who may have cases?

The fruits of these labors were consistent. Almost every conversation I had with almost every evaluator elicited a response like: "What a great idea. This happens to me all the time. Do I ever have material for you!" But responses were few when it came to asking people to submit cases. I have several explanations for this outcome, but no data to support any of them. One possibility is that surprise threatens evaluation less often than I thought, despite people's verbal assurances that the phenomenon was ubiquitous. Another possibility is the difficulty of writing on this topic without admitting failure as an evaluator, that is, copping to being an evaluator who executed an inadequate evaluation plan. The third possibility I can think of is that it is hard to discuss this topic without casting one's sponsors in a negative light, as a group of people who could not make up their minds, or who meddled in the evaluation, or who could not implement the program they had planned. Finally, there is the possibility that the discovery of unintended effects of program action requires a long-term view of program operations, and as we shall see, few of those kinds of evaluations were revealed with the sampling plan I used. Whatever the explanation, I am convinced that we will all be better evaluators if we amass as many cases as possible and use the collection to build a corpus of knowledge. My hope is that the small number of examples presented in this book will stimulate others to add to the collection.

Although I started with a plan to map real cases into my original typology, the mapping exercise forced me to extend my thinking about what "surprise" meant and how it should be handled. One major extension was the realization that "evaluations" and "programs" are similar social phenomena in that they are both collections of resources and processes that are embedded in a social/organizational setting for the purpose of accomplishing specific objectives. I came to understand that the same dynamics that generate surprise in programs also affect the evaluations themselves. (Chapter 8 is the start of a detailed explanation of these surprises.) A second realization was the extent to which efforts to buffer evaluation against surprise can become counterproductive as each buffering tactic incurs overhead costs in time, money, human capital, and management attention. (Chapter 7 delves into this topic in detail.) I realized how important it is to implement a great many methods to deal with surprise, but also how important it is to choose wisely.

As I reviewed cases and developed frameworks, I realized that I needed two different methods to use cases to illustrate the points I wanted to make. The first was to draw on the contributed cases. These were valuable because they highlighted the actual experience of evaluators working in real-world settings. To aid in drawing lessons from the cases and comparing them, I asked the contributors to present their cases in three main sections: (1) description of the case, (2) unexpected events, and (3) responses to the unexpected events.

The second method of using cases was needed because often no single case juxtaposed all the aspects of evaluation that I needed to make a point. For instance, in order to make a point in Chapter 5 I needed to illustrate the relationship between a program in a single department of an organization and similar programs that sprang up independently in a different part of the same organization. No such situation arose in the cases, so I constructed an example involving a safety training program for managers and its interaction with a companywide Lean Six Sigma quality improvement initiative.[1] I don't know of any evaluation like this, but I know of evaluations of safety programs and other evaluations of quality improvement programs. It is not much of a stretch to imagine the evaluation consequences of such programs operating simultaneously. The scenario has verisimilitude to real experience. Many of us would be able to think of that scenario and say, "I can imagine having to evaluate a situation like this." Or, "I have not done this kind of evaluation, but it makes sense to me. I have done things like it."

GUIDING PRINCIPLES

I am writing this book from a distinct point of view. It seems only fair to articulate that point of view to help you judge what is coming and its applicability to your own work. The arguments that follow emanate from a variety of perspectives that have guided my work for a long time: complex systems, innovation and organizational behavior, life cycle change, the dictates of practical action, and my role as an evaluator.

Complex Systems

As I have designed and implemented evaluations I have come to see my work as an exercise that takes place in a universe where control and authority are distributed, where the course of seemingly unambiguous action is uncertain, and where relationships are constantly changing. How many bosses have you met who can say: "I can tell people how to run this organization and they do as they are told"? Beyond immediate subordinates, almost nobody has this level of control. Organizations are just too big and too complicated for tight centralized control to be possible or desirable, particularly over extended periods of time across multiple subgroups. I believe that we all know this intuitively. The principles of complex system behavior provide a theoretical underpinning to this intuitive understanding, as can be seen from some of the core principles of the adaptive system approach. (This list is adapted from Wikipedia's excellent overview of the essential elements of complex systems; *en.wikipedia.org/wiki/Complex_system*).

1. Complex systems show nonlinear relationships among their elements. Thus, small perturbation may cause a large effect, a proportional effect, or even no effect at all.

2. Complex systems contain multiple damping and amplifying feedback loops.

3. Complex systems have memory; that is, they change over time, and prior states may have an influence on present states.

4. Complex systems may be nested; that is, components of a complex system may themselves be complex systems.

5. Boundaries are difficult to determine.

6. Emergent phenomena may be present. (Think of a beehive. Its architecture, functioning, and output result from the behavior of many bees, but the hive cannot be understood by any summation of the actions of particular bees.)

Innovation in Organizational Settings

Evaluation is intimately bound up with innovation both because innovation is often the object of evaluation, *and* because the act of evaluation can itself be regarded as an innovation. Thus the behavior and characteristics of innovation are important. For instance, we know that characteristics of an innovation affect how it is implemented and its chances for success. We act differently depending on the innovation's degree of compatibility with existing values, complexity, trialability, and observability (Rogers, 1983). To illustrate the similarity between programs and their evaluations, consider a mental health program and a plan to evaluate that program with a randomized design. With respect to the program, we may observe that a behaviorist approach may not jibe with the values of service providers who are committed to psychodynamic therapies. With respect to evaluation, we may observe that a design based on randomization and control groups may not fit the values of either the service providers, or the evaluators, or both. In both scenarios, implementation of the innovation—whether the program or its evaluation—suffers from the same problem, in this case, a values disconnect between various stakeholders.

For the most part, the innovations we evaluate are embedded in organizational settings. Thus we must appreciate organizational behavior in order to implement evaluations and also in order to apply evaluation in the service of understanding change. I tend to see organizations as complicated entities that pursue multiple (and often conflicting) goals, which must allocate scarce resources, are beholden to multiple stakeholders, have formal and informal structures, shifting stores of intellectual capital, changing environments, tensions between goals of service and goals of self-preservation, and interorganizational relationships. Into this setting are cast innovations and their evaluations, which are themselves partially nested and partially overlapping.

Life Cycle Change

Life cycle changes are driven by developmental processes that produce highly predictable consequences. Life sciences are one obvious field where life cycle change is an important concept, but the notion can be found in many other fields as well. A few examples are: organizational development (Sherman & Olsen, 1996), research and development (R&D) project management (Pillai & Joshi, 2001), innovation management in companies (Koberg, Uhlenbruck, & Sarason, 1996), organizational growth and financial performance (Flamholtz & Hua, 2002), strategy formation (Gupta & Chin, 1993), alliance behavior (Lambe & Spekman, 1997), software development (Boehm & Egyed, 1999), and innovation adoption (Adner, 2004).

Two aspects of a life cycle are noteworthy. First, stages are predictable and invariant. Once we know what stage an entity or process is in, we can predict what the next stage will be. (This is not *always* so, but when stages are not followed the results are rare and noteworthy.) Second, the way in which an entity is managed, and how it interacts with its environment, is affected by life cycle stage. For instance, programs in a start-up phase are likely to undergo fast-paced change that calls for rapid feedback evaluation methodologies that are not appropriate for assessing outcome once the program is stable. In this book I take the perspective that both innovations and evaluations go through life cycles, and that interactions between evaluation and innovation depend on where each is in the life cycle.

Practical Action

I believe that, above all, evaluation must be practical. It must inform action in real-world settings. I do not mean that evaluation use must only be instrumental, but I do believe that evaluation must guide practical action. In this sense evaluation is a technological endeavor (Morell, 1979, Ch. 5). As Jarvie (1972) puts it: "The aim of technology is to be effective rather than true, and this makes it very different from science." Evaluation should focus on program theory and design elements that will be powerful enough to make a difference in real-world settings, and what can either be manipulated by a program or taken into consideration by a program in order to take action that will have practical consequence. I believe that evaluation can be practical because while change is ever present and the future is always unknowable, time horizons can be set at which a reasonable degree of certainty exists and within which evaluation can provide a reliable guide for further action. John Maynard Keynes recognized the importance of setting appropriate time frames in a famous and eloquent statement. What was true for economics in 1923 is true for evaluation today.

> The long run is a misleading guide to current affairs. In the long run we are all dead. Economists set themselves too easy, too useless a task if in tempestuous seasons they can only tell us that when the storm is past the ocean is flat again. (*A Tract on Monetary Reform*, retrieved from *www.quotationspage.com/quote/38202.html.*)

My Role as an Evaluator

My view is that programs represent investments in a course of action that are designed to achieve specific objectives. Investors have a right (and an obligation) to ask whether their investment has paid off. Evaluators have the obligation to answer that question. I believe that the best approach to getting the needed information is almost always to begin with careful identification of measures and rigorous advance planning. An important source of evaluation surprise is the inescapable fact that evaluation must conform to a basic assumption that is made by program planners: that their programs as designed will make a difference. We may be able to influence planners' thinking about what those differences may be, and we may have some wiggle room to include outcomes that were not envisioned by the planners. We must do so whenever we can, and we should practice the art and craft of constructing as much of that wiggle room as possible. But in the main, we are contractually bound (if not duty) bound to measure program behavior relative to the goals of the program's designers and funders. That said, programs do change in their structure, function, intent, and impact, and evaluators do need to stay abreast of those changes.

HOW TO READ THIS BOOK

Working through the Chapters

This book consists of 13 chapters that I have written and 18 cases contributed by people working across a wide array of methodological proclivities, programs, and geographical areas. Case titles were chosen to reflect these attributes. Table 1.1 contains the case numbers and case titles. Each time I refer to a case I provide the case number and the case's beginning page.

Chapters 2 though 7 are heavy on theory and draw on the cases to illustrate various points I tried to make. Chapters 8, 9, 10, and 11 focus on the cases and show how the previously discussed theory can be applied. Chapter 12 draws from all the previous chapters in an effort to explain how evaluators can handle unexpected program outcomes. Chapter 13 contains my concluding remarks.

Chapter 2 categorizes different kinds of surprise. It can be read in stand-alone fashion. Chapter 3 addresses two questions: (1) When is the probability of surprise high? and (2) When is surprise disruptive to evaluation? It, too, can be read as a stand-alone. Chapters 4, 5, and 6 should be read together because they progress through different degrees of surprise, all the while suggesting tactics that may help evaluators conduct their business. Chapter 7 is a cautionary tale about the perils of heeding too much of my advice. It argues that any tactic for dealing with surprise brings its own risks, and that the more that is done, the greater the risk. Although Chapter 7 draws on the previous chapters, knowing what went before is not a requirement for raising one's consciousness about the risk of making research design too complicated. Chapters 8, 9, 10, 11, and 12 discuss cases, but draw heavily from the earlier material. These chapters have tables and figures to illustrate various points or to summarize information. Just reading the titles of those tables and figures may help convey a sense of what this book is about. Table 1.2 provides numbers and titles for all the tables and figures that are to come.

TABLE 1.1. Overview of Cases

Case	Page	Title
1	197	Grasping at Straws and Discovering a Different Program Theory: An Exercise in Reengineering Analysis Logic in a Child Care Evaluation Setting
2	200	Shifting Sands in a Training Evaluation Context
3	204	Evaluating Programs Aimed at Promoting Child Well-Being: The Case of Local Social Welfare Agencies in Jerusalem
4	210	Assessing the Impact of Providing Laptop Computers to Students
5	214	Quasi-Experimental Strategies When Randomization Fails: Propensity Score Matching and Sensitivity Analysis in Whole-School Reform
6	219	Unexpected Changes in Program Delivery: The Perils of Overlooking Process Data When Evaluating HIV Prevention
7	224	Evaluating Costs and Benefits of Consumer-Operated Services: Unexpected Resistance, Unanticipated Insights, and Déjà Vu All Over Again
8	231	Keep Up with the Program!: Adapting the Evaluation Focus to Align with a College Access Program's Changing Goals
9	235	Assumptions about School Staff's Competencies and Likely Program Impacts
10	241	Mixed Method Evaluation of a Support Project for Nonprofit Organizations
11	244	Evaluating the Health Impacts of Central Heating
12	249	Recruiting Target Audience: When All Else Fails, Use the Indirect Approach for Evaluating Substance Abuse Prevention
13	253	Unintended Consequences of Changing Funder Requirements Midproject on Outcome Evaluation Design and Results in HIV Outreach Services
14	258	Generating and Using Evaluation Feedback for Providing Countywide Family Support Services
15	263	Trauma and Posttraumatic Stress Disorder among Female Clients in Methadone Maintenance Treatment in Israel: From Simple Assessment to Complex Intervention
16	270	From Unintended to Undesirable Effects of Health Intervention: The Case of User Fees Abolition in Niger, West Africa
17	277	Unintended Consequences and Adapting Evaluation: Katrina Aid Today National Case Management Consortium
18	281	Evaluation of the Integrated Services Pilot Program from Western Australia

Getting Acquainted with the Content of the Cases

The 18 cases that evaluators so graciously contributed to this book contain a great deal of information about evaluations that used many different methodologies to support a wide variety of stakeholder needs in a variety of substantive domains and geographical areas. As I draw on specific cases I will provide snippets of contextually appropriate material about that case. As you read, you may find in these snippets all you need to maintain a sense of how the case illustrates the point I am trying to make. Or, you may find it more comfortable to use either of two other approaches. The first is to take the time to read (or skim) through the whole case when I refer to it. Second, you may want to read (or skim) through all the cases now, before descending into the detail that is to follow. Any of these approaches, in various combinations, may work for you. Do what feels best.

IN SUM

In this chapter I tried to make the case that we would be better off if we moved our efforts to deal with surprise from the realm of crisis management to the realm of systematic inquiry. I summarized what the fields of planning and systems tell us about where surprise comes from and how it behaves. I tried to show that what is known about surprise from those disciplines is a useful foundation for us, but that knowledge from those other disciplines is not sufficient because it does not touch on evaluation's particular need to collect and analyze empirical data. Finally, I laid out the intellectual foundations that have forged my sense of how a systematic understanding of surprise can be integrated with evaluation methods. These are the intellectual threads that I spin in the rest of this book.

NOTE

1. By "Lean Six Sigma," I refer to the collection of process improvement methodologies and tools that populate the field of continuous process improvement.

TABLE 1.2. Index to Tables and Figures

Chapter 2

Structure of the Unexpected

So far I have used the terms "unexpected" and "surprise" as if they were simple and unitary, that is, that either something happened that was expected, or that something happened that was not expected. Either we are surprised, or we are not. In fact, surprise can come in shades of gray. The notion that surprise occurs for different reasons is a critical aspect of the approach advocated in this book. Surprise can be divided into two broad categories: (1) events that might have been foreseen (to a greater or lesser degree) had proper mechanisms been in place, and (2) events that, for theoretical reasons, can never be foreseen. Different procedures are needed to buffer against each kind of surprise. Of course, in real-world settings this dichotomy is actually a matter of degree, but looking at pure cases makes for a good beginning and clear explanation.

WHERE DOES SURPRISE COME FROM?

To say that an unexpected occurrence "might have been foreseen" is to say that sharper foresight could reasonably have been factored into evaluation planning. It is not to say that specifics and detail could have been known in advance, but it does mean that by applying existing knowledge we stand a better chance of preparing our evaluations to assess a greater number of likely outcomes. To illustrate, let's look at two examples, one a large-scale policy change and one a limited organizational innovation.

The policy example is the No Child Left Behind (NCLB) legislation. (I realize that by the time this book comes out this example will be overtaken by events, but the example still works.) At the heart of NCLB is high-stakes testing in math and reading, a requirement that imposes a narrow set of outcome measures on the multifaceted institution known as a school system. Any of several theoretical perspectives or bodies of research knowledge could alert us to what might happen. Systems theory tells us that whenever such impositions are made, the system will adjust to meet those objectives at the cost of other goals. For short times in extraordinary circumstances, exclusive devotion to one goal can be an adaptive response, but it cannot be sustained in the long run. Educational research parallels this insight with data showing that when pressured to produce narrow results, teachers will "teach to the test," no matter how deleterious doing so will be to other aspects of education (Firestone, Schorr, & Monfils, 2004). We also know that when outcomes matter, those with a stake in the outcome will do what they can to game the system to their advantage (Ginsberg, 1984). Finally, NCLB provides ample opportunity for gaming because each state gets to set its own performance criteria. None of these insights about the behavior of NCLB speaks to whether NCLB is a good policy or a worthy method of forcing needed change in school systems. It is to say, however, that applying these perspectives in advance would drive better evaluation because it would highlight a set of potential process, outcome, and sustainability issues that need to be considered.

For the second example consider Case 16 (p. 270). Case 16 is an evaluation of a nongovernmental organization's (NGO) effort to improve antenatal (postnatal) health service utilization by new mothers. Prior to implementation, the health service program staff sold "health record books" for their own profit. As part of the new program all material fees were abolished. As the program unfolded, various unexpected changes took place. For instance, other fees crept in. Also, the NGO that supplied materials to the clinics was not informed when stocks were running low, thus necessitating special purchases by clients. Experience with similar programs in similar settings indicates that the psychology of self-interest and common sense would predict the same outcome. In fact, literature was available to the program planners (but not used) that did discuss these kinds of behaviors. I do not believe that anyone could have foreseen precisely how this particular situation would unfold, because context specificity has such a strong hold on the workings of principle. On the other hand, I believe that proper attention to existing literature and the experience base would have alerted the planners to the possibility, and thus would have alerted the evaluators to program behavior that was worth investigating.

In contrast to unexpected but foreseeable events, there are events that are not just difficult to discern, but for theoretical reasons are *impossible* to discern. These are the kinds of events that flow from the behavior of complex systems—nonlinear interactions, feedback loops of different lengths, evolutionary adaptation to continually changing circumstances, sensitive dependence on initial conditions, and rich cross-linkages. Because of these dynamics, complex systems can exhibit self-organization, emergence, and phase shift behavior as they continue to adapt to ever-changing circumstances. To say that the future behavior of such systems can be predicted (i.e., that unexpected events will not occur) is akin to claiming that all relevant aspects of an open system can be fully specified. This cannot be.

Extending the NCLB example illustrates these kinds of truly unforeseeable events. So far, I have considered NCLB in a narrow context—what teachers, schools, and school system bureaucracies would do when faced with a need to narrow the outcomes for which they are accountable. What happens to my simple example when we expand the boundaries of the systems involved? Consider some of the many factors that would be at play. Looking at each stakeholder individually, there is the matter of their relative power with respect to one another. I can't imagine any good way to predict how those relationships would fluctuate over time for the Department of Education, various school reformers with different political philosophies, supporters of charter schools, teachers' unions, state legislators, suppliers of educational materials, and student tutoring services. Nor can I imagine a way to know what coalitions these groups would form, the ability and willingness of the current presidential Administration to defend its educational policy, and the ability and willingness of government officials to fund corrective actions, to name only some of the factors that might come into play.

The unpredictability of all these events and relationships is intuitively oblivious, but it also helps to use an adaptive system perspective to see why the intuition is correct. A system this big and complicated will have no central control. Absent such control, there will be self-organized behavior that will develop over time in response to changing conditions. For instance, the formation of coalitions may depend on beliefs about what position the Department of Education will take on changing NCLB, on emerging data on student achievement, on positions held by Democrats and Republicans in Congress, and on teachers unions' beliefs about their bargaining power. There would be complicated linkages among the drivers of the system. (For instance, how might data on student achievement affect teachers' ability to lobby Congress?) There would be feedback loops of different lengths affecting this rich network of linkages. For instance, student achievement data over several years may affect the public's beliefs about the meaning of yearly data, both of which may interact with strategic planning decisions made by publishers of school materials and advocates of charter schools. As initial positions were staked out by various parties, support and opposition by others may lock in what was initially an uncertain stance. Thus sensitive dependence on initial conditions may set a developmental path in the politics of NCLB.

The future of U.S. foreign policy is uncertain; but imagine that there was an unexpected decline in our spending on overseas military operations. Depending on the amount of money freed up, government spending to stimulate the economy, and the inclusion of educational spending as part of infrastructure development, there may be a sudden influx of resources, thus suddenly allowing choices that were previously impossible. In essence, we might see a phase shift in the sense that very suddenly a whole new set of choices would become possible. Finally, all these possibilities would be taking place over time, on a continual basis. It is not as if there was a single time for change, after which we could expect a reasonable steady state to come into existence. Rather, the possibility of needing to adjust to sudden change would be ever present as all the dynamics described above were continually playing themselves out. No matter how clever we were, no evaluation planning would be able to discern such a development trajectory.

The NCLB example described above deals with a major social issue that is playing out in U.S. society on a grand scale. However, the same issues can be seen in smaller scale evaluation settings. Consider Case 16 (p. 270), which involves changing access fees in a health care setting for new mothers. Impact was assessed with short-term measures of use and satisfaction. Let's spin possibilities beyond the time horizon experienced by the evaluators. What (of a very great many) things don't we know? Did increased access improve child health? Did healthier children affect family structure or functioning? Did similar programs spring up? Were efforts made to help clinic staff replace their lost income? If such efforts were made, what were the consequences for the lives of those people? Did the program affect the funding agenda of the NGO sponsor or other NGOs? Was government policy or funding affected? As with the NCLB example, here we have numerous stakeholders that may align with each other in various ways, depending on what changes were perceived and the value attached to those changes. Feedback loops of different lengths would be at play. For example, immediate local impact on health may affect short- and long-term decisions by the NGO sponsor, other NGOs, and the government. Over time that policy might circle back and influence the NGO's priorities. Early resistance by health care workers might make it just a little bit harder to start up other demonstrations, but the added difficulty might be just enough to turn the NGO's attention to other projects. Thus a local change might have a major impact on a long-term funding agenda.

Looking at both the NCLB and Case 16 tells us something about scale in systems. NCLB is a major policy change—the extension of federal power into the detailed workings of every school board in the country. Case 16 was a significant change, but it only took place in a limited setting. In both scenarios the same issues are driving our inability to glimpse what is likely to happen.

BEYOND SIMPLE DISTINCTIONS

The discussion in the previous section conveys an overly simple view of the problem facing evaluators because it implies a sharp boundary between which events may be foreseeable and which are truly unpredictable. Most evaluation situations are messier. To illustrate the mess, consider Case 13 (p. 253). In that evaluation, a regulatory change affecting service in an HIV program eliminated the need for follow-up interviews with clients. Eliminating the follow-up may have made a lot of sense from the point of view of program cost or the quality of treatment, but it wiped out a critical data collection point for the program's evaluation. Can one imagine an evaluation team that identified this specific change as a potential problem and planned for it? Sure. Can one imagine an evaluation team that was prescient enough to identify this change as a *likely* problem? Not I, or at least, not unless someone gave me a hint. If a little voice whispered in my ear, "Keep an eye on service regulations, there may be changes that will affect your follow-up data collection," then I might have defined critical events in the evaluation, mapped them to regulations governing service, and wondered what would happen to the requirement for a 12-month client follow-up. But in the real world, such hints are few and far between. (Although there are ways to search for them, as we will see in Chapter 5.) If the evaluators in Case 13 (p. 253) worked at it, I bet their fevered brains would have generated dozens of nightmare scenarios. I am also sure that no matter how many they thought of, more reflection would have revealed more nightmares. We are clever folk, and we will always be able to conjure more eventualities than we can identify and plan for. It would help, though, if we could distinguish problems that were flights of fancy (those residing at the "unforeseeable" end of the continuum) from more realistic possibilities that we might want to take seriously. For those, we could make intelligent decisions about whether, and how, we should act. Thus we would do better evaluation if as many potential surprises as possible were driven as far as possible toward the "foreseeable" end of the continuum. We can't get them all, and we can't overly complicate our evaluations by accounting for all the ones we do know about. But despite these limitations, the more we know, the better we will be at making wise choices about evaluation design.

I visualize the situation as an exercise in herding invisible cats. We are faced with invisible cats wandering within poorly defined boundaries. Our challenge is to herd as many of them as possible into a particular corner of the territory. I like the cat metaphor because it keeps me from slipping into a mode of discourse that says: "Of course this problem occurred. I should have seen it coming. Had I been appropriately vigilant, I would have implemented such and such a tactic to prevent the problem." Or worse: "Had I really not been able to anticipate this eventuality, I should have been clever enough to build an evaluation methodology that could handle the surprise." Thinking about having such prescient insight is dangerous, though, because it implies that we can discern a particular causal chain that will lead to a particular occurrence, and by knowing that, we can break the chain and avoid the problem. This kind of reasoning is flawed because, as we know from fields like accident analysis, in retrospect a causal chain can often be detected in very complicated settings (Dekker, 2002, 2007). Our problem is that we are looking into a future in which multiple causal chains can lead to the same outcome, and in which chance events can change what seemed like a sure thing. From the point of view of foresight, our vision is dim and appropriate choices are difficult. Furthermore, if we try to deal with too many eventualities, we risk either severely limiting design choices or producing an evaluation plan that was complicated and unworkable. Choices must be made between the need to buffer against surprise and all the other design constraints (e.g., time, money, expertise) within which we develop our evaluation plans. (I say a lot more about these trade-offs in Chapter 7.)

The discussion so far has skirted an important issue: Can we know in advance how much surprise to expect? It is one thing to know that a particular problem might pop up. It is something else to know how many problems will pop up, how frequently, and what their potential ramifications will be. So what can we expect in the way of surprise? This question is both unanswerable and important. It is unanswerable because innovations are embedded in complex systems, complete with interacting feedback loops of various lengths, dense network nodes, self-organization, shifting environments, co-evolution of programs and their fitness landscapes, and all the other aspects of systems that induce uncertainty and make prediction impossible. (Lest you think it can be done, just look at the history of commodity prices over the last 10 years.) The question is important because it has implications for methodology.

If we really cannot predict how a program will unfold, or what impact it will have, or how the program will affect an evaluation plan, then we should favor evaluation plans that combine "quick-hit" methods (short cycle time from design to findings), with an emergent design approach to inquiry. Short evaluation cycle time and emergent design are not the same. Short-cycle approaches can provide rapid feedback to help planners and evaluators adjust to changing circumstances. There is nothing to preclude these designs from being rigid and fixed. Emergent designs can be used in long-term evaluations. (In fact, that is where they are most useful because the more protracted the evaluation horizon, the greater the likelihood that programs, or their boundaries, or their environments, will change.) Because emergent designs are built to be flexible, they can be used to explain why a program is operating as it is at any given point in time, and how it got there.

To illustrate why both short cycle time and an emergent orientation are important, imagine an evaluation of an initiative to introduce Web 2.0 collaboration processes into a part of an organization, say, a government agency within a department, or an operating division in a company, or a school within a university. ("Web 2.0" is shorthand for the collection of tools that are fueling the expansion of social networking and collaboration on the Internet.) Because the innovation is so novel, there would be great uncertainty if, how, and for what purpose people would use it. At least in the beginning we would expect a great deal of change. What might the evaluation look like? We might want to collect qualitative data from interviews with both users and nonusers, and do textual analysis of blog posts and posted documents. Quantitative data might include counts of the number of people using the system, the number of interest groups that formed, the stability of those groups, movement of people into and out of those groups, dollars spent by the organization on ideas that were generated from the collaborations, the number of ideas considered by management, the number of bottom-up and top-down changes made, and changes in the ratio of ideas for making existing processes more efficient to the number of true innovations. All of this evaluation could be done on a fast clock; that is, data could be collected and analyzed continuously and reports could be turned out monthly. The process as described so far would provide rapid feedback about how well the program was working. What it would not do, however, is provide insight as to *why* the results were as they were. For instance, we might want to know whether the quality of deliberations changed as group membership changed in terms of numbers of members or the number of points of view they represented. If anonymous postings were allowed, what affect might that have? How much value was derived from information exchange versus true collaboration? How did existing information that the organization collected (e.g., statistics on time to accomplish tasks) play in deliberations? How much recommended action could be accomplished within existing stovepipes in the organization versus a need for cross-boundary collaboration? Did this ratio change over time and was it related to the trust built up in the virtual communities? All of these questions (and many more we could think of) represent hypotheses that would surely develop over time as we tried to extract meaning from the data through an inductive, grounded theory-like approach (Thomas, 2006). To really help decision makers, the evaluation would have to be both timely and explanatory.

The example above has focused on a program in its start-up phase, and thus has emphasized the need to combine rapid feedback with understanding why the program worked as it did. To continue the example, imagine that the program had been operating for a year and had nestled into the organization's culture and operating procedures. At that point evaluation could determine whether the collaboration initiative had a noteworthy affect on the organization: Did it affect profitability for companies, rule making and enforcement for the government agency, or scholarly output for the school? To answer this question it would be necessary to move from fast turn-around evaluation designs to approaches that took longer to yield results, but which could provide a greater range of methodological tools. For instance, it would be possible to use long-term trend data and control groups (e.g., other divisions in the company, other agencies, or other schools) that could not be easily incorporated into an evaluation design whose priority was to provide results at frequent intervals, and which was constantly changing.

As the collaboration example illustrates, evaluation designs should differ based on the degree of uncertainty we have about how programs operate and what they accomplish. But other than a hint that a program's life cycle stage might be an indicator of uncertainty, we still don't have guidelines to answer the question: How much surprise should we expect? The answer is both important and unanswerable. So what to do? As in many unanswerable questions, it is still useful to seek an answer. The struggle itself provides guidance. Here is my answer. When I look at a prospective evaluation I think in terms of five questions.

1. How rich and tight are the linkages among major elements of the program? Rich, tight linkages make for unpredictability in system behavior.

2. What is the "size" of the program relative to the boundaries of the system in which it lives? Small programs have less of a chance to behave in ways that will perturb the systems in which they reside.

3. Where is the program in its life cycle? Programs in the start-up phase may change rapidly.

4. How stable will the environment be between the time we implement the innovation and the time we expect results?

5. How robust is the innovation across time and place?

The last question can be answered empirically *if* we have enough experience with similar programs. But outside the world of simulation it is impossible to get good measurement to answer the others. Moreover, even if we did have decent measurement we would be unlikely to have criteria for interpreting the numbers. Consider what we don't know each time we size up a particular evaluation scenario. What does it mean to say that a program is "big" with respect to the system in which it is residing? How many and what pattern of linkages qualify as "rich"? What feedback latency do we need in order to say that a feedback loop is "tight"? What does it mean to say that environmental change is "fast" with respect to a program's life cycle? To complicate matters even more, contrary system behavior is always possible. Rich linkages can make a system extremely stable because threats to any one element would be resisted by multiple elements. Small change can be revolutionary. Mature programs can change quickly. Unstable environments can change in ways that support a program's status quo. Still, despite my uncertainty about the direction of change, and the fact that my answers are only intuitive, I have found that the exercise of trying to answer these questions leads to some pretty good insight as to whether a lot of surprise is in store. If I'm lucky I get a chance to combine my intuition with the intuition of others. Including others has two advantages. First, the combined insight is almost always better than mine alone. Second, the exercise of thinking about the topic can lead stakeholders to a better understanding of unrealistic assumptions they may be making. As unrealistic assumptions are tempered, evaluation surprise decreases.

IN SUM

It is useful to think of surprise in evaluation as spanning a continuum. At one extreme are surprises that we can expect to discern (at least in general terms), if we invoke a well-defined set of techniques. At the other extreme are surprises that are impossible to foresee because their behavior is a function of complex systems. As we move away from the "foreseeable" end of the continuum, our vision of surprise becomes hazier and hazier until it blurs into invisibility. Because we are smart and experienced, we will always be able to conjure more surprises than our methodologies and our resources will be able to accommodate. Add the truly unforeseeable to the problem of identifying many more possibilities than we can manage, and our task seems futile. Still, making the effort is worthwhile. There are techniques we can apply to minimize surprise and to maximize adaptability to what we cannot predict. I hope to convince you of the truth of this assertion in the chapters to come.

Chapter 3

Placing Surprise
in the Evaluation Landscape

When is the probability of surprise high? When is a high probability of surprise a challenge to evaluation? In this chapter I try to answer these questions and show how the answers lead to a categorization scheme that can help us understand what we can do to anticipate surprise and to react to the surprise that we cannot avoid.

WHEN IS THE PROBABILITY OF SURPRISE HIGH?

Design, implementation, and management are exercises in foresight. They involve actions taken now with the intent of either eliciting a future state, or responding to likely future states. The essence of our problem with surprise is the disconnect between how planners must behave and how the world really works. Because planners have this problem, evaluators do, too.

The disconnect between planning behavior and how the world really works arises because powerful solutions to many problems require coordinated (or at least joint) action in several domains, but the only practical way to effect change is to constrain action within a limited set of boundaries. For instance, we may believe that improving the quality of life in certain geographical areas or populations requires substantial improvement in health care *and* education *and* economic development. But from a practical point of view, any single organizational entity (e.g., government agency, NGO) is able to take substantial action in only one (or at most a few) domains. Furthermore, even within a narrow set of boundaries (e.g., health care *or* education *or* economic development), time, money, expertise, political will, and competing demands all conspire to limit the number of attempts to change the status quo. The practical realities are such that we end up with one program, having one mode of operation, chasing a limited number of outcomes. Planners may consider multiple designs, different priorities, and coordinated action, but eventually they settle on a single program.

Funders often have good reason to believe that a single, well-defined program is indeed the best. Belief that a particularly successful approach can be identified is the premise behind evidence-based medicine and, more broadly, the evidence-based movement in general (Weiss, Murphy-Graham, Petrosino, & Gandhi, 2008). The Campbell Collaboration has been busily conducting reviews and meta-analyses to document interventions that work (Petrosino, Boruch, Soydan, Duggan, & Sanchez-Meca, 2001). But if a program is really proven with respect to efficiency and effectiveness, there is little need for evaluation. Much of what we do is in settings where a program is not proven, where outcomes are uncertain, and where alternate approaches are sensible. This is the realm of innovation that cannot be understood or controlled with traditional approaches to planning and management (Stacey, 1992). It is the realm where, because little is simple and much is either complicated, complex, or chaotic, "best practice" has less applicability than we would like (Snowden & Boone, 2007). And yet, even under these conditions of uncertainty, single-solution programs are implemented. Why?

I am sure that funders and planners know better than to pin their hopes on a narrow set of processes to address messy real-world problems. So why do they do it? I believe it is because a confluence of limitations leaves them no choice. Windows of opportunity for getting programs approved are narrow. Competition for resources demands fast action and bold claims. Resource owners have narrow interests. (How much do congressional committees with oversight over health really care about education or transportation?) The expertise available for program design and planning is limited. The organizational locations of program advocates limit their choices. Collaboration across organizational boundaries is difficult because opportunity for personal contact is limited, because joint funding mechanisms are scarce, and because the complexity of coordination increases as more and more organizational boundaries are crossed. And herein lies our problem. Planners surely know that things will not work out as intended when a narrow artificial construct that we call a "program" is expected to behave in predictable ways in real-world conditions. But if planners are competent enough to get a program implemented, they are smart enough to know that they must adopt narrow solutions to broad problems if they are going to get anything done at all.

Context affects how the above issues play out. For instance, consider the effects of organizational culture, economics, and organizational behavior.

- *Organizational culture*—policymakers in government agencies may see themselves as stewards of public resources, and their actions as part of a democratic process that is beholden to the public will as expressed in the election cycle. From that point of view, civil servants may feel a particular obligation to place bets on programs that are likely to be successfully implemented and which can show success in the short term. Foundations, on the other hand, may see their unique contribution in terms of *not* having to take short-term perspectives. Their organizational culture may orient them to longer-term, more comprehensive solutions.

- *Economics*—people may be justified in implementing limited solutions when a relatively small amount of money is available, and a choice has to be made between doing something or doing nothing.

- *Organizational behavior*—Coordination becomes more difficult with increases in the number of organizational boundaries that must be crossed, the social distance among the stakeholders, differences in their incentives, and dissimilarities among their paradigms. These differences do not have to get too large before the sum total of their effect makes coordinated action impossible.

No matter how these kinds of contextual factors play out, no planner or policymaker can escape them entirely. There will always be pressure to succeed. Attempts at cross-organizational coordination will always be risky. Long start-up times will always make implementation vulnerable to changing circumstances.

Where do all these cultural, economic, and organizational complications leave us? They leave us with narrow programs, guided by simple program theories, pointing to a small set of outcomes. This happens despite the fact that those programs touch many outcomes in a complicated world. When I contemplate this situation I find it useful to visualize an evaluation landscape composed of simple programs embedded in larger systems, and of evaluations that can take different perspectives on how programs can lead to long-term outcomes. My schematic notion of the situation is depicted in Figure 3.1.

The real situation is much more complicated, but the essential message comes through in the simple view. The center of the bottom part of the diagram (gray box) is a typical logic model showing how internal program operations relate to each other and to program outcomes. Surrounding the program are a variety of other programs and environmental characteristics that affect the program being evaluated. The top of the

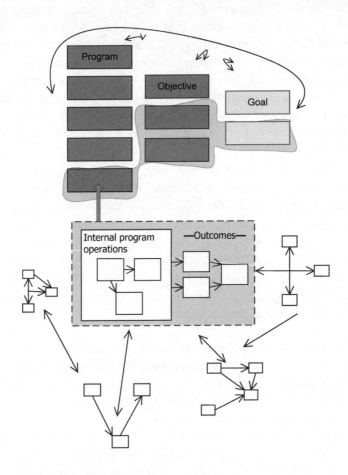

FIGURE 3.1. An evaluation landscape.

diagram shows a world of multiple programs focused on a smaller number of intermediate objectives, which are in turn focused on a smaller set of long-term goals. Programs, objectives, and goals can interact with each other in strange and unpredictable ways. In theory, any evaluation can take a slice through this terrain, and include various combinations of programs, objectives, and goals. (The irregular gray region indicates what one such slice might look like.) For the reasons discussed above, however, most evaluation works on single programs, as indicated by the thick vertical arrow mapping the program in the bottom half of the diagram to one single program in the top. The programs at the top are what most policymakers are actually able to implement—one program, in isolation, at a time. Evaluators follow by evaluating what is implemented. Is it any wonder that things happen that were not planned for?

Despite the inevitability of surprise, it is also true that some programs are more trustworthy than others. If we can understand the reasons why, we can begin to develop effective tactics for anticipating and reacting to events that threaten the integrity of our evaluation plans. To develop those plans, it is helpful to think about the accuracy of foresight in program planning in terms of research and development (R&D) content, robustness, fidelity, time between implementation and effect, and knowledge of context.

High R&D content implies that we are dealing with unproven systems. These are situations where we incur risk because a need has arisen that requires applying proven knowledge in novel settings, or drawing on uncertain knowledge, or dealing with a novel phenomenon. To illustrate, consider an example of each possibility.

Proven Knowledge in a Novel Setting

I have been evaluating cooperative labor-management problem solving in an industry with historically very poor labor relations, a blame-based culture, and a legal framework that feeds the "blame game" when an accident occurs. To make matters even more problematic, the program I have been evaluating focuses on collaboration to find the root cause of human-factors-caused accidents and precursors to accidents. To succeed, it requires workers who observe dangerous conditions to report what they have seen in sufficient detail that a proper analysis can be done. These kinds of close-call reporting programs are common in many sectors (Barach & Small, 2000; Phimister, Oktem, Kleindorfer, & Kunreuther, 2003; Suresh et al., 2004). But they are novel in the organizational culture and liability-based setting where I am working. It was by no means clear that what could be implemented in other settings could be made to work here.

Uncertain Knowledge

The example of Case 7 (p. 224) is a useful example of this concept. This example evaluated the consequences of augmenting "traditional mental health services" (TMHS) with "consumer-operated services" (COS). COS are provided by service recipients rather than traditional mental health service providers, and include peer counseling, patient education, advocacy skills, housing assistance, legal counseling, and case management. As the author puts it: "Prior to this, evaluations of COS outcomes had involved small samples and often conceptualized COS as an alternative to TMHS rather than as a possibly useful addition." Here, the value of the innovation itself was untested. An elegant multisite random-assignment design was planned.

Novel Phenomenon

It is only relatively recently that widespread use of social networking has become common, driven by a combination of low-cost communication, high bandwidth, inexpensive hardware, and networking standards. It is even more recently that the concept of Web 2.0 has emerged. Web 2.0 refers to the idea that many users are able to draw on many sources of information and rich communication in a way that transforms social interaction and how work is done (IBM, 2007). Many large organizations are beginning to look to the Web 2.0 concept as a way to improve their operations by using it to enhance knowledge sharing, collaboration, and decision making among its workforce (Prasarnphanich & Wagner, 2008). In this case any evaluation of efforts to apply the Web 2.0 concept is dealing with a novel phenomenon. Of course, Ecclesiastes was right. In some sense there is nothing new under the sun. Any evaluation of Web 2.0 efforts would certainly include concepts drawn from the writings on learning organizations, management under uncertainty, traditional networking behavior, collaboration, communications, and the behavior of complex adaptive systems. But it is one thing to claim that these fields can help us understand Web 2.0 behavior. It is quite something else to claim that Web 2.0 is a familiar type of social behavior for which we can find ample precedent. We can't.

As R&D content decreases, risk becomes a function of Carol Mowbray's definition of "fidelity": "the extent to which delivery of an intervention adheres to the protocol or program model originally developed" (Mowbray, Holter, Teague, & Bybee, 2003). The problem with "fidelity," though, is that it is quite a leap of faith to assert that we know all the relevant program characteristics individually, and also that we understand how they interact during real-world operation over an extended period of time. We do not and we cannot.

For minimal surprise we need to combine fidelity with robustness. To say that a program is "robust" is to say that it has proven itself under a wide range of approximations to essential program elements, operating in a wide variety of settings. We have confidence that the program will work as intended because experience has given us confidence that despite our meager ability to control or influence actions and events, our actions will still fulfill our expectations. The parallel to the notion of "robustness" in statistics is apt. Robust statistical tests are those whose conclusions are not unduly affected by violations of assumptions about the characteristics of the data. The situation is similar here. Robust programs are based on assumptions that do not break easily. Another way to look at robustness is to think in terms of external validity and generalizability. Imagine an experiment that has been replicated multiple times in poorly controlled settings, and each time with lax attention to the experimental protocol. A research design like this might constitute a bad experiment, but if results were consistent, one would have high confidence in the results of the next implementation. We implement programs in settings that we believe are appropriate for the program to work. Each implementation of the program is never exactly the same, nor is the environment in which the program is implemented. Some programs (and some statistical tests) will remain trustworthy when the assumptions are violated to varying degrees. Some will not. Robustness is a desirable program characteristic because it acts as insurance against lack of ability to specify with high precision various aspects of fidelity, that is, to control both the internal process by which a program operates, and the characteristics of the settings in which the program is implemented. While we cannot specify what makes a program robust, a general knowledge of system behavior tells us that programs will be robust under conditions of powerful interventions, multiple supporting interventions, stable environments, and multiple characteristics of those environments that support program effectiveness. And of course, it always helps if intervention is based on a tested program theory.

The discussion of robustness presented above takes an overly simple view because it assumes that "robustness" is a black box—that we cannot specify the circumstances in which a program will have an effect. (The Realist camp in our field is working hard to make those black boxes as small as possible; Henry, Julnes, & Mark, 1998.) If we had such knowledge we would not have to rely on robustness alone. To illustrate, imagine an effort to improve a product design process by teaching collaboration skills to engineers, shifting rewards from an individual to a group basis, supporting cross-departmental interaction, and providing much greater input on customer needs. Now, imagine implementing this program in two separate companies that varied with respect to the extent to which employees with different functions were co-located (an ecological variable), the company's history of success in implementing innovative work processes (a change management variable), and the extent to which the company was subject to government regulation (an environmental variable). It is not hard to think of many reasons why any of these differences would have an effect on the success of efforts to improve product design. If we understood these factors, we could temper our reliance on robustness alone as a way to decrease evaluation surprise. This is, in fact, the kind of analysis that drives efforts to synthesize knowledge about program effectiveness with a context-specific understanding of why programs that may be effective on average across many settings, differ in how they behave in any given setting (van der Knaap, Leeuw, Bogaerts, & Nijssen, 2008). The more we can apply such knowledge the better, but we will never get it completely right because to do so implies that we can fully specify a model of program operations.

Time erodes predictability because time acts as a window that continually widens to admit the effects of shifting environments, longer feedback loops, changes in programs' internal operations, new customer needs, shifts in stakeholder demands, and the multitude of other factors that make open systems unpredictable.

This section began with the question: When is the probability of evaluation surprise high? The answer is that surprise increases with the amount of R&D content and the length of time between action and observation. The likelihood of surprise decreases with fidelity to proven program models, robustness, and knowledge of operating context. Thus we have answered the first question that began this chapter. But we do not care about surprise for its own sake. This knowledge may be useful to planners, but for our purposes we need to address the second question as well. We need to explain when surprise becomes problematic for the conduct of evaluation. As evaluators, we need to understand both the conditions in which uncertainty is high *and* the conditions in which uncertainty poses difficulties for doing good evaluation. Once those situations are identified, it becomes possible to develop appropriate evaluation tactics.

WHEN IS SURPRISE DISRUPTIVE TO EVALUATION?

Whatever else evaluation requires, it requires data and it requires methodology. Data are needed because evaluation is an empirical endeavor, and thus requires some kind of real-world indicator of program activity. Methodology is needed because methodology is the logical structure in which data are embedded. Methodology allows one to look at data and answer the questions "Compared to what?" and "How can I explain what is happening?" Both data and methodology may take numerous qualitative and quantitative forms, but in one way or another, both have to be present. Thus one way to ask the question of when evaluation is threatened by unanticipated change is to ask the question: Under what circumstances will program change make it difficult for the evaluator to use data and methodology in the service of assessing a program? A useful answer to this question emerges by setting evaluation within two different frameworks, each of which provides a different perspective on when and how unexpected events might threaten the integrity of an evaluation: (1) a life cycle view, and (2) a social/organizational view.

The Life Cycle View

Life cycles are characterized by behavior that is governed by invariant phases that follow each other, with each phase having predictable characteristics which follow from what went before. (Terms like "invariant" and "predictable" are dangerous because there can always be exceptions. What is important in the life cycle perspective is that exceptions are rare occurrences.) The life cycle view of change has proved to be a powerful guiding concept in many different fields, and it will prove useful here for understanding how surprise affects evaluation.

In Chapter 1, I mentioned that one of the realizations I had while writing this book was that programs and their evaluations can both be seen as related innovations that are jointly placed in social/organizational settings. As innovations, they both have life cycles. As joint innovations, they have intersecting life cycles. (Let's leave aside for the moment the complication that evaluations and programs are seldom independent of each other. Looking at the life cycles as independent will get us a long way.) Figure 3.2 depicts the joint life cycles of programs and their evaluations.

Programs go through a life cycle beginning with "inception" and either terminating at some point, or continuing into the indefinite future (*X* axis in Figure 3.2). During that life cycle there are formal events in which change can be institutionalized. Examples include annual budgets, hiring staff, submitting strategic plans, and publishing requests for proposals. In addition to the formal change events, there is also a continual stream of influences, large and small, that move the program about. These are depicted by the cloud that stretches throughout the program life cycle. The reason for the trapezoidal shape of the cloud is because even small changes early in the life cycle may have larger affects than similarly sized changes later on. Early small change can have large effects for two reasons. First, small changes have a way of subtly influencing a series of decisions that can amount to major change

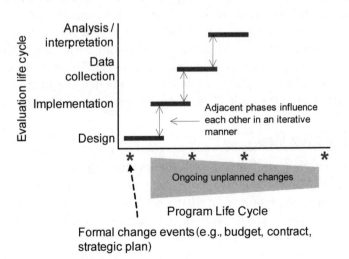

FIGURE 3.2. Evaluation × program life cycles.

over time. The more time these small changes have to work themselves out, the greater the overall impact. Second, as programs mature, they become more stable as novel processes become proven and expectations about services, objectives, and customer needs become tested.[1]

Superimposed on the program life cycle is an evaluation life cycle (Y axis in Figure 3.2). The evaluation life cycle may be shorter or longer than the program life cycle, depending on stakeholders' needs for information and the longevity of the program in question. For the moment, the situation is deliberately simplified by making both life cycles approximately equal in length. No matter what the end points, though, evaluation almost always (despite the fondest hopes of evaluators) begins some time after initial planning for the program has begun. Evaluation life cycle stages progress through four broad phases: design, implementation, data collection, and analysis/interpretation. In the real world these stages can follow more of a spiral than the waterfall model depicted in the figure, and in the extreme the stages can overlap to the point of it being difficult to distinguish one from the other. But always, conceptually and with some time lag, each stage is visible. One useful way to think about change to evaluation is to consider the relationship between a program's life cycle and the life cycle of its evaluation. Figure 3.3 builds on Figure 3.2 by showing the range of possibilities of how program and evaluation life cycles may relate to each other.

With respect to the problems posed to evaluation by a program's unexpected change, one key question is the relative lengths of the program and evaluation life cycles. Scenario 1 is a situation in which multiple sequential evaluations are nested within one program life cycle. Scenario 3 is the opposite. There, one long evaluation extends past the life cycle of the innovation being evaluated.

Scenario 1 depicts a continual testing of small changes within a program. Continual testing of small changes would be appropriate if there were short times between program action and observed change. The situation is similar to a continuous improvement, or rapid prototyping methodology; that is, approaches in which small innovations, or small tests of process, are continually tested and revised. In scenario 3, evaluation is focused on long-term program impact. Thus a single, long stage of data collection and a complementary evaluation methodology are needed.

The shorter the evaluation life cycle with respect to the program life cycle, the lower the probability that surprise will challenge the

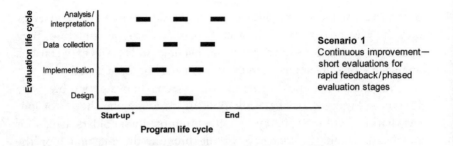

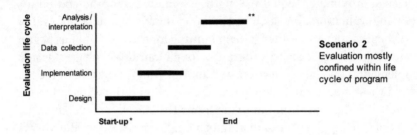

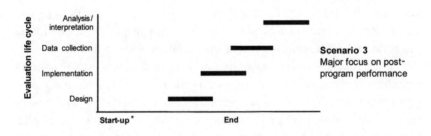

FIGURE 3.3. Three scenarios for program × evaluation life cycle relationships. *In practice, program stages also overlap, but for our purposes it is the evaluation stage overlap that is most relevant; includng program stage overlap would make the figure overly complicated.
**For the sake of simplicity, all life stages are shown as being equal in length.

integrity of the evaluation design. The reasons for the lower probability touch on both the logistics and the methodology of evaluation. Looked at through the lens of logistics, surprise is minimized because rapid cycling of evaluation provides more opportunity to revise an evaluation methodology. If one source of data dries up, another may be substituted for the next iteration. If one methodology (e.g., records review) proves impractical, another (e.g., observation or interviewing) may be substituted. If the spread of an innovation spoils cross-group comparison opportunities, other groups, or a greater use of historical data, may be brought to bear. In methodological terms, rapid-cycling evaluation design puts less of a burden on assessing causal relationships. The burden is lower because the shorter the time between measurements, the less chance there is for outside factors to affect observations, and controlling for outside influences is one of the main reasons for having to keep an evaluation design intact over time. The more intact the design has to be, the more brittle it is, and thus the more problematic unanticipated changes become.

A second way to interpret scenario 1 is that it represents a single protracted evaluation that is more like scenarios 2 and 3, the difference being that the evaluation in scenario 1 has a series of sequential stages, each of which provides information to inform the next stage. Case 10 (p. 241) is an example of this style. There, three phases were designed to build up to a data collection exercise that would give the sponsors the information they needed. Interviews and focus groups identified relevant issues. These led to a structured questionnaire to identify each organization's level of satisfaction with the support services they received. The third stage was another round of focus groups to understand why high- and low-satisfaction organizations were so rated. The three stages in this case exhibited two characteristics. First, each stage provided useful information to stakeholders. Second, the critical question about what differentiated high- and low-satisfaction organizations required a series of three efforts. Each could not have been designed without input from the preceding one.

In some sense almost all evaluations can be said to fit scenario 1 because any complicated effort will almost certainly include some kind of pretest or feasibility assessment. The classification is a matter of judgment. Compare Case 10 (p. 241) with Case 5 (p. 214), which began with an historical analysis of test scores in order to establish sample size. Using historical data to estimate sample size was a prudent first step, but the overwhelming reason for its use was to provide technical guidance to the evaluators. It was not an exercise in which two evaluations were linked.

In addition to the length of an evaluation life cycle, it is also useful to consider the timing of an evaluator's entry upon the scene. Scenario 2 shows a fairly typical situation in which an evaluation begins after initial program planning and implementation have taken place, and continues until about the end of the program or shortly thereafter. The later in the program life cycle that the evaluation begins, the more stable the program will be because the fog of start-up will have subsided. As program stability increases, there is a corresponding decrease in the chance that an unexpected occurrence will challenge the integrity of the evaluation. Also, as the program matures, stakeholders will have a more accurate understanding of how the program operates, a clearer vision of its outcomes, and a more realistic understanding of what evaluation designs may be feasible. At the extreme, evaluation shifts to a major focus on postprogram impact, as shown in scenario 3. There, program operations will have minimal (or no) affect on how evaluation can be carried out, and stakeholders will have a very good idea of what the program has done, irrespective of their initial beliefs.

Earlier I claimed that two essential elements of evaluation are data and methodology. Their characteristics bear on what role the "program: evaluation" life cycle relationship plays in threatening an evaluation plan. In terms of data, what matters is the importance of measuring specific, well-defined variables. In terms of methodology, what matters is the extent to which an evaluation design has to remain stable over time. The greater the need for specialized measurement and long-term design stability, the more brittle the evaluation plan will be. The problem is most acute in scenario 2. Because of the short evaluation life cycles, scenario 1 easily accommodates the need to change evaluation design. Scenario 3 represents a largely retrospective view of innovations that are either very mature, or over. Thus change in programs or environments will not have much of an influence on the conduct of the evaluation. But in scenario 2 there is ample opportunity for program or environmental change to challenge an evaluation design that spans a large part of the program between its beginning and its end.

Another use of the life cycle approach is to compare the evaluation stage at which surprise is detected to the stage of the evaluation where corrective action would be (or would have been) most appropriate. Table 3.1 shows a framework for this mapping.

To see how it works, compare Case 1 (p. 197) with Case 2 (p. 200). Case 1 took place in a child care setting. The sponsor's primary interest was the ratio of the number of caregivers to the number of children. Policy restricted the caregiver-to-child ratio, leaving the number of children and caregivers within the purview of day care centers. This restriction meant that within capacity limits (i.e., no need to expand

TABLE 3.1. Difficulty of Dealing with Surprise as a Function of the Evaluation Life Cycle

Stage where corrective action most useful	Stage where surprise discovered			
	Design	Implementation	Data collection	Data analysis
Design	Case 2			Case 1
Implementation				
Data Collection				
Data Analysis				

infrastructure), financial considerations argued for groups to be as large as possible. The result was a narrow gap between the high and low "caregiver-to-child" ratios that could be analyzed. The evaluation design was built on the assumption that the ratio across implementations would be broad enough to show effects. When data analysis proved that assumption wrong, the evaluation had to change its major question from the impact of the ratio to the absolute number of children in the group. Here, a problem with the evaluation design was discovered in the analysis phase of the evaluation life cycle. Case 2 (p. 200) involved a computer training curriculum. What seemed like a straightforward assignment during negotiations with the sponsor turned out to be a web of misunderstanding, suspicion, and competing interests. Design was continually reworked as these conflicts were negotiated. In this case all the surprise occurred during the design stage. There was plenty of rework, but none of it required contorting the evaluation into something it was not intended to be, or of revisiting long-settled decisions.

The Social/Organizational View

The social/organizational view identifies the location in the social system where an unintended occurrence begins and traces that event to its impact on evaluation. Figure 3.4 illustrates the possible paths.

The origins of change are divided into two broad categories: program related (top left in Figure 3.4), and evaluation related (bottom left in Figure 3.4). Program-related elements can in turn be subdivided into changes in a program's operating environment (e.g., funders, regulators, needs of clients and customers) and changes that are internal to the

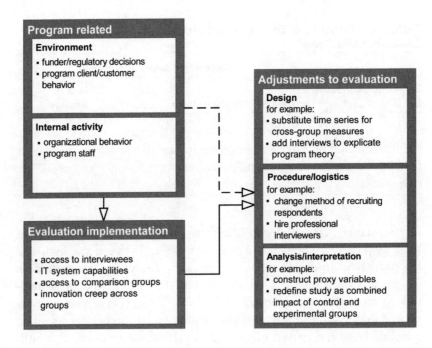

FIGURE 3.4. Where does surprise occur?: The social/organizational view.

program (e.g., organizational behavior, staff behavior). A change in any one of these can lead directly to a change in evaluation. As an example of how the nature of a program can directly affect the evaluation, consider Case 17 (p. 277). This was an evaluation of a case management system designed to coordinate the aid that was provided to people who were displaced by Hurricane Katrina (the hurricane that devastated New Orleans and much of the rest of the Gulf Coast in 2005). A key element of the program was a case management database that was used by case managers to help coordinate services provided to people scattered across many states, and under the care of many different agencies and organizations. Utility of the case management database grew as data accumulated and users' familiarity with the system grew. Evaluation of the impact of the database had to accommodate by adding measures. In this case there was no interference in how the evaluation was conducted. Compare this situation with those about to be described.

The broad category in the bottom left of Figure 3.4 is "evaluation implementation." This category recognizes that although program change may affect an evaluation, it is also possible that a program remains largely intact, but that its operation cannot accommodate an evaluation as the evaluation was originally planned, either in terms of accessing data or implementing methodology. Examples of data problems might be an unfilled promise to make staff available for interviews or discovery that a database cannot produce data at the granularity that is needed for time series analysis. Examples of methodology problems would be a delay in implementation that spoiled a pretest, or failure to provide entry into nontreatment comparison groups. To see some of these problems in operation look at Case 18 (p. 281). That case describes an evaluation of an innovative effort to provide an integrated set of humanitarian services to refugees in western Australia. The evaluation design was built on the assumption that baseline interviews could be conducted; that is, that service recipients could be contacted when the new program first started. In fact, it was not possible to contact these people until some time after the beginning of the program. Unlike Case 17 (p. 277), the problem had nothing to do with how the program was conducted. Rather, the problem was that evaluators were promised a corpus of data that turned out to be unavailable. The program being evaluated did not change, but the evaluation had to. These challenges to the integrity of an evaluation can result in three broad types of responses by evaluators: (1) design, (2) logistics, and (3) data analysis and interpretation.

Design

This type of response involves changing the traditional elements of design, for example, which groups will be compared, what outcomes will be assessed, who will be interviewed, or how case studies will be aggregated. Case 8 (p. 231) is a good example. This case describes an evaluation of college access assistance programs in Ohio. The evaluation was designed based on the funder's belief that the various participating college access assistance programs had data that could be used to determine their success, and further, that the data kept by the various programs existed in such a form that the data could be compared and aggregated. This assumption about data availability turned out not to be the case. The result was a shift in the evaluation design from an emphasis on outcome to an emphasis on the progress that participating programs were making with respect to three strategic goals—sustainability, advocacy, and program development.

Procedures and Logistics

Evaluators can change the procedures they use to implement and conduct an evaluation. A good example is Case 13 (p. 253). In this situation evaluation data collection required interviews with participants
in a drug rehabilitation program for injection drug users. Successful
data collection required interviewers who were sensitive to the needs
and lifestyles of the people being interviewed. The best interviewers
were themselves individuals in recovery. Given the nature of the program and the clients, all of the people involved—both interviewers and
respondents—were likely to have had criminal records. As the evaluation was going on, new policies about hiring appeared that required
criminal background checks, which made it very difficult to allow the
interviewers unsupervised contact with the clinic's clients. The evaluators' solution was to use the experienced interviewers to train others who were eligible to do the needed data collection. There was no
change to design or analysis. There was only a new set of procedures
that assured a new cadre of qualified data collectors.

Analysis and Interpretation

Here the evaluators' response is focused on how data are manipulated
and analyzed. Case 6 (p. 219) is an example. This evaluation was tightly
integrated into a specific treatment schedule that allowed the use of a
traditional quasi-experimental design. When client demand required
a change in the planned schedule, the design fell apart and had to be
replaced with the use of whatever data were available to eke out knowledge of how the program worked.

   Of course, real cases are more complicated than a diagram such as
Figure 3.4 can show, because many elements can be at play simultaneously and can affect each other. For instance, a change in resources might
affect the kind of staff that could be employed, which would in turn affect
the draw of the program to different groups of clients, which might then
require a change in what data need to be collected. But the simple view
depicted conveys a sense of the roots, paths, and end points of change.

IN SUM

Two questions are important for evaluators: When is the probability of
surprise high? When is surprise disruptive to evaluation?

The base level of surprise will always be high because strong organizational, economic, and political considerations foster "single-solution" programs to address multifaceted problems. Departing from this baseline, the amount of surprise we can expect will vary with respect to (1) a program's R&D content, (2) its fidelity to design parameters, (3) its robustness with respect to effectiveness in a variety of settings, (4) our knowledge about program context, and (5) the time between implementation and observed outcome.

Two frameworks are useful for understanding when surprise will disrupt evaluation. One framework relates stages in the evaluation life cycle to stages in the life cycle of the program being evaluated. The second framework is a "social/organizational" view that has two paths. One path leads directly from the program being evaluated to changes in some combination of an evaluation's design, execution, data analysis, or data interpretation. In the second path these aspects of evaluation are changed because program operations affect how an evaluation is implemented, for instance, affecting data availability, access to comparison groups, or the distribution of services across group boundaries. These implementation problems, in turn, lead to changes in design, execution, or analysis.

NOTES

1. This statement assumes that the program is operating in a stable environment. More precisely, it assumes that the internal capacity of the program is sufficient to protect it from whatever changes in the environment may arise. It also assumes that the internal structure of the program is such that the program is not brittle in the face of change; that is, that it will take a very rare event to cause a radical change in the program. It is always possible for any system to be affected in a way that will require sudden change. But from the practical point of view of everyday program functioning, it makes sense to think in terms of stability of proven systems. In my experience sometimes there is radical change, but most of the complaints I hear (and make myself) is that programs are too stable and do not change when they should.

Chapter 4

Minimizing Foreseeable Surprise

This book began by making the case for treating evaluation surprise as a topic in its own right that is worthy of systematic discussion. It then developed a continuum of surprise (unforeseen ↔ unforeseeable) and presented two typologies (life cycle and social/organizational) to classify cases. In this and the next two chapters I discuss tactics that evaluators can use to keep surprise from weakening their evaluation plans. These tactics are divided into eight categories: (1) theory, (2) exploitation of past experience, (3) limiting time frames, (4) forecasting and program monitoring, (5) system-based logic modeling, (6) data choices, (7) agile methodology, and (8) retooling program theory.[1]

The discussion to come presents these tactics in a rough order along the continuum of applicability from "foreseeable" to "unforeseeable." This chapter sticks close to the "foreseeable" end of the continuum. Chapter 5 wanders through the middle of the continuum. Chapter 6 deals with evaluation tactics for situations in which surprise is inescapable. To illustrate, "theory" is presented first because it can be used in evaluation planning stages to get a sense of what program outcomes need to be measured, while "monitoring" comes later because it is useful for detecting leading indicators of unexpected change.

Of course, these eight categories are by no means pure. For example, it is impossible to consider future scenarios without drawing on past experience, to develop logic models without an appreciation of time frames, or to monitor program activity without considering the availability of data. But these categories are useful as ways to consider the core intellectual contribution of various approaches.

As a reality check and a caution lest all the possible courses of action seize our imaginations, these three chapters are followed by one dedicated to the evils of excess; that is, an explanation of why too much effort to deal with surprise is counterproductive. Then, in Chapter 8, I turn to the real-life cases that appear on pages 197–292. Using them, I try to show how the problems caused by these surprises have been blunted.

THEORY: USING EXPLANATORY POWER
AND SIMPLIFIED RELATIONSHIPS

Theory is used to explain a set of related observations.[2] As such, using theory in evaluation can be useful in two ways. First, if it is applied early enough in a program's life cycle, it might affect the program's design, and thus help both program planners and evaluators avoid surprise. If the evaluation begins once the program design is set in stone, theory can help the evaluators prepare for program behavior that was not anticipated by the program's planners.

Because of its explanatory power, theory can be useful in pointing us in the right direction to get a sense of what might happen. The list of possibly useful theories is endless. Later I discuss the challenge of which one(s) to pick.[3] In this section I present four examples to show how theory can help us anticipate surprise: (1) life cycle behavior, (2) free-market characteristics, (3) systems theories, and (4) program theory as articulated by planners and stakeholders. I am not presenting these particular examples to plug their respective virtues, but only to use four very different examples to make a general point.

Example 1: Life Cycle Behavior as a Driver of Change

Change is often a function of life cycle behavior. Van de Ven and Poole (1995) categorize the fundamental reasons for change as falling into four general categories: teleology, life cycle, dialectic, and evolution. The first two are particularly useful for helping to reveal possible consequences of a program's action. (The last two are good reasons why unexpected events can never be eliminated. Dialectic change is the product of conflict resolution and evolutionary change comes from adaptation to environments.) "Teleology" has a rich history in the study of cause and has been subject to debate since the birth of Greek philosophy. But for our purposes, we can think of it as a view that design is dictated by purpose, or put another way, that "each kind has its own final cause, entities are so constructed that they tend to realize this goal" (Audi, 1995). This notion of teleology is apparent in most of the evaluation that we do. We ask program planners to articulate what they want to achieve and to specify how their actions will achieve their ends. We (or at least they) expect their programs to unfold in a way that promotes the desired result. As evaluators, we have developed ways to help stakeholders define these relationships. Working with stakeholders this way is the essence of logic modeling. One of the defining characteristics of logic modeling is the goal of getting stakeholders to articulate workable methods of achieving specific objectives. In other words, we ask stakeholders to develop programs that can reasonably be expected to be the causes of specific end states.

We are not as good, however, at using life cycle dynamics as an evaluation tool for discerning the likely course of events. Life cycle changes are driven by developmental processes that produce highly predictable consequences. Life sciences are one obvious field where life cycle change is an important concept, but the notion can be found in many other fields as well. A few of many examples are: organizational development (Sherman & Olsen, 1996), R&D project management (Pillai & Joshi, 2001), innovation management in companies (Koberg et al., 1996), organizational growth and financial performance (Flamholtz & Hua, 2002), strategy formation (Gupta & Chin, 1993), alliance behavior (Lambe & Spekman, 1997), software development (Boehm & Egyed, 1999), and innovation adoption (Adner, 2004).

To be sure, evaluators do recognize the importance of life cycles. In a review of empirical research on sustainability, Scheirer (2005) argues that: "Evaluation researchers conducting studies of sustainability need to have some background in the literature on organizational behavior to understand the organizational influences that operate across the life cycle of project start-up, implementation, then sustainability and other potential longer-term outcomes." Altschuld, Thomas, and McColskey (1984) map evaluation strategies to stages in the development of training programs (e.g., follow-up procedures are needed once a program is deployed, but not before). Fetterman (1994) discusses the importance of judging a program's accomplishments relative to its stage of development (e.g., small achievements in a program's early stages mean something different than small achievements when a program is mature).

Gajda (2004) employs a developmental stage model to the evaluation of strategic alliances. Implicit in the work of these evaluators is the idea that a knowledge of life cycle behavior can help evaluators anticipate program behavior they might miss had a life cycle view not been taken. What I have not been able to find are situations in which the life cycle idea was specifically applied to avoid surprise.

A good illustration of how a life cycle perspective can be useful comes from an evaluation I am doing of a major quality improvement effort in several large companies. Part of the data collection involves interviews with line workers about their views of the value of the program. As one worker put it (in paraphrase): "I have seen lots of these kinds of programs. They all last about 5 years, and then the company goes on to something else." The "flavor of the month" phenomenon is an obvious point that I should have thought of, but did not. Had it occurred to me, I would have made that trajectory a part of the sustainability assessment part of the evaluation. I would have (or at least I'd like to think I would have) built an evaluation that looked for influences of the program on any new programs that moved in to take its place.

A second illustration is hypothetical, but plausible and illustrative. Imagine two community college programs, both designed to prepare students for employment. The first requires mastery of a mature technology, such as welding or construction. The second requires mastery of a fast-changing technology, such as animation or search software. In both cases outcome evaluation might follow a logic model that asked the following questions: Is there an employment shortage in this field? Are the necessary skills incorporated into the curriculum? Is the instructional design sound? Do students acquire those skills? Does the program have strong links to industry that will help students find employment? Do the students find jobs? Do students succeed in their jobs once they are employed? These questions are reasonable for both scenarios. However, they are not sufficient to explain a pattern that might occur in the software scenario. Suppose early results showed successful skill acquisition by students and high employment rates, followed over time by continued successful skill acquisition, continued high demand for employees, and lower employment rates for the program's graduates. How might these results be explained? Evaluators might have been prepared to answer this question if they were sensitive to the rapid life cycle changes that characterize the applications in which students were being trained. Had a life cycle view been taken, the evaluation design might have addressed questions such as: How quickly are new applications introduced? How does that life cycle compare with the life cycle of technology refresh rate at the community college? Addressing these questions would have resulted in choices of measures and the timing of observations that could explain the fate of the program.

Example 2: Free-Market Behavior

The field of economics provides a set of concepts that can reveal unique insight into a very wide range of human and system behavior. Moreover, intuitive understanding is often all that is needed to apply these concepts in a useful manner (Frank, 2007). Thus evaluators can apply these concepts with stakeholders in a common search for explanation about program functioning and estimates of program outcome.

To illustrate the value of the economic lens, consider the activity going on based on the assumption that making health care outcome information freely available will decrease cost and increase quality.[4] To illustrate this contention, consider the mission statement of the Consumer–Purchaser Disclosure Project:

> The Consumer–Purchaser Disclosure Project is a group of leading employer, consumer, and labor organizations working toward a common goal to ensure that all Americans have access to publicly reported health care performance information. Our shared vision is that Americans will be able to select hospitals, physicians, and treatments based on nationally standardized measures for clinical quality, consumer experience, equity, and efficiency.
>
> Improved transparency about performance will improve both quality and affordability. Driving this improvement will be (1) consumers using valid performance information to choose providers and treatments, (2) purchasers building performance expectations into their contracts and benefit designs, and (3) providers acting on their desire to improve, supported with better information. (*healthcaredisclosure.org*)

Many useful theories could be used to inform evaluation of programs based on the Disclosure Project's premises. One might apply a psychological perspective, and consider people's relationship with their physicians, or their beliefs in the value of science. One might take an organizational view and assess the constraints imposed by health insurance companies on people's choice of health care providers. One might take a communications perspective and assess how relevant information is disseminated. All these are valuable. But the economic perspective leads to choices that might not be readily apparent with other theories. Also, the economic view leads to an overarching structure for organizing material that emerges from other frameworks. To see why an economic perspective is so useful, consider what we learn by applying the characteristics of a "perfect market" to the situation.[5] In a perfect market: (1) there is a large number of buyers; (2) there is a large number of sellers; (3) the quantity of goods bought by any individual transactor is so small relative to the total quantity traded that individual trades leave the market unaffected; (4) the units of goods sold by different sellers are the same (i.e., the product is homogeneous); (5) all buyers and sellers have complete information on the prices being asked and offered in other parts of the market; and (6) there is perfect freedom of entry to and exit from the market.

Using these characteristics of a perfect market, an evaluator could implement a design that specifically assessed whether each condition developed, and why. For instance, the principle of "homogeneous product" speaks to the information dissemination that the purchase disclosure effort is seeking to advance because information is needed to understand which products (services, in this case) are actually the same. But the "information availability" characteristic does not consider the profound psychological aspects of doctor–patient relationships, which will surely affect a patient's choices. "Perfect freedom to enter the market" assumes that all services are equally available; that is, that there are no geographical barriers, or that there are no time constraints keeping a patient from purchasing services from one or another provider. "Entry freedom" is certainly not real. Innovations in medical practice begin in constrained areas; even in the same geographical areas, scheduling constraints may make services from some providers more available than services from others. Any one of these issues could be explored by applying a noneconomic lens. The psychology of the doctor–patient relationship is one issue; another might be an organizational view of constraints imposed by insurance companies. But while several different frameworks can be invoked, there is a twofold advantage to including the perfect market perspective. First, it speaks to the role of "information," which is a bedrock principle in the change effort that is being attempted. Second, it provides an overall framework that can help knit many disparate evaluation findings into a coherent explanation.

Example 3: System Theories

Another stock of useful theories can be drawn from the domain of "system thinking." Consider, for example, an application of system theory to the evaluation of a learning organization. While no all-inclusive definition of a "learning organization" exists, many different definitions converge on a few key themes[6]:

1. They place heavy emphasis on knowledge held by people, and collectively by groups.

2. There is a sense that knowledge at the organizational level is something other than the collective knowledge of individuals.

3. The value of having a learning organization is that it helps an organization achieve its goals.

4. Open communication and common understanding are important.

5. There is a reliance on "systems thinking" as a theoretical foundation as to why organizational learning can result in a learning organization. To vastly oversimplify, systems thinking focuses on analysis of how organizational performance can be made more powerful by thinking of organizational activity in terms of part–whole relationships and the operation of feedback loops of various lengths and degrees of nesting.

Let us consider what an evaluation of a program to produce a learning organization would look like if it were based on the perspective outlined above and then extend the example by adding the insight generated by adding a complex adaptive systems (CAS) view. Without CAS, the evaluation would address the following questions: Were people trained in appropriate forms of problem solving and group interaction? Did they apply those methods? Did they do so effectively? What proportion of the employees, spread across the organization, acquired these skills? Did collaboration take place across organizational boundaries? Was information available? Were organizational goals accurately transmitted to employees? Did the organization achieve its goals? Did the organization thrive in its environment?

Now, let us add CAS to the mix. The importance of adaptation to environment is most certainly evident in the traditional view of the learning organization. However, adaptation is not *central*, nor is the notion of adaptation considered in a rigorous manner. Furthermore, the *relationship* between internal states and adaptation is not dealt with in depth. How might the measurements in our evaluation be expanded if there were a greater focus on adaptation? To answer this question it is useful to refer to the discipline of CAS, and in particular to what it has to say about stability, chaos, and the border between stable and chaotic states.[7] For our purposes, a few elements of CAS are relevant. First, states of systems vary along a continuum of stability. Deeply stable systems are highly resistant to change. As long as stability will serve their interests, highly stable systems will function well. The problem is that because they are so stable, they do not adapt easily to rapid change. At the other end of the continuum are highly unstable systems that cannot maintain themselves for very long. A critical question is where a truly adaptive system will exist on the continuum. To address this question, CAS applies a model that relates a system's internal structure to the characteristics of its environment. These are known as NKCS models. N is a measure of the number of elements within a system. As examples, these may be people, departments, coalitions, or interest groups. K is a measure of the richness of linkages among the systems. In low-K systems, each element directly affects only a few others. In high-K systems, a change in any one element will directly affect many others. S represents the number of entities (e.g., organizations, species) with which a system interacts. C is a measure of the degree of interdependence among the entities in the environment.[8]

Computer simulations are used to show how systems behave under different NKCS values. For instance, these simulations have shown that systems tend to be stable under conditions of high internal complexity and an environment characterized by low competition among a small number of elements. One can see how this variation in stability makes sense. Think of an industry that is highly specialized internally and operating in a stable environment. Automobile manufacturing comes to mind. (Or at least, it did when I began to write this book.) Until recently, no serious competition to the internal combustion engine existed. Within an automobile manufacturing company efficiency derives from a complex interrelationship among elements. The delivery of parts is exquisitely tuned to manufacturing schedules. Marketing and design work together to make sure new products will sell. Design and manufacturing are coordinated to make sure that designs can be built. Design and manufacturing both work with the supply base to make sure parts will be available with the right functionality and at the right price. And so on. Under these conditions, the company that does the best job of complex internal coordination will win the competition with other manufacturers who are similarly, but not quite as well, internally organized. But what happens when changes in the environment get too big? Once the shock becomes large enough the organization cannot easily adapt because all the linkages among parts of the system are self-reinforcing.

What would happen if we added a CAS perspective to our evaluation of the program to promote a learning organization? None of the measurements already specified would be dropped, but new ones might be added. With a CAS view, the definition of how well an organization learns can be cast as a measure of how well an organization adapts to its environment. At the same level of linkages among elements, an organization may be adaptive or not depending on what is happening in its environment. Thus the evaluation might add assessments of internal organizational dependencies and environmental flux. Consider how adding a CAS view would affect unexpected findings. Without CAS the evaluator might rate an organization highly on a learning organization scale only to suddenly discover that the organization was incapable of coping with a sudden change in its environment. How might this disjunction between rating and behavior be explained? Why would a seemingly high-learning organization suddenly become a low-learning organization? Without measures of both changing internal structure and environmental characteristics, such a rapid change could not be explained. With the CAS view, the findings make sense.

Example 4: Program Theory

Program theory has a long history in evaluation and its precursor fields. Leeuw (2003) has traced it back to Karl Manheim, who in 1935 argued for identifying the assumptions that lay behind "social planning" (Manheim, 1935/1967). The rationale for using program theory is that if underlying assumptions about a program's operations and outcomes can be identified, the knowledge can help both planners to design better programs and evaluators to produce information that will lead to program improvement. Program theory has a strong stakeholder orientation; that is, it places great emphasis on what stakeholders believe about why a program should be constructed as it is and what effects the program can be expected to have over time.[9] The reason why program theory can be useful for unearthing surprise is that assumptions about program operations can be used as a starting point for considering a range of possible program effects. A good example of this can be seen in Case 16 (p. 270). The surface assumption in that program was that by eliminating user fees for prenatal care, women's use of health services would go up, with a consequent improvement in mothers' and children's health. Perfectly reasonable, but not complete. An underlying assumption was that other than the reduction of fees, the health care system would remain unchanged. This assumption was false because the old system provided income to service providers that was eliminated in the new order of things. It might not have been possible to predict exactly what would happen, but confronting that assumption would certainly have prepared planners and evaluators to confront the possibility of some kind of reaction that would affect program operations and outcome.

Use of program theory has a unique place in evaluation because of its value in engaging stakeholders. But there are two reasons why I do not think it should be used exclusively in the hunt for lurking surprise. First, it is limited to the perspective of stakeholders. To draw on the previous example of community college training, I have no trouble imagining that, left to their own devices, stakeholders would not consider life cycle changes with respect to software. Another reason not to rely solely on program theory is that program theory can be wrong. This is precisely what happened in Case 1 (p. 197). That evaluation ran into trouble because the range of the caregiver-to-child ratios was too restricted to reveal differences in the outcome of interest. But as the author of that case states, " ... for a variety of political, bureaucratic, and theoretical reasons, the project stakeholders concluded that important effects would be observed even under the restricted range of the key independent variable."

Choosing Theories

Theory may be useful, but which theory to choose? It will never be practical to choose more than a few, because each theoretical perspective added to the evaluation mix increases both the number of constructs that require measurement, and analytical complexity. Soon enough the evaluation exercise would become unwieldy. My proposed solution boils down to four principles.

1. One is better than none.
2. A few are better than one.
3. It does not matter which ones are chosen.
4. More than a few are dysfunctional and impractical.

To see how these principles would work in practice, consider the following thought experiment.

1. Establish a group of stakeholders to help design the evaluation.
2. Consult with a few trusted experienced advisors and generate a list of 10 candidate theoretical frameworks that in their best judgment are relevant for the evaluation at hand. (To work, the choice must include experts with diverse bodies of expertise.)
3. Pick one at random and use it to inform the design of the evaluation.
4. Perform the evaluation.
5. Pick another of the frameworks.
6. Repeat steps 3 through 5 several times.

I believe that if this thought experiment were carried out, two results would ensue. First, there would be a great deal of similarity across all the evaluations. Why? Because in each case the program is the same, the stakeholders are the same, and the program goals are the same. Second, all the evaluation designs would be better than the design that used none of the theoretical frameworks. Why? Because programs are social activities that are subject to the same human, social, economic, and organizational dynamics that have been probed and tested by generations of social scientists. Any group of those probers is likely to have come up with insights that are worth considering.

The above advice notwithstanding, the choice of particular theories does matter over the long run. The choice matters because, over time, any particular theoretical orientation will guide an evaluation in a particular direction. Looked at in the middle or toward the end, it will be obvious that the evaluation design evolved in a path-dependent manner. Path dependence is consequential enough for the evaluation in its own right. It is even more consequential when we factor in any impact the evaluation may have had on the development path of the program being evaluated. Thus step 2 in my thought experiment—consult with a few trusted experienced advisors and generate a list of 10 candidate theoretical frameworks—takes on special importance. Theories chosen at random may very well result in evaluations that do not serve the best interests of either evaluators or their customers.[10]

EXPLOITING PAST EXPERIENCE: CAPITALIZING ON WHAT WE ALREADY KNOW

Few social problems are so unique that previous experience cannot be used to decrease evaluation surprise. But while it may be trite to recommend an old-fashioned literature review or to suggest a discussion with people who have dealt with similar problems, these are still good ideas. It really does help to systematically scan previous knowledge when preparing an evaluation. (There is nothing new in this idea. It was proposed in 1971 in a classic evaluation book by Francis Caro; Hyman & Wright, 1971.) Past experience can be used in two ways. The first is to understand process, for example, "What tends to happen to programs like this at election time?" Or, "How will government hiring rules affect the implementation of our new initiative?" The second provides domain knowledge, for example, "What do we know about why diabetics stop monitoring their blood sugar levels?" One way to think about domain knowledge is to adopt the view that history has already done an experiment for us about how predictable program activities and impacts are in different settings. Our job is to find and interpret the data. As I explain the use of this knowledge, I draw on specific examples. At the end of this section I address the question of how to identify the relevant domains and how to choose among them.

Process Knowledge

By "process knowledge" I mean knowledge about the conditions under which a program is operating, regardless of what the program is designed to do. What follows are three examples of how this kind of knowledge can reveal how a program may change over time. The three examples are: (1) political context, (2) organizational growth, and (3) R&D.

Political Context

The closer an innovation's start-up is to an election, and the more politically value-loaded the service, the greater the likelihood that changes in political climate may come into play to affect the program. As an example, contrast the likely fate of an innovation designed to promote immunization against childhood diseases with an innovation designed to improve sex education. The structure and specific aims of the former will be acceptable to any political ideology, while the structure and specific aims of the latter are likely to be closely tied to a specific political and social ideology. As a second example, consider an innovation designed to help schools meet the requirements of No Child Left Behind (NCLB). The context of that innovation (i.e., the NCLB legislation) could be assumed to be stable were implementation done at the beginning of the Bush administration. The closer to the end of the administration (and as the administration's power to defend its agenda weakens), the greater the likelihood that our innovation might have to adapt to new circumstances, find new ways to serve its clients, or accommodate a different set of school priorities and programs. (I know this example will be overtaken by events by the time this book comes out, but it still works as a good illustration.)

Organizational Growth

Ample research (and common sense) indicates that as organizations move through the stages from start-up to maturity, each transition represents a crisis that must be met (Flamholtz & Hua, 2002; Macpherson, 2005; Scott & Bruce, 1987). Or put another way, moving from stage to stage can be seen as moving from one internal state to another, with quite a bit of turbulence at the boundaries. What might knowledge of boundary conditions say for designing evaluations of innovations in organizations? To illustrate, let's return to the example of an effort to transform an organization into a "learning organization" that was presented earlier in this chapter.

Five key themes describing learning organizations were laid out: (1) learning organizations are heavy on knowledge held by people, and collectively by groups; (2) knowledge at the organizational level is something other than the collective knowledge of individuals; (3) the value of having a learning organization is that it helps an organization achieve its goals; (4) open communication and common understanding are important; and (5) reliance on "systems thinking" is an important concept for understanding why organizational learning can result in a learning organization. Let's assume that the program being evaluated took place at any stage in the organization's life cycle other than its terminal stage; that is, that the innovation was implemented at a time when the organization might be expected to encounter the turbulence that appears during the stage transitions. What might an evaluator do in planning the evaluation, given his or her knowledge about the problem of stage transitions? As a minimum, he or she would expect threats to the implementation and running of the program. These problems might be as obvious as difficulty in scheduling training sessions, or as subtle as small delays in the organizational consultants' access to higher-level management. The evaluators would be sensitive to these kinds of problems and always be on the lookout for them. The formative evaluation plan might end up with more interviews done more frequently, a greater number of open-ended questions and focus group sessions, and a set of specific questions about the extent to which stage transition uncertainty was affecting the program's operations.

Other than garden-variety implementation issues, stage transition might affect the key elements of what a learning organization is. For instance, what would happen to people's (and groups') efforts to make decisions that were in alignment with the organization's overall goals, as the internal structure of the organization became more differentiated and more formalized? With those changes would come a larger and more heterogeneous set of local goals that had to be aligned. Widespread communication of what those goals were would also become more of a challenge. The problem of jointly optimizing multiple goals would be harder. I can't prove it, but I'd be willing to bet that under such conditions the "learning organization" might differentiate into a group of more localized "mini-learning organizations," each of which had greater or lesser degrees of overlap with the others. Such an event might be either functional or dysfunctional, but it would certainly be an unexpected outcome. If evaluators began their efforts with an inkling that this kind of differentiation might take place, they would have the opportunity to embed tasks to track and assess these developments. If I were doing this evaluation, I would be thinking in terms of social network analysis, shifts in overlap of groups over time, and an analysis plan that put a greater emphasis on the relationship between local goal alignment and overall organizational performance.

R&D

The greater the uncertainty in a program (i.e., the less tested the program and the greater its R&D content), the more likely it is that the program either will not develop as expected, and/or that it will have different consequences than expected. Moreover, the more a program's uncertainties affect each other, the worse the problem. To illustrate, imagine a school system that is implementing two separate innovative math and language curricula. Both are untested and both rely on untested methods. There is plenty of opportunity for either innovation to have unintended effects, but any outcomes from one would be reasonably independent of outcomes from the other. Contrast this scenario with an innovation in which various curricula—math, science, social studies, and language arts—all drew on one another for common material and common themes. Here, there are major dependencies in the innovations, and we would expect the effectiveness of any one to cascade through the system. I don't mean to imply that there are no dependencies in the first scenario. A school is only so big. At some level there is only one faculty, one administration, one body of students, and one group of parents. None of these can deal with too much change at a time, and attitudes about the change process or the effectiveness of change in one large innovation are bound to affect the other innovation that is taking up the same space. Still, from a process point of view, the first scenario and the second differ dramatically in the strength, richness, and immediacy of their respective dependencies. As with the example above on learning organizations, here too there are implications for methodology. For instance, how important would it be in each scenario to develop a strong quantitative model of the relationships among achievement scores in the various topics? It would be nice to have that kind of data for both scenarios. But I wouldn't go out of my way to get one if I were working in the first scenario. I'd make every effort to get the data to develop such a model if I were working in the second. How important would it be to understand the indirect system effects of the total amount of change going on within the school? Again, it would be nice to have that knowledge in both scenarios, but I'd put a lot more effort and resources into obtaining that knowledge for the first scenario than I would for the second.

Domain Knowledge

By "domain knowledge" I mean knowledge about the specific topic under investigation, for example, depression in a mental health program, collaboration in a Web 2.0 initiative, or circadian rhythms in a fatigue minimization effort. Many examples can be found. I'll illustrate with two.

Richard et al. (2004) provide a case study of implementing an ecological approach to tobacco control programs. In the ecological approach, focused efforts are set within a range of related health behaviors and elements of personal functioning. As the authors put it: "Planners and practitioners have been urged to use this approach by implementing programs that integrate person-focused efforts to modify health behaviors with environmental-focused interventions to enhance physical, political, and sociocultural surroundings" (pp. 409–410). The problem they faced was that little was known about how to successfully implement such programs. Their approach was to begin with a literature review of the extensive work that has been done to identify the determinants of successful ecologically based programs (e.g., multidisciplinary teams, expertise in health promotion programs). Then they developed a theory-based evaluation to investigate mechanisms that linked the various correlates of successful ecological implementation.

The previous example dealt with research that was immediately related to the program at hand. Broader knowledge can be included as well. An evaluation by Grella, Scott, Foss, Joshi, and Hser (2003) focused on gender differences in outcome with respect to a drug treatment program in Chicago. The raison d'être for this evaluation was an appreciation of a vast research literature that indicated different patterns of substance abuse for males and females entering substance abuse treatment. That knowledge led this study to use path analysis to evaluate the differential long-term outcome of the program on males and females. Some of the information they used was directly related to service utilization. For instance, they used data on treatment history and referral source, both of which seem obvious candidates for evaluating the impact of substance abuse treatment. Much of their data, however, dealt with substance abuse differences that described the populations, but which had no immediate relationship to treatment or treatment programs. For instance, they included data on living arrangements, mental health status, and criminal history. These findings did not come from program evaluation. They came from research on substance abusers, but were deemed by evaluators to be potential explanatory factors in a program evaluation exercise.

One way to look at what these evaluators did is to think of two sets of relevant information that may affect treatment. One set includes evaluation studies of entry into treatment and treatment outcomes. The second set includes more general research on differences between males and females with respect to substance abuse. The two sets only partially overlap, even though both sets of information are plausible candidates for explaining the differential effects of treatment.

Choosing Appropriate Bodies of Knowledge

The same problem exists here as was presented in the discussion of theory. Any given evaluation faces myriad choices for what knowledge to actually use. How can these be identified, and from them, which few should be picked? My proposed solution is the same, but with a substitution of "body of knowledge" for "theory." Use a diverse group of experts to nominate a long list of relevant candidates. Randomly pick a few and use the knowledge to help design the evaluation. Replace and pick again. Continue. Compare each evaluation design to the "control" design, which relied only on interaction with stakeholders. I am convinced that each of the designs that used expert input would reveal more lurking surprise than would the control condition. There may not be a way to know which sets of expertise would be best, but any would certainly be better than none.

LIMITING TIME FRAMES TO MINIMIZE THE OPPORTUNITY FOR SURPRISE

One way to reduce the probability that an unexpected event will spoil an evaluation is to reduce the "distance" between the innovation being evaluated and the outcomes that are measured. This statement is intuitively obvious, but as is often the case in life, it is sometimes worth taking a systematic look at commonsense understanding. First, let me restate why "distance" matters. If we believe that the programs we evaluate are embedded in an open, complex system, then the program is subject to all the dynamics operating that keep systems from moving smoothly along a single predetermined trajectory. Self-organization, adaptation to changing environments, multiple feedback loops operating at different latencies—all these and many other factors bring uncertainty into any predicted development path. The greater the opportunity for these forces to operate, the greater the likelihood of unexpected change. Decreasing "distance" between implementation and measurement decreases opportunity for system forces to come into play. We now have to define "distance."

I believe that it is useful to define "distance" in two ways—temporal and causal. Temporal distance introduces uncertainty because the longer the time period between innovation and observation, the greater the likelihood that some set of system dynamics will perturb an expected development trajectory. (Of course, not all system dynamics will have this affect, but some will. Also, it is certainly possible that some changes will make the program more stable, but I think that assuming change is the prudent course.[11]) Causal distance refers to the number of events in a causal chain between the innovation and an outcome of interest. Shorter time frames and few steps are less susceptible to unexpected change than are long time frames and multiple steps. To illustrate these relationships, consider the following example. I envision four versions of a program that is designed to improve safety in an industrial setting. The program is designed to improve safety by changing managers' ability and willingness to work with the people they supervise to improve safety behavior on the job. Different chains of logic and different expected latencies for observing change are operating in each case. The situation is depicted in Figure 4.1.

Each scenario can be characterized by three parameters: (1) time frame between innovation and desired change, (2) number of elements in the causal chain affecting the desired outcome, and (3) opportunity for outside forces to affect the system. (The case assumes that environmental influences are evenly distributed over time, but let's accept this simplification.) The most predictable scenario is 1 because it ranks low on all three parameters. The least likely scenario is 4 because it ranks highest on all three parameters. Not only is the time frame longer in 4, but it includes a new element in the logic model (safety culture). For the program to work in scenario 4, more stages have to succeed than in the other versions. As influences impinge on the system, they can act in two ways. First, they might directly affect how the program is run. For instance, increased sales may increase demands on managers, and thereby decrease the amount of coaching they were scheduled to receive. Second, they might influence the outcomes, as might be the case if greater sales increased the workload, thereby souring labor–management relations and decreasing workers' willingness to recognize change in managers' behavior. Another way outside events may affect the evaluation is through their impact on feedback loops. For instance, the logic model shows that managers' behavior is a function of both the program and of their reaction to change in workers' behavior. It is

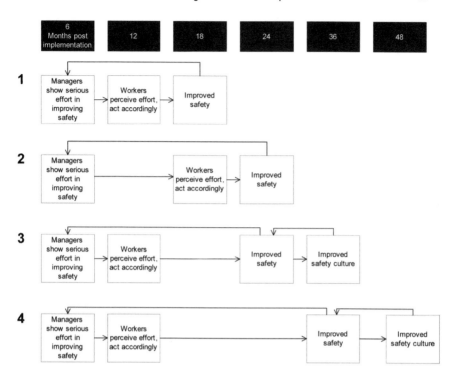

FIGURE 4.1. Temporal and causal distance between program and effect.

not hard to imagine that without some relatively rapid change by the workers, managers would conclude that the program was not worth the effort. If those increased sales decreased the pace of implementation, the time between program implementation and worker change would lengthen, thus decreasing managers' beliefs that participating in the program was worth the effort.

Combining "time frame" and "length of causal chain" allows us to recast Figure 4.1 as Figure 4.2. The evaluator's task is to reduce unpredictability by decreasing distance along both dimensions. The closer one can get to the origin in Figure 4.2, the less the chances of surprise affecting the design, data collection capacity, or objectives of the evaluation. With respect to the temporal dimension, it is often possible to get clients to agree to shorter time frames because they so frequently begin their interest in evaluation by focusing on the large-scale, long-range change that was touted during the political and bureaucratic struggles

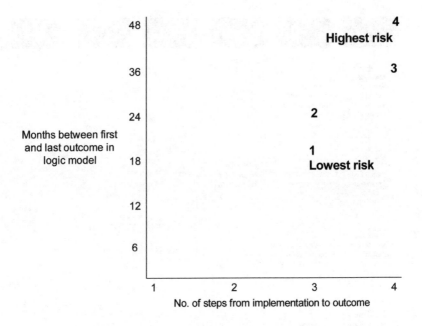

FIGURE 4.2. Risk as a function of time × length of causal chain.

that were needed to get a program funded. In such cases an argument such as the following often works: "I am a really good evaluator. If you pay me to evaluate your program relative to those goals, I will. But do you want to stake your reputation and credibility on showing that what you are doing in this program will achieve those goals?" Sober reflection often focuses the mind and brings about a willingness to measure shorter-term goals over a shorter time frame.

Sometimes, however, the temporal distance cannot be reduced. It may be that commitments have been made by program champions, or that it is critical to get an answer about a particular long-term outcome, or that shortening the time frame trivializes study of an important problem. In such cases the desired tactic is to keep the original time line, but to add intermediate outcomes. Essentially, the plan is to decrease temporal distance by moving down the causal chain.

Before leaving this discussion, some words of caution are in order. First, causal chains can be scaled to any degree of granularity one wishes. It will always be possible to insert more elements. Thus the notion of shortening or lengthening a causal chain has to be thought of in terms of some reasonable level of programmatic steps that most managers would consider realistic in terms of how they plan the expenditure of time and resources and the scheduling of milestones. Second, changing the scale of a logic model is not an exercise that should be taken lightly. Each added element can generate five types of complications to program theory.

1. The added element itself represents a hypothesis about program operations. That could be wrong.
2. Any one-to-one or one-to-many relationships that are posited between the added element and other elements in the model are also hypotheses about program theory. They too can be wrong.
3. Any feedback loops added may be misplaced, creating more room for error.
4. Increasing granularity represents a belief that lower levels of detail can explain higher-level operations. This view of aggregation may be incorrect.
5. All these errors can pile up and interact.

Overall, adding elements to a logic model can be hubris, the overbearing pride that brings destruction. Let us not think that we know more than we do.

IN SUM

Three tactics are particularly useful near the "foreseeable" end of the continuum: (1) use of theory, (2) use of past experience, and (3) limiting time frames. *Theory* is useful because it can provide predictions about what will occur and explanations of why a program may work as it does. As long as informed choices are made, any theory will be better than none when it comes to first designing an evaluation. However, initial choices of guiding theories will have increasing influence over time because the choices will influence path-dependent developments in evaluations, programs, and interactions between them.

Exploiting past experience informs evaluation by providing specific, trustworthy information about the behavior of programs that are similar to the one being evaluated. Two kinds of knowledge about past experience are useful: knowledge about the conditions under which a program operates (process knowledge), and knowledge about specific programs that are similar to the one being evaluated (domain knowledge).

Limiting time frames is useful because as "distance" between program and outcome is extended, opportunity for unpredictable change increases. "Distance" has both a temporal and a causal dimension. The temporal dimension takes in the "time" aspect of distance; that is, the longer the elapsed time, the greater the chance for change. The causal dimension defines distance in terms of the number of events in a causal chain between program activity and outcomes of interest. The greater that number, the greater the opportunity for perturbation in any one to affect those that follow.

NOTES

1. In the field of evaluation, "logic models" are "a diagram and text that describes and illustrates the logical (causal) relationships among program elements and the problem to be solved" (*www.epa.gov/evaluate/glossary/l-esd.htm*).

2. Consider some definitions of "theory":

   • "A set of statements or principles devised to explain a group of facts or phenomena, especially one that has been repeatedly tested or is widely accepted and can be used to make predictions about natural phenomena (*The American Heritage Dictionary of the English Language, Fourth Edition*).

   • "Theory, in scientific or technical use, refers to a general principle or set of principles, based on considerable evidence, formulated to explain the operation of certain phenomena (*www.yourdictionary.com/theory*).

   • "A well-substantiated explanation of some aspect of the natural world; an organized system of accepted knowledge that applies in a variety of circumstances to explain a specific set of phenomena (*dictionary.die.net/theory*).

   • "Systematic ideational structure of broad scope, conceived by the human imagination, that encompasses a family of empirical (experiential) laws regarding regularities existing in objects and events, both observed and posited. A scientific theory is a structure suggested by these laws and is devised to explain them in a scientifically rational manner" (*www.britannica.com/EBchecked/topic/528971/scientific-theory*).

3. In making this distinction I am glossing over an old (and still current) argument over the extent to which program theory should be based on social science theory versus the theories of program operation that are held by stakeholders (Christie & Alkin, 2003). Personally, I can't get

excited about this argument. As far as I am concerned, both should be used as needed. If a use of theory is helpful to deal with surprise, that is good enough for me.

4. Many thanks to Laura Leviton of the Robert Wood Johnson Foundation in helping me to develop this scenario.

5. This list comes from *www.lse.co.uk/financeglossary.asp?searchTerm=perfect &iArticleID=1095&definition=perfect_market*, but a search of the Web will find many similar explanations.

6. To see where these themes come from, consider a few summaries of what learning organization is.

• A review by Infed (*www.infed.org/biblio/learning-organization.htm*) presents three definitions of a learning organization: (1) "Learning organizations [are] organizations where people continually expand their capacity to create the results they truly desire, where new and expansive patterns of thinking are nurtured, where collective aspiration is set free, and where people are continually learning to see the whole together" (Senge, 1990, p. 3). (2) "The Learning Company is a vision of what might be possible. It is not brought about simply by training individuals; it can only happen as a result of *learning at the whole organization level....* A Learning Company is an organization that facilitates the learning of all its members and continuously transforms itself" (Pedler, Burgoyne, & Boydell, 1996, p. 1). (3) "Learning organizations are characterized by total employee involvement in a process of collaboratively conducted, collectively accountable change directed toward shared values or principles (Watkins & Marsick, 1992)" (*www.infed.org/biblio/learning-organization.htm*).

• In their analysis of the relationship between scenario planning and the characteristics of learning organizations, Chermack, Lynham, and van der Merwe (2006) state that "for the purposes of this study, it is important to clarify that a learning organization is an organization thought to be capable of continuous learning and adaptation" (p. 770).

• In their research on measures of learning organizations in schools, Bowen, Rose, and Ware (2006) assert that "in our definition, learning organizations are associated with a core set of conditions and processes that support the ability of an organization to value, acquire, and use information and tacit information from employees and stakeholders to successfully plan, implement, and evaluate strategies to achieve performance goals" (pp. 98–99).

7. The topic of CAS takes in a huge amount of information that can in no way be dealt with here in anything approaching a comprehensive manner. For a good overall discussion of CAS, see Kauffman (1995). Marion (1999) provides an analysis of how various organizational theories (e.g., contingency theory, organizational learning, functionalism) would look through the lens of CAS. Stacey (1992) provides CAS as a heuristic for managing in times of uncertainty.

8. In this discussion I am committing the same sin that characterizes a great deal of the discussion of CAS in the organizational literature. I am using quantitative terms as if they can be dealt with qualitatively. K, for instance, is a parameter in a mathematical simulation that has a very specific value. To say that K is high is meaningless without knowing the simulation scenario. What could be a high K in one context may be low in another. I do believe, however, that intuitive understandings of these concepts is useful. If we know the settings we are dealing with we do, for instance, have a sense of what rich and sparse linkages are, or what a fast-moving environment is. If I had my way (I'm working on it) there would be an effort in our field to integrate true CAS simulation with evaluation. The evaluation would provide empirical data to feed the simulation, and the simulation would provide the evaluation with insight on how a program was likely to develop.

9. Of course, this statement is a broad generalization. One of the modern era's seminal books on evaluation theory (Chen, 1990) argues for an emphasis on basing program theory on social science research. Christie and Alkin (2003) provide a good example of beginning with a literature review prior to engaging stakeholders. Still, the major emphasis in most contemporary writing on program theory orients evaluators toward the importance of discovering the assumptions that stakeholders make about why their programs might work as planned. Many different approaches are advanced for helping stakeholders identify assumptions. Much of Patton's work on user-focused evaluation is very sensitive to the difficulties that stakeholders have in understanding why they make the decisions they do (Patton, 2008). This is also true in many of the systems approaches (Williams & Imam, 2007). Donaldson (2007) provides a casebook on how program theory is used in eight different evaluations. Leeuw (2003) provides cases illustrating three different empirical approaches to reconstructing program theory.

10. Special thanks to Deborah Wasserman for pointing out this critical point, which, I admit, I had not thought of in earlier drafts of this book.

11. This conversation skirts the question of what "stable" means. The field of CAS contains the notion of stability existing in different states, from systems that are highly stable but breakable in dramatic ways, to systems that can continually adapt to environmental change.

Chapter 5

Shifting from Advance Planning to Early Detection

The methods discussed in the previous chapter—use of theory, use of empirical evidence, and limiting time frames—have their primary value in the early stages of evaluation design, that is, when fundamental decisions are made about the scope and purpose of the evaluation. If a credible job is done in the beginning, then it seems unlikely that more attention to theory, or further investigation of previous findings, will make a big difference in decreasing surprise once an evaluation is established. As to the question of time frames, that determination is a fundamental scope decision that must come from serious negotiation between evaluator and funder. Given its implication for funding levels and contract end dates, it is unlikely that changes will be made once an evaluation has begun. Because these methods are most useful early in an evaluation life cycle, their primary value is for anticipating surprise that is close to the "foreseeable" end of the continuum that separates the "highly foreseeable" from the "impossible to predict."

The methods I discuss here begin to have a greater range of application. They are applicable along the evaluation life cycle, and begin to shift from an emphasis on advance planning to early detection of the need for change. I begin with a discussion of detecting and using leading indicators of change. I conclude with a discussion of system-based logic modeling, which can be useful in its own right, and also valuable as a method of organizing leading indicator data.[1] Chapter 6 completes the three-chapter journey by discussing methods that will increase evaluation's responsiveness to unfolding events. Following that I explain why using too many of these suggestions is guaranteed to be counterproductive.

LEADING INDICATORS

A great deal of change is preceded by a collection of signs and indicators that, if detected and interpreted correctly, would presage the impending new circumstances. Detecting, interpreting, and reacting to those indicators are tall orders. (My goal is to elevate the process a step or two above reading entrails.) Complete success is impossible in the open systems in which we operate. Partial success is difficult. But with the proper approach some success is possible, and the more success the better, because the more time evaluators have to prepare for shocks to their designs, the better they will be at performing evaluation. Some occurrences happen so quickly that it is truly fair to say that one had no time to react. By "no time" I mean that the response time for any practical reaction is longer than the time allowed by any practical means of detecting the need to change. These kinds of events are a fact of life. Still, there are tactics that can provide a longer-range view, and in so doing, open windows of opportunity to change an evaluation before its integrity is compromised. I'll explain these tactics in three steps: (1) forecasting to discern what should be observed, (2) monitoring to map observations into understandings of program theory, and (3) organizing the evaluation enterprise to detect and react to change.

Forecasting

Forecasting is needed because the essence of dealing with unexpected events is to detect impending change as early as possible. Thus any method to help with early detection is worth consideration. To identify those methods I turn to the field of planning, where the challenge of forecasting future developments is a core challenge. Planning is a prospective exercise. It seeks to answer the question: What can we do now to bring about a desired state in the future? Planners are acutely aware of the difficulty of answering this question and have developed techniques that can be used along a project's life cycle to detect deviations from plans. It is true that traditional planning has come in for a good deal of justified criticism because of its determinist flavor and its assumptions about the operations of large systems (Stacey, 1992). But as with any tool, planning methods have their advantages as well as their limitations.

In one way or another, planning methods begin with a vision of the future and then posit ways to get to that vision. Scenario planning is a common approach to this kind of forecasting (Godet, 2000; O'Brien, 2003). Here, planners posit likely multiple futures and try to discern development paths that will lead to those futures. Another approach is backcasting, in which desirable futures are assumed and the question is asked: How did we get here? (Drenborg, 1996). Both of these approaches can be applied in highly systematic ways. For instance, Assumption-Based Planning (Dewar, 2002) begins by identifying critical assumptions that must be realized if a plan is to be effective. It then goes on to identify load-bearing assumptions (those that are susceptible to breakage by future events), signposts (leading indicators of potential problems), shaping actions (used to support uncertain assumptions), and hedging actions (to prepare for the possibility of failure). These methods can be focused either on the program being evaluated or on the evaluation itself. For instance, the planning exercise may indicate that population needs are changing, which may drive a change in how services are provided or what services are provided. If such changes were to take place, evaluators may realize that they need to add outcome measures or find another set of comparison groups. Or these methods might look at the evaluation itself. For instance, environmental scanning may reveal that participants in a control group are beginning to find alternate means of finding services similar to those offered by the program being evaluated. The use of alternate means of obtaining a service does not change the program, but it certainly has implications for the evaluation design. These planning methods can be useful in detecting evaluation surprise by applying them continually (or at least at defined intervals) as an evaluation proceeds; that is, they need to be embedded in a systematic program-monitoring process.

Monitoring

The application of systematic, ongoing program monitoring as an evaluation approach is well established. Traditionally, program monitoring can be thought of as assessing the degree of conformance between a program's activities and its logic model (Kaplan & Garrett, 2005). The emphasis that program monitoring places on systematic and ongoing observation well serves evaluators' need for vigilance with respect to unanticipated change. To detect incipient change, however, the traditional framing of monitoring in terms of a logic model is insufficient. Two additions are necessary. First, the same processes used to develop the logic model in the first place must be used to revisit the model at periodic intervals. Second, relevant developments in the program's environment need to be systematically scanned.

Most logic models contain an "if–then" logic; that is, they provide insight on what is likely to happen if particular program elements are implemented or outcomes achieved. But because program logic may change over time they can lose their ability to foreshadow coming events. To correct this weakness, the scope of monitoring needs to be extended from observation of program activity to observation of its underlying logic as well. (Of course, older generations of a program's logic models should not be abandoned, because they serve as a test of the original program theory, and also because changes over time constitute useful information.)

As models are revised, understanding will emerge as to how the evaluation design must be modified. To illustrate, let's expand on the examples provided in Figure 4.1. All four scenarios in that figure posit the theory that change in manager behavior will affect worker behavior for one reason only—that managers' demonstration of their concern for safety will affect workers' safety-related behavior. Assuming a single reason for success is reasonable because the program in question is completely focused on training managers to interact with workers around issues of worker behavior. But what actually might happen? First, it seems likely that as group discussions proceeded and awareness of safety increased, managers would begin to attend to safety improvements not directly related to worker behavior. For instance, they may become more sensitive to the limitations of existing safety equipment or procedures and act on that awareness. Second, it is not unreasonable to think that, as managers changed their style of interaction with workers, labor would begin to engage in other activities to improve productivity. To complicate matters still further, safety itself is a component of productivity. What has happened? The original program theory has been shown to be wrong (or at least too simple). Now we have an additional intermediate outcome, additional longer-range outcomes, and additional feedback loops. The new situation is depicted in Figure 5.1. (Original = white fill, solid lines, open arrows. Revised = gray fill, dashed lines, solid arrows.)

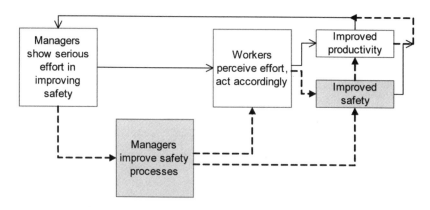

FIGURE 5.1. Self-organized behavior as a complication to a simple program logic.

By monitoring the changing program logic, evaluators would be alerted to these developments and could adjust the evaluation design accordingly. Two changes might ensue. First, the new logic model would provide feedback to stakeholders about their program theory. Second, it would alert the evaluators of the need to retool their designs to account for the unexpected effects of the program.

The changes in program logic between Figures 4.1 and 5.1 focus on activity that is internal to the program being evaluated. But surprise can also be driven by factors external to a program. Again to draw on the previous example, imagine that while our safety program was going on, but completely independent of it, two events took place within the company. First, the quality assurance department embarked on an enterprisewide Lean Six Sigma quality improvement program.[2] Second, the labor relations department instituted a new discipline policy that required workers' compliance to rules to be monitored more closely. (Who says companies have to act consistently to make sure their policies align?) The model now looks like Figure 5.2.

There is now both an added input to drive managers' safety improvement efforts and an added input to improved safety. There is also a new policy that may depress workers' willingness to cooperate and which might sour their relationships with their managers. With the new policy comes much greater uncertainty in the program logic. Figure 5.2 indicates that the new discipline policy will have a negative impact. So far so good. But will it have that negative impact by work-

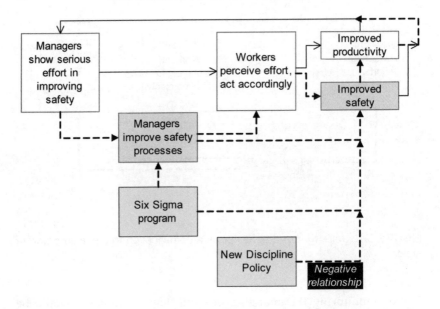

FIGURE 5.2. External change as a complication to a simple program logic.

ing directly on "improved safety" (as I posited in the model), or might it affect "worker perceptions," or both? Perhaps the new policy made the managers' jobs more unpleasant and thereby depressed their enthusiasm for taking proactive action. The possibilities are numerous, and I doubt that either previous research or querying stakeholders would shed much light on the matter.

With the addition of the companywide program and the new discipline policy, it becomes much more difficult to test the original program theory, that is, that teaching managers how to interact with workers can improve safety. More difficult, but not impossible. Evaluators could assess the value of the Six Sigma program as a way of testing its impact on the safety training program. They could try to determine how much the new rule-compliance policy affects workers' willingness to cooperate with safety initiatives. Or they could conclude that parsing the effect of the training program from all the other changes has become too complicated and too expensive and shift their focus to a "black box" assessment of safety change over a fixed period of time. But any of these options would require them to negotiate with stakeholders and to institute change in evaluation procedures. The better the monitoring, the more time evaluators will have to get it right.

Organizing Evaluation to Detect Change

The above discussion of Figures 5.1 and 5.2 has left out an important bit of process. How do the evaluators know whether these activities are occurring? And even if the evaluators did find out, how might they determine whether the changes were worth paying attention to? No doubt the importance of the new quality program would become evident once it was deployed, but by then the evaluators would have lost valuable opportunities to retool their evaluation design. The same is true for the discipline policy. Our goal, after all, is to anticipate events and to prepare for them, not to get hit over the head and then have to react. To complicate matters, in big companies many different activities and policies are always being started, stopped, and modified. How is one to know in advance what important changes are brewing? The traditional advice to include all stakeholders in logic model development is insufficient because so much surprise grows from activity that lies outside of the population of a program's stakeholders. To continue with the example in Figure 5.2, I would not have included the labor relations department as a stakeholder in a safety training program because of the program's exclusive emphasis on safety training. I don't think I would have ever thought to consider the quality assurance department. I'd rush to include them once the Six Sigma program and the new discipline policy were implemented, but by then my chance to anticipate would have been lost.

The solution parallels the suggestions given earlier with respect to choosing relevant theories and sources of past experience. It suggests that we identify all the relevant domains in the setting that might affect the program being evaluated. Not all of these domains will contain program stakeholders, but they may contain people with relevant insight about activities in the company that might affect the program being evaluated. If this exercise were carried out rigorously (and with a good deal of brainstorming from a diverse group of people), the result would probably be a larger pool of domains than could be reached within the constraints of time and budget. To prune the list, I find it useful to split the group into those domains where I can see a clear connection to the program I am evaluating and those that lie further afield. I try to include all of the first group and a sample of the second. Any sample will be better than none. In any case, it is truly impossible to get them all because it is impossible to know in advance where change may come from. Because the sources of change cannot be predicted, it is also useful to monitor a different sample of domains over time.

When I think about organizing my evaluation work in a manner that will help me detect surprise as early as possible, I return to the notion that both evaluations and organizations are agglomerations of people, resources, and processes brought together into a recognizable entity for the purpose of accomplishing specific objectives within larger social settings. Looked at in this way, threats to an evaluation are akin to what any organization must do to react to unexpected change. Building on this similarity, we can apply the principles of "high-reliability organizations" to the evaluation enterprise and think in terms of "high-reliability evaluations." Weick and Sutcliffe (2001) offer five characteristics of organizations with reputations for being able to react successfully to undesirable surprise. First, they have a preoccupation with failure, whether large or small. Any deviation from plan is taken seriously. Efforts are made to detect them and to interpret their meaning. Second, there is a reluctance to simplify. They employ diverse expertise and viewpoints to provide different perspectives. Third, they maintain high degrees of situational awareness within their organizations, fueled by open communication between those closest to unfolding events and other members of the organization. Fourth, high-reliability organizations are committed to keeping errors small and to developing alternate methods of keeping their operations going. To do this, they draw on deep knowledge of their operations. Finally, in high-reliability organizations there is respect for expertise. Diverse viewpoints are used not only to detect problems, but also to formulate solutions. With respect to high-reliability evaluation, these principles can be applied by means of forecasting and monitoring.

SYSTEM-BASED LOGIC MODELING

I hesitate to wade into the morass of "systems in evaluation" because this topic is subject to so much discussion and debate about what systems are, how they can be used as evaluation tools, how systems themselves can be evaluated, and what conceptualizations of systems are useful under what circumstances. (For those wishing to engage this literature I recommend: Williams, 2005; Williams & Imam, 2007; Cabrera, Colosi, & Lobdell, 2008; and the responses to Cabrera: Cabrera & Colosi, 2008; Datta, 2008; Forrest, 2008; Hummelbrunner, 2008; Midgley, 2008; Nowell, 2008; Reynolds, 2008; Rogers, 2008; Wasserman, 2008.) Nevertheless, there are some generally accepted notions of systems that can be extremely useful in helping to scout for surprise.

1. Systems are assemblages of components that interact with each other to serve some identifiable function (or functions).

2. Boundaries around systems can be identified. At a sufficiently granular level any border becomes indistinct, but at the level of routine functioning the contours that separate one system from another can be determined.

3. Systems stand in different relationships to each other. They can be nested, adjoining, overlapping, or remote.

4. Boundaries among systems can be more or less permeable.

5. Systems can have different types of influences on each other. Influence can be direct or indirect. The strength of the influence can vary.

Latencies can be different; that is, there can be variation in how long it takes for a change in one to be felt by another. Impact may be symmetrical or asymmetrical. To illustrate these relationships, contrast three pairs of systems: (1) a school and the school's central administration, (2) health care and mental health care, and (3) health care and schools. I can see a debate as to whether the "schools–central administration" pair are closer than the "health–mental health" pair, but either way, there is less distance within these pairs than there is between "health–schools." What about strength and latency? As a general rule I'd say there are more actions a central administration can take that will rapidly have a noticeable impact on a school than there are actions a school can take that will have rapid and noticeable consequences for central administration. Because of this difference it would also be fair to say that the direction of influence is asymmetrical. (Many exceptions and idiosyncrasies are possible, which is why making a decision about system relationships must be based on a sample of actions in a system rather than on the selection of any particular action.) An implication of these characteristics of systems is that a logic model of their relationships can be constructed. (Wasserman, 2010, provides a good explanation of how these kinds of models can be constructed.)

To see how system-based logic models might be useful for dealing with surprise, imagine a school pondering the impact of two kinds of changes taking place in its operating environment: (1) decreases in mental health services and social services in its community, and (2) change in Board of Education policies. Over time, deterioration in mental health services may well affect what happens in schools, but these changes would be longer term, more gradual, and more diffuse than policy changes at the Board of Education. If nothing else, evaluators would have a time frame to help determine when surprise might appear and a general sense of what kinds of changes might take place.

As with the other suggestions I am offering, a few cautions are in order. The first is that constructing elaborate models risks committing one of the biggest sins in systems approaches—losing the power that comes from stripping away detail and complication. I believe, though, that prudence can lead to reasonable decisions about what to include and what to exclude. To extend the example used previously, let's consider the relationships between schools, health, and mental health by adding three other programs: one to improve defense R&D, one to improve social welfare, and one to improve the national economy. I think most people would agree that if we started with mental health, there would be disagreement only about social welfare. Leaving social welfare out, the progression would be: (1) mental health, (2) health, (3) schools, (4) defense R&D, with (5) national economy having an overarching affect on all. Some people might place welfare before or after schools or health, but in the main, consensus could be achieved.

Once that consensus was achieved, decisions could be made about the boundaries of the evaluation. Eliminating defense R&D would be an easy decision. While in some sense everything is connected to everything else, the relationship between the mental health system and the defense R&D system is so tenuous that it would have no discernable influence on a mental health program. If I were doing the evaluation, I'd also leave out the programs dealing with the national economy. I would agree that the state of the economy affects people's stress, which might in turn have some impact on my mental health program. But many other factors influence people's stress levels as well. I might include measures of stress in the evaluation, but I would not put any effort into analysis of how programs aimed at the economy might influence the mental health program I was evaluating. Health care, on the other hand, might be an important part of the evaluation. If nothing else, many patients have multiple problems that require coordinated care across different specialties. Changes that increase or decrease access to a wide range of health care services might plausibly affect either participation in the mental health program, or the outcomes of its services, or both. Returning to the issue of surprise, what does this system-based logic modeling exercise say about the design of the evaluation? It says that if I want to account for unexpected change in the effectiveness of the mental health program, one of the things I'd better do is keep an eye on changes in the health care system. Why go through this exercise? Doesn't everyone know that health care affects mental health care? In one sense, yes, everyone does know that. But does knowing that lead to a systematic decision about the design of an evaluation of a mental health program? Probably not. System-based logic modeling will lead to a methodical identification of many systems that may be relevant and to a decision process that winnows those candidates to the few that are worth absorbing evaluation resources.

The second major problem in looking at relationships among systems, as I have been advocating, is that it assumes a stability that may not endure. Using system-based logic modeling will always be vulnerable to the unpredictability of complex system behavior (i.e., to the threat that unpredictable changes in relationships might appear). How might my neat arrangement of systems change if an unexpected organizational shift brought the health and mental health systems under one commissioner, or if the previously unified bureaucracies were split apart? But even in the face of unpredictability there is value to using the limited deterministic systems view I am advocating. First, many systems do operate in a stable manner over long periods of time. Within those limits, the simple view can provide a lot of useful information. Second, by expanding the horizons of observation, there is a greater chance of detecting early signs of truly unexpected change.

IN SUM

This chapter shifted the discussion about surprise in evaluation from minimizing surprise through advance planning to methods for detecting surprise as programs and their evaluations become operational. The key is to use methods that will supply evaluators with as much lead time as possible about impending problems. Three types of methods were proposed. The first was to adapt forecasting techniques used by planners. The second was to expand the traditional evaluation view of program monitoring to include changes in program logic and activity in the program's environment. The third was to expand logic models to include the systems in which a program is embedded.

NOTES

1. As noted in Chapter 4, in the field of evaluation, "logic models" are "a diagram and text that describes and illustrates the logical (causal) relationships among program elements and the problem to be solved" (*www.epa. gov/evaluate/glossary/l-esd.htm*).

2. As noted in Chapter 1, by "Lean Six Sigma," I refer to the collection of process improvement methodologies and tools that populate the field of continuous process improvement.

Chapter 6

Agile Evaluation

Much in the previous two chapters has been a discussion of how evaluators can act in order to know what might happen. Missing has been a discussion of the characteristics of an evaluation that make it adaptable to change. How can an evaluation be designed to change? What makes it agile? The answers to these questions lie along the three dimensions of agility—data, methodology, and the ability to retool program theory.

As we delve into the intricacies of agile evaluation, it is worth keeping in mind what part of the evaluation business I am in. Put overly simply, evaluators can try to answer one of two questions: (1) How can I provide information to help planners innovate in constructive ways as needs and circumstances evolve? and (2) How can I provide information to help planners know how well their predetermined decisions are working? Let's leave aside the philosophical question of whether any program can ever have enough stability to be worthy of a consistent evaluation plan over time, and assume that, depending on their predilections and funding opportunities, evaluators can address either question. Evaluators who address the first question need approaches such as those advocated by Patton (2010), who advances a developmental evaluation methodology. Agility is needed when there is a reasonable amount of program stability and goal consistency over time.

DATA

The data available to an evaluation define the boundaries of what can ultimately be said about the program. The choices are critical. To all the reasons for choosing one dataset over another, it is useful to add the potential for dealing with surprise. I never assume that data that are useful for assessing stated purposes of a program will be applicable to assessing changing circumstances. Foresight is needed because often choices about data are locked in early in an evaluation life cycle, and once made are difficult to change. For instance, consider three scenarios where changes in data collection plans may be difficult, expensive, and time consuming: (1) custom scales need to be developed and validated; (2) gatekeeper approval is required (e.g., the Office of Management and Budget, the Air Force Survey Office, the Human Resources department of a large corporation); and (3) data collection requires custom programming for access to a database or integration across multiple databases. Generalizing from these examples, we can identify two aspects of data that need to be considered: (1) characteristics of the data itself and (2) processes for data acquisition.

The primary issue with the data itself is whether we can find high-quality substitutes if the data we planned on getting prove to be unavailable. The pillars of quality are the traditional criteria—reliability, validity, and generalizability for quantitative measures; and credibility, transferability, dependability, and confirmability for qualitative measures (Patton, 2002). But what other considerations are important? I see three questions that must be asked as we vet data options:

1. Are substitutions available? For instance, compare an evaluation that relied on a carefully validated scale, to one in which it were possible to substitute "total cost" for "direct cost."

2. Are alternate means of collecting the data acceptable? For instance, an evaluation that required evaluation of students' interest in particular course modules might substitute interviews for direct classroom observation.

3. If substitutes are acceptable, is it practical to use them?

To illustrate, consider an evaluation that relied on training teachers to make particular kinds of observations about their students' behavior. Once that training is done and teachers have incorporated the observations into their routine work life, it would be difficult to retrain them to make different kinds of observations. Or what if a lengthy Office of Management and Budget approval process resulted in permission to obtain particular data, from a defined sample, in particular ways, with a predetermined burden on responses?

Some of these problems are illustrated in the cases. Consider Case 8 (p. 231). There, an initial objective of the evaluation was to aggregate data across different college access assistance programs. An implicit assumption was that the various programs had client tracking data that could be aggregated across programs, thus allowing an overall assessment. When it turned out that the tracking systems (such as they were) could not be integrated, that entire objective of the evaluation had to be changed. Compare this situation with Case 13 (p. 253), in which evaluators were able to use data from a clinical records system when a change in service requirements eliminated a follow-up interview that was also used to collect evaluation data. That was a good example of substitution.

Both the nature of data and the social setting in which the data acquisition is embedded can combine to make it very difficult to change data collection plans once they are set in place. For these reasons it may be desirable to establish data plans that are inherently flexible, that is, evaluation plans in which: (1) the switching costs from one dataset to another are low, and (2) making the switch does not harm the intent of the evaluation. Flexibility is high when development costs for new data, data collection burdens, and switching time are all low.

By "development cost" I mean the cost of determining what data to collect, constructing data collection instruments, and implementing collection procedures. Costs are high when evaluators cannot reuse existing instruments and procedures. The most obvious case of high cost is constructing and testing of new scales and questionnaires. But costs for archival data can be high as well. For instance, it can take a great deal of expertise, time, and money to answer six technical questions about data that reside in information technology (IT) systems.

1. What do data fields really mean? (Names can be ambiguous and code books incomplete.)
2. Is it possible to index data across files and systems?
3. Do the data actually indicate the constructs of interest to evaluators?
4. Have the definitions of data fields changed over time?
5. How far back can the data be retrieved?
6. How accurate is the information?

In addition to these technical problems, information in data systems can be sensitive because of privacy concerns or because they touch on topics such as an organization's costs and performance. Thus even getting to the point of being able to investigate the value of information in a database may require extended negotiations with data owners.

"Burden" refers to the amount of work needed to collect data. While "burden" can be defined as total work for the evaluation team plus program staff, I tend to discount the portion attributed to the evaluators. I have two reasons for this. First, I see it as the evaluators' job to make sure that data get collected. I don't mind adding to their workload, but I find it problematic to divert service providers and managers from doing their routine work. Second, any added effort imposed on program staff has costs beyond the actual time spent because the added effort may sour the relationship between evaluators and staff, thus causing all manner of problems as the evaluation proceeds.

"Switching time" is the calendar time needed to move from collecting one dataset to another. The importance of "switching time" depends on the width of the windows of opportunity that are available for collecting data. To illustrate, consider two versions of a health care service outcome quality evaluation, one of which relied on clinical records, and the other of which relied on patients' opinions immediately after treatment. What would happen if a problem arose in collecting data in each scenario? Supposing a data field denoting the date of entry into treatment was discovered to be unreliable? It is not clear from the information I have given whether the evaluators could combine other data fields to make up for this deficiency. It is clear, however, that taking the time to figure it out would not harm the evaluation because whatever data were available would continue to be available as the evaluators worked out solutions. The data are not time sensitive. The evaluation that relied on patients' opinions at the end of treatment, however, is extremely vulnerable to any delay in timing the interviews to the conclusion of treatment. Opinions are ephemeral. If the interview were found to be wanting and had to be redesigned and validated, a great deal of outcome data would be lost.

As another example, imagine two versions of an evaluation of a new school curriculum—one that relied on routinely administered tests, and one that relied on a checklist of teachers' observations that is filled out at the end of the school year. Here, too, there is a big difference in the time sensitivity of establishing data collection routines. If anything, the education scenario is even worse than the health example because patients are continually beginning and ending treatment at different times. A delay in developing a new scale may require missing some patients, but it would not lead to missing them all. In the educational case there is only a single window of opportunity for data collection—the end of the school year. If that opportunity were missed, a large percentage of the needed data would be lost.

AGILE METHODOLOGY

By "methodology" I mean the logic in which observations are embedded. Whether the data are quantitative or qualitative, some such logic is needed to interpret the data. By "agile" I mean the ability to change quickly in the face of new circumstances. With respect to dealing with surprise, agile methodology either employs an analysis logic that can encompass a wide range of evaluation needs, or has an organizational structure that can be reconfigured to meet new needs, or both.

I regard evaluation as an organizational entity—a collection of processes, resources, and structures constructed in a manner that allows both a logic of analysis to exist and a data acquisition mechanism to feed the analysis. Looked at in this way, part of agility is the ability to change the organizational nature of an evaluation. From the point of view of agility, the worst case would be a narrow analysis logic coupled with an evaluation structure that was difficult to change. To illustrate how these concepts may play out, let's go back to the scenario in Figure 5.1 and inspect what might happen at different points in the evaluation life cycle. In that scenario a program that began as a test of training managers to interact with workers about issues of safety morphed into a program that had two effects on the managers. First, it did indeed teach them how to talk to workers about safety. But it also gave the managers a chance to discuss safety with each other, thus leading to safety changes that had nothing to do with their conversations with the labor force.

What might the evaluation have looked like as designed for the original program? Without designing the entire evaluation, some of its elements may well be as shown in Table 6.1. Elements of the design (as shown in the rows of the table) vary considerably with respect to their agility. Let's look at three levels: (1) inflexible, (2) some malleability, and (3) flexible.

TABLE 6.1. Rigid and Agile Elements of the Training Program Depicted in Figure 5.1

Data: Formative	Data: Summative	Design	Implications for Agility
1 Pretested, validated assessment of managers' beliefs about workers and safety; used to assess quality of training		Two administrations, at beginning and end of training	• Development time, cost, and access to test populations make it difficult to change instrument. • Timing of administration to training schedule is critical to determine pre–post change due to training as opposed to events that may transpire after training.
2 Semistructured questions used to explain why managers are or are not changing their views		One administration about halfway through training; used to determine how training may be improved	• Minimal development time and effort needed to determine questions. • To be useful for improving training, data must be collected not too far past the midway point. But some variation earlier or later is acceptable.
3	Pretested, validated scales to measure safety culture, one of the primary intended outcomes	Three administrations, at start of training, 6 months and 1 year after end of training, and 6 months after training	• Development time, cost, and access to test populations make it difficult to change instrument. • First two administrations must be tightly synchronized with training schedule. Third administration can be moved somewhat earlier or later.
4	Interviews with employees when safety issues arise; used to explain why manager behavior affected safety behavior	Keyed to occurrence of accidents	• Minimal development time and effort needed to determine questions. • Very tight synchronization with accident is critical.
5	Safety and accident statistics	Retrieved from company IT system	• Available any time during the evaluation. • No tight coordination with training or accidents required.
6		*Design 1:* Control groups using parts of company not involved in program	• Difficult to implement. Considerable negotiation and justification needed.
7		*Design 2:* Historical time series data of safety and accident trends	• Available from IT systems. Available any time during the evaluation.

Inflexible Design Elements

Using carefully validated questionnaires precisely at the beginning and ending of training (row 1) is a brittle tactic. Because it would take time to revise the instrument, any effort to do so would risk missing the narrow time constraints during which the data needed to be collected. Interviews whose timing is tightly connected to the occurrence of accidents (row 4 of Table 6.1) is also problematic because people's recollections are ephemeral, and knowing why people thought they acted as they did is an important part of assessing program outcome.

Malleable Design Elements

Contrast these evaluation elements above with the safety culture measures that are taken at the start of training, and then 6 and 12 months after the training (row 3 of Table 6.1). Agility here is still restricted because it would take time to change the instruments and because the first administration does have to be tightly coordinated with the beginning of training. Furthermore, losing the initial data would inhibit our ability to make causal inference. On the other hand, the 6-month delay in the second test does provide some room to maneuver. If reasons were compelling enough, the time could be used to redesign the culture scales. (It might not even matter that much if the 6-month administration slipped a bit.) Not having baseline data would be troubling, but the ability to track change between 6 and 12 months after the program could contribute to conclusions about the program's effectiveness.

Flexible Design Elements

The comparisons identified in rows 6 and 7 combine to offer quite a bit of latitude with respect to changes in the design. Because causal inference comes both from control groups and historical data, losing either one might not be catastrophic. (Of course, this would not keep me from fighting tooth and nail to keep both.) This redundancy makes the design inherently agile. Also data that can be retrieved from IT systems has minimal dependence on time frames. Thus if problems with access or data integrity were encountered, the time might be available to find alternate ways of working with the data.

As the above discussion implies, evaluations are not categorically "agile" or "not agile." Rather, different elements of an evaluation have different degrees of agility. The real question is whether enough of the design is agile enough to allow adaptation to unforeseen circumstance. By thinking of evaluation in this way we will be led to deliberate efforts at identifying specific aspects of our evaluations that affect their agility. We could work at making our designs more, rather than less, agile. Or at least, we would enter the evaluation with our eyes open to the risks. How can we make these assessments? By trying to answer three questions about any design we consider: (1) What are the dependencies? (2) What are the boundaries in the innovation being evaluated? and (3) How much can evaluation activities be partitioned? These three questions are not truly independent and separate, but for the sake of exposition it is helpful to discuss them as if they were.

Dependencies

Some evaluation plans are more forgiving than others with respect to how a change in any one element affects the overall functioning of the plan. (This is true of all systems, but this book is about evaluation.) Evaluations that consist of many close dependencies are not agile because too much change would take place if any one part of the plan were modified to deal with an unanticipated circumstance.

When I devise evaluation plans I find it useful to think in terms of sequencing and cross-linkage timing. *Sequencing* comes down to the question of how many critical path activities are in the evaluation and the length of the critical path.[1] For example, if interviews were necessary to get the material needed to develop a questionnaire, the interview task would be on the critical path for questionnaire development. The greater the number of critical path activities, the harder it would be to change any one activity to meet an unexpected need. To extend the previous example, imagine that the surveys were needed to collect baseline data, and that the baseline data were needed to execute an important pre–post analysis. The pre–post analysis would depend on three activities (interviews, surveys, baseline data), each of which depends on one of the others. Contrast this scenario to one in which the surveys were needed to get a contextual understanding of the setting where an evaluation was taking place, and pre–post comparisons came from routinely collected data in information systems. The interviews are on the critical path of the survey, and access to records is on the critical path to the pre–post comparison. But if either the interviews or the data access were compromised, part of the evaluation could still be carried out. This lack of dependency means that if unforeseen circumstances warranted a change in the interviews (e.g., content, timing, respondent population), that part of the evaluation could be changed without spoiling the part of the evaluation that depended on the pre–post analysis.

Case 4 (p. 210) is a good example of dependencies that can be problematic. That scenario played out in a school system and required that data be collected from the beginning of the school year to the end. Thus a full test of the intervention required the introduction of the innovation and the beginning of data collection to occur early in the term. Critical aspects of that program were to provide students with laptop computers and teachers with the professional development they needed to help the students work with the computers. "Lead teachers" were assigned to provide professional development and to do classroom observations. All of these activities had to be finely timed. If the timing were missed a great deal of data would be lost because if observers were not in place, observation of a whole classroom would be lost. Case 6 (p. 219) is another example. There, the pre–post design depended on HIV services being provided according to a very specific schedule— three sessions, one per week, for 3 weeks. When client demand resulted in a change to that schedule, planned comparisons in the evaluation design could not be carried out. Both of these examples involve dependency between the way the program was carried out and the way the evaluation was carried out.

Not all problems with dependencies hinge on critical path activities. The problem may simply be a function of how many noncritical path *linkages* are in the evaluation plan.[2] Even without a critical path, changing one element of an evaluation may require time, effort, and thought to rejigger the others. To illustrate, let's revisit the critical path described above: interviews → questionnaire → baseline data → pre–post comparison. Imagine what might happen if at about the time of baseline data collection, evaluators suspected that the program may have some outcomes that were not originally considered. Suppose that they could go back and do more interviews and redesign the questionnaire in order to expand the pre–post comparisons that could be made. They may have the time and money to do it, but would they? Doing so would consume resources that might be spent in other ways and cause delay that might narrow windows of opportunity for executing other tasks, thus making the evaluation vulnerable to other unforeseen circumstances.

Boundaries

The borders of the organizational setting in which an innovation is being tested are one kind of boundary that affects agility. Any design requiring a control group, for instance, requires crossing such a boundary. Case 11 (p. 244) illustrates one aspect of this kind of problem. That case was an evaluation of a central heating assistance program for households that did not already have central heating. As the program progressed, households in the control group found other ways to acquire central heating, thus contaminating the experimental–control comparison.

Case 11 (p. 244) is an example of problems that involved the maintenance of boundaries. Another type of boundary problem involves negotiating across boundaries. To illustrate, imagine an evaluation that required obtaining comparison group data from departments in a company that would not directly benefit either from the innovation being tested or the knowledge that derived from the evaluation. The risk of relying on groups like this depends on how distant they are from the group using the innovation, the data burden, and the sensitivity of the data. To illustrate, compare two possibilities. In the first scenario, all the control and experimental departments have a common leader, the data come from information systems (no burden on the departments), and the topic is not sensitive. In the second scenario the groups are far removed from each other organizationally, data collection requires taking people's time, and the subject is touchy. Negotiating agreements in the second scenario would be much more difficult and much less certain than it would be in the first.

To complicate matters, once these kinds of agreements are established, effort is needed to nurture and maintain them over time. Agreements of this kind are not instantiated in formal organizational process, culture, or structure. Rather, they come together at particular times, among particular people, for context-specific reasons. Maintaining agreements reached like that cannot be left to chance.

Partition

I find it useful to think of partitioning in two ways. First, there is the idea of partitioning the evaluation itself, that is, of breaking it into phases, each of which can inform the one succeeding. These are situations in which the breaks in the parts of the evaluation can be thought of as being for the convenience of the evaluator and as a tactic for quality assurance. Aside from having to meet an overall deadline, the break points are not closely keyed to critical events in the program that is being evaluated. The cases amassed in this book are replete with this kind of compartmentalization. Well they should be, because no complicated undertaking can be successful without discrete tasks, milestones, and sequences. Case 2 (p. 200) went through a task of early negotiation with sponsors about scope. Case 5 (p. 214) began with a preliminary historical analysis of school performance in order to estimate sample sizes. Prior to implementing a training program, Case 9 (p. 235) tested the baseline skills of participants to check on the suitability of the training. Case 10 (p. 241) used interviews to develop a survey, and the survey to drive another round of focus groups. Case 12 (p. 249) used a survey to assess whether physicians would be willing to participate in an innovative substance abuse prevention program.

To all the reasons why evaluation plans are phased in this manner, another could be added, that is, as a step in the process that increases the capacity of the evaluation to adapt to new circumstances. To illustrate, let's revisit the evaluation design shown in Figure 5.1 and Table 6.1. The evaluation plan calls for semistructured interviews to get information on why managers are changing their views on safety improvement. It calls for these interviews to take place once, about halfway through the training program. This kind of interview schedule is an entirely reasonable step, but it could be modified for the sake of improving agility. The sample could be split, with half the managers interviewed earlier, and half shortly after the training concluded.[3] There is a downside to either of these plans. Presumably, the original plan was developed because the evaluators had good reason to want as much information as possible midway through the training. The new plan decreases that data, and it probably also complicates the evaluators' scheduling logistics. But it does have the advantage of providing a previously unavailable opportunity to determine whether the program is unfolding according to plan.

Another aspect of the evaluation in Figure 5.1 and Table 6.1 is the extraction of outcome data from the company's IT systems. Once obtained, this data could be analyzed at whatever interval made sense for the time series analysis. But the plan says nothing about how often the data are downloaded. From a strictly logical point of view it would be fine to get all the data toward the end of the evaluation. To support agility, however, it might make sense to download the data at several different times in order to get a sense as to whether unexpectedly large or small changes are taking place. As with the interviews, there are disadvantages to too many downloads. Each requires an analysis in its own right, and each may be an extra task for the company's IT staff. Thus for both the interviews and the data downloads there are pros and cons to various data collection approaches. What I am advocating is that when these decisions are made, the contribution of the various options to support agility should be explicitly considered.

The second approach to partitioning an evaluation comes into play when the innovation being evaluated can be conceptualized as a series of micro-level changes, each of which must succeed for the overall innovation to be successful. (Program planners themselves often recognize this, but it is also possible for evaluators to help them to see it by means of logic modeling and related exercises.) In situations such as these, evaluation is inherently agile because it consists of a series of micro-level studies keyed to the program phases. When done this way, the structure of the evaluation echoes the worldview of continuous improvement (CI; e.g., Lean Six Sigma, Theory of Constraints).

It is certainly possible to find discussions of CI in the evaluation literature, but those discussions are not as numerous or well developed as I think they should be. A search of evaluation journals finds quite a few articles that advocate for a continuous improvement approach to evaluation, but only a small number actually draw on the tools and methodologies that come out of the continuous improvement tradition (Green, 1999; Morell, 2000; Posavac, 1995). It is difficult to find evaluation articles that deal with the application of tools such as benchmarking, value stream mapping, root cause diagrams, control charting, and quality function deployment, to name just a few. But most important is the lack of discussion about the logic of CI analysis and how that logic fits with the logic that evaluators traditionally employ in their methodologies. In fact, the two logics are highly compatible, and from the point of view of dealing with surprise, the logic of CI has some particularly appealing features. That logic is embodied in the term "continuous improvement"—it is a term that implies that in order to meet some overall objective it is necessary to monitor and react to a never-ending flow of change; that is, it will always be necessary to adjust to new circumstances that intercede between what is happening now and what is needed to attain a long-term objective. In a sense, one can look at the CI approach as a type of emergent evaluation design in that successive changes in the design are not planned in advance. Rather, it is assumed that the evaluation design will be made known as the program, the evaluation, and the interaction between the two develop over time. (While some aspects of CI are valuable in evaluation, I do not mean to imply that the entire approach should be adopted whole cloth.) Other important aspects of CI include a focus on reducing "waste" (a technical term having to do with whether an activity adds value to an end product) and a focus on improving standard processes. These might sometimes be useful in evaluation, but the overall emphasis on efficiency and standardization does not serve the purpose of much evaluation, which is to promote the process of innovation.

As with all tactics I have suggested, CI has its limitations for helping evaluators deal with surprise. It is not useful in cases of long latencies between program action and impact, or when an external assessment of a program is required, or when tight cooperation between program and evaluation staff is not practical or desirable. But tight coordination between evaluator and program staff is common in our field, and rapid feedback is often appropriate. In these cases CI methods are useful to deal with surprise because the essential logic of CI is to rapidly respond to emerging trends. As a methodology, CI is inherently agile.

Collective Treatment of Dependencies, Boundaries, and Partitioning

While it may be useful for the purposes of explanation to discuss dependencies, boundaries, and partitioning separately, actual design for agility must consider these topics jointly. For instance, the notion of critical and noncritical path activities (a dependency issue) is closely tied to what elements of an evaluation can be partitioned, because as projects are divided into smaller discrete components, there is greater concern about dependencies among the components. As another example, any plan to stagger treatment as a way of having control–experimental comparisons (a boundary issue) is likely to have implications for the timing of data collection, which is a dependency consideration.

RETOOLING PROGRAM THEORY[4]

The arguments presented above imply that there is a time at the beginning of an evaluation when all efforts should be made to anticipate as much of the "foreseeable" as possible, and that thereafter, effort should be focused on early detection of surprise and adaptation to it. In large measure this is a productive view because so many fundamental decisions are made early on. Without this view, one is guaranteed to get into trouble. However, a second view can be useful as well. In this other view the "beginning" is a moving target. At any time during an evaluation one can think about opportunities to retool it. In this view there is always some leeway to think in terms of the continuum of foreseeable to unforeseeable and make adjustments.

Of course, this approach has severe limits. First, choice does decline along the evaluation life cycle. Evaluators do have more choice when data collection is just beginning than they do after all data are collected and stakeholders' expectations are firmly set. Second, too much change will result in delay and cost, which will make it impossible to complete any evaluation. Third, ethical issues may exist. What should be evaluated—the program as originally designed, or the program as is? The answer depends on contract provisions and stakeholder needs. Sometimes the message to evaluators is: "We are testing model X but we really want to know if what we are doing is working, whatever that turns out to be down the road." Sometimes the message is: "We want to know if X is working."

Assuming that it is possible and ethical to redesign an evaluation, *how might it be done efficiently?* I have found it extremely useful to involve stakeholders in a two-stage logic modeling exercise (see note 1 on p. 99). The first step is retrospective. Here, we revisit the current status of the program and redesign the logic model to fit the program theory as it is actually operating. As a minimum, comparison between the original and new models provides extremely useful evaluation information. It also provides a common understanding to take stock of how the program is likely to unfold in the future. If the stars align during this kind of exercise, one can almost think in terms of a new beginning for the evaluation.

To illustrate the value of revisiting logic models, recall the example in Figure 4.1. That example began with a truly simple logic model for an industrial safety program: Managers are trained to work at improving safety. Labor perceives managers' behavior and acts accordingly. As a result of change by labor, safety improves. There is a feedback loop between safety and managers' behavior as the managers perceive that their efforts are bearing fruit. The example then posed three variations: (1) latency periods between the program elements change; (2) the training program turns out to have value not only because of the training, but also because it gives managers a chance to interact with each other; and (3) the company implements an enterprisewide comprehensive Six Sigma program and a new discipline policy, both of which affect managers' behavior and safety improvement. What might happen if periodic exercises in logic model revision revealed these complications as they arose after the training program was launched?

If a revised logic model picked up on these changes, what might evaluators do? They might change their timing for measuring changes in safety. They might work with stakeholders to alter expectations about when change would occur. They might change their analysis of sustainability by adding linkages among related activities. They might add to their outcome measures by including assessment of the managers' training on related programs. Knowledge of the parallel safety programs might prompt evaluators to reassess the value of different comparison groups and time series analyses based on when each program was implemented in which location. Evaluators might conclude that the evaluation as planned was hopelessly contaminated by the new programs, thus requiring a reconceptualization of the evaluation, changing it from a focused assessment of a single well-defined intervention to a black-box assessment of the combined impact of a group of related interacting innovations. In essence, by revisiting the logic model, opportunity arises to reassess how a program is operating, what is affecting its development, what needs to be measured, and what designs are needed to make sense of that measurement. As these realizations dawn, a new range of foreseeable consequences come into view, and detection plans for new sets of unforeseeable change can be laid.

In addition to improving the technical aspects of evaluation, revisiting the logic model also serves the needs of knowledge use. It serves those needs because the act of revisiting the model facilitates a collaboration between evaluators and stakeholders that focuses attention on evaluation findings. My experience is that periodic reassessment of logic models can be built into evaluation project plans. It works particularly well to schedule these events to coincide with formal milestones and phases, for example, beginning of new phases in a program, submission of interim evaluation reports, strategic planning, or budget reviews.

Finally, let us keep in mind that revisiting logic models is a ploy, but not a requirement for reassessing an evaluation methodology.

There may be perfectly sound reasons not to use a logic model, but even then, milestones or interim analyses in an evaluation project plan can be perfectly good platforms for reviewing the adequacy of a methodology in light of current circumstances and making appropriate changes.

AGILITY AND STAKEHOLDER NEEDS

Agility must be considered in light of stakeholders' requirements. It is entirely possible (indeed, it is likely) that too much agility will produce an evaluation that will not give stakeholders what they need to support their own decision making and their accountability to others. For instance, specific control groups or well-developed scales may be critical in particular situations. It might be easy enough to design an evaluation that did not use those groups and scales, but it may be difficult or impossible to do so while providing the information needed to support a decision-making process.

The entire discussion in this chapter has treated "agility" as if it only depended on various aspects of methodology. In fact, the question of whether an evaluation is agile also depends very much on both the context in which the evaluation is being carried out and the nature of the program being evaluated. These relationships are tightly related to assessment of unintended consequences of program action. I return to them in Chapter 11, which is devoted to those cases that exhibited unintended consequences.

IN SUM

Despite all our efforts to anticipate and minimize surprise, some surprise is inevitable because programs and evaluations are embedded in complex systems. Therefore, when we develop our evaluation plans, one of the characteristics to consider is agility, that is, the capacity of an evaluation to change to meet circumstances. Three topics are important when thinking about agility: (1) data, (2) design, and (3) program theory.

• *Data:* Efforts to make designs agile include choices about the sources of data with respect to (1) development cost for new data sources, (2) data collection burden, and (3) switching time from one data source to another.

- *Design:* Determinants of a design's agility are (1) the richness of dependencies among different aspects of the design, (2) the number of organizational boundaries that need to be crossed to conduct an evaluation, and (3) the extent to which an evaluation design can be partitioned.

- *Program theory:* The greater the possibility to revise program theory in light of new circumstances, the greater the opportunity to change an evaluation design.

While it is useful to think of each of all these aspects of agility separately, each characteristic of agility can affect the others. Thus design for agility requires an integrated approach that considers the unique and common effect of data, design, and program theory. Finally, it is important to consider the effect of agility on meeting stakeholder needs. Depending on circumstances, greater agility can either support or inhibit the potential of an evaluation to meet those needs.

A complete understanding of agility must consider relationships among three aspects of evaluation—methodology, program context, and the program being evaluated. These relationships are closely bound to the matter of evaluating unintended consequences of program action, and are dealt with in Chapter 12.

NOTES

1. Technically, a critical path is defined as the "longest sequence of activities in a project plan which must be completed on time for the project to complete on due date. An activity on the critical path cannot be started until its predecessor activity is complete; if it is delayed for a day, the entire project will be delayed for a day unless the activity following the delayed activity is completed a day earlier" (*www.businessdictionary.com/definition/critical-path.html*).

2. Rather than "dependency" one can think in terms of cross-linkages. In system terms rich cross-linkages are not an unalloyed evil. Linkages can support each other and thus make a system resistant to shocks. In the case of evaluation designs, however, I believe that cross-linkages are much more likely to be problematic. Maybe I take this view because in my personal experience it is too easy and too common for events to occur that challenge, rather than support, the ability to execute an evaluation according to plan.

3. There is always the possibility of not splitting the sample and collecting all the data twice. But it is more interesting, and probably more realistic, to assume that constraints are operating to preclude this. Perhaps there are cost issues, or limits on the evaluators' time, or worry about burden on respondents.

4. Program theory is "the set of assumptions about the manner in which the program relates to the social benefits it is expected to produce and the strategy and tactics the program has adopted to achieve its goals and objectives" (*www.epa.gov/evaluate/glossary/p-esd.htm*).

Chapter 7

How Much Is Too Much?

APPRECIATING TRADE-OFFS
AND MANAGING THE BALANCE

There is an assumption in most of the tactics discussed previously that more is better. More theory, more environmental scanning, more monitoring, more data, more intermediate outcomes, more adaptation to change—the more of these we have, the greater will be our ability to contend with surprise in evaluation. This assumption is true, but only up to a point. As Mathie and Greene (1997) point out in their case studies of diversity in participatory evaluation, "too much diversity may stall or subvert the transformative aims of participatory evaluation because time and resources are rarely available to work through and resolve the complex range of voices and perspectives." What is true about participatory evaluation is true of all evaluation. Any tactic that can be invoked to minimize the impact of surprise on an evaluation carries the risk of making things worse.

Another assumption I have made is that sometimes less is better; that is, that if we limit time frames along conceptual and temporal dimensions, we will do better evaluation by decreasing the likelihood of surprise. This assumption is also true, but only up to a point. The more we limit our scope, the less we can tell decision makers and stakeholders. At some point we reach the boundary of evaluations that are executed according to plan, are valid, and yet are useless.

The point at which more, or less, becomes counterproductive can only be learned through experience. No formula can be specified. The situation is akin to exercising clinical judgment. Repeated practice and application of principle leads to decision making that to outsiders may appear effortless and devoid of logic, but which actually combine principle and expertise in ways that lead to wise choices.

To illustrate the kinds of judgments that have to be made, let's play out a seemingly simple scenario of an evaluation that had to rely on the cooperation of a program's staff to fill out questionnaires describing their activities and the results of 6- and 12-month posttreatment follow-ups with clients. It is plausible that despite the assurance of the evaluation's funders and the program's administrators, staff might resist filling out what they saw as onerous forms that did not contribute to service quality. What choices does the evaluation team have if they suspected that this problem might arise? They might eliminate the requirement for filling out forms for one of the follow-ups. Eliminating the follow-up data recording would lower the burden on staff, but would it decrease the burden enough to assure their cooperation? The answer is by no means obvious. In any case, would eliminating follow-up data trivialize the evaluation? Quite possibly.

A different approach that the evaluators might take would be to dispense with all the forms in favor of reliance on data from the program's information systems. Exclusive reliance on information systems might work, but this, in turn, raises a host of other pitfalls that would need to be considered. As with promises about the cooperation from staff, there is ample reason to suspect assurances from funders and administrators about the quality of data systems. For instance, data field definitions may have changed over time, accuracy may differ across evaluation sites, indices to link service recipients with services may be imprecise, the ability to retrieve data from past years may be limited, system documentation may be missing, system architecture may limit the ability to execute complicated queries, or experts who understand the system might have gone on to other jobs. In short, it would be a considerable effort to vet the information system to make sure it met the needs of the evaluation.

Suppose the evaluation team suspected these problems, but did not have the time, resources, or local knowledge needed to do anything but a cursory job of checking. If this were the case, the evaluation team might opt for redundancy by constructing an evaluation that could use either staff surveys, or the information system, or both. Using both is appealing. First, it buffers against problems with either information source. Second, each source is likely to produce some information the other won't, so the range of information for the evaluation would increase. Finally, for those cases where the information overlaps, two separate measures would provide opportunity to check on reliability and validity.

All very nice, but there are costs to using the two data sources. It would take longer to design and implement the evaluation. Conducting the evaluation would be more expensive. A greater diversity of expertise may be needed on the evaluation team. Maintaining the integrity of the evaluation design over time would be more difficult. Relations with a greater number of program staff (service delivery personnel and information managers) would be required.

This example illustrates two aspects of the problem. First, there is the additive problem of resources. More complicated evaluations require more people, more money, more time, and more expertise. But there may also be nonlinear complications that, like complicated programs, cannot be predicted in advance. For instance, more management resources invested in maintaining the integrity of the design might reduce the hours that technical experts could put into actually doing the evaluation work. One can only guess at all the problems that might crop up if the structure of design were maintained, but the intellectual quality of the work diminished even slightly, but continually, over the entire life cycle of the evaluation.

A FRAMEWORK FOR APPRECIATING DESIGN TRADE-OFFS

While there is no formula for making judgments about how elaborate or complicated an evaluation plan should be, there are guidelines. The essence of the challenge is reflected in the relationships depicted in Figure 7.1.

The rectangles on the top row indicate that many of the suggestions proposed in this book can increase the time it takes to do an evaluation, the cost of the evaluation, or the complexity of the evaluation. By "time" I mean the length of time from the beginning of a task (or an entire evaluation) to the end. By "resources" I mean whatever combination of money, labor hours, and expertise is needed to conduct an evaluation. By "complexity" I mean the number of groups that have to be dealt with, measures used, entities that have to be coordinated, relationships that have to be analyzed, bodies of knowledge that have

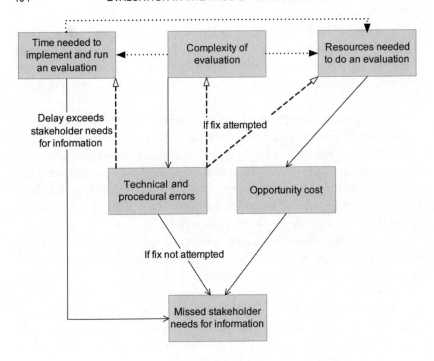

FIGURE 7.1. Trade-offs among tactics for dealing with surprise.

to be considered, and the linkages among them. The bottom row of Figure 7.1 represents the problem evaluators always try to avoid—not meeting stakeholder needs. What happens in between? The answer is represented by the three types of arrows in the figure. Black arrows with open arrowheads indicate the "flow-down" from time, complexity, and resources to the ultimate problem of not meeting stakeholder needs. Dashed arrows with closed white arrowheads indicate feedback processes as one moves from the top to the bottom of the figure. Dotted arrows with closed black arrowheads indicate interactions among time, complexity, and resources.

Any change in time, complexity, or resources has the potential to affect some of the others. Anything that makes an evaluation more complex is likely to increase either the time, or the resources, or both. Increases in time are likely to increase cost because projects need continual maintenance, and will thus consume resources even if the actual evaluation work remains unchanged. Furthermore, longer time lines increase the possibility that unexpected events will arise that demand attention. (See the discussion surrounding Figure 4.1.) One might try to throw enough resources at the work so that it can all be done in the original time frame, but such efforts might increase complexity by tightening the linkages among elements of the evaluation, thereby increasing the likelihood of errors that will cascade through the system.

What might happen if increases in time, complexity, or resources did occur? The biggest problem with increasing time is the risk of not meeting stakeholders' windows of opportunities for using evaluation results. The main problem with increasing complexity is an increased chance of making some kind of technical or procedural error, that is, an error of omission or commission in some aspect of the evaluation's methodology or project execution. Any resources diverted to tactics for dealing with surprise divert resources from other evaluation objectives, thus incurring opportunity costs. Perverse feedback is possible. Any effort to deal with a new technical or procedural problem has the potential to increase some combination of time, complexity, and resource use. Finally, the combined effects of error that may build up, or of missed opportunity costs, can have the consequence of not fulfilling stakeholders' needs for information. Let's explore how these dynamics might play out with respect to the tactics for dealing with surprise that I have been advocating in the previous chapters. As we work through the discussion to come, keeping an eye on Table 7.1 might be helpful. It summarizes my explanation of Figure 7.1.

Evaluation gets more complicated, more difficult to implement, harder to maintain, and more expensive as it tries to incorporate additional theoretical perspectives, domains of expertise, and measures. For instance, depending on the underlying theory or domain of expertise, there may be good reasons to add different types of comparison groups or sets of measures. But with each addition comes the added work of eliciting cooperation, maintaining that cooperation, developing measures, and acquiring data. Furthermore, as cost and complexity increase there will be a corresponding decrease in ability to change the evaluation in light of truly unforeseen events. As the planning gets more complicated, the design becomes more brittle because there will be more to coordinate, tighter linkages, and more dependencies. At some point, efforts to buffer against surprise become counterproductive.

I claimed that adding intermediate measures can buffer against surprise. This is true, but the tactic carries its own risks. With respect to intermediate outcomes in a logic model, each addition increases

TABLE 7.1. Summary of Trade-Offs among Tactics for Dealing with Surprise

Element in Figure 7.1	Definition
Time	Elapsed time from the beginning to the end of an evaluation task or the evaluation as a whole
Resources	Whatever combination of money, labor hours, and expertise are needed to conduct an evaluation
Complexity	Number of groups, measures used, entities to be coordinated, relationships to analyze, bodies of knowledge to be considered, and the linkages among them
Technical/procedural error	Error of omission or commission in evaluation methodology or project execution
Opportunity cost	Loss of benefit that could have been obtained had resources not been consumed elsewhere
————⟶	Flow-down from time, complexity, and resources to the ultimate problem of not meeting stakeholder needs
— — ⟶	Feedback process to upper levels of Figure 7.1 as one moves from time, resources, and complexity to missed stakeholder needs
·················▶	Interactions among time, complexity, and resources

the chance for error. After all, each element in the model represents a hypothesis about relationships. We might be wrong, and the greater the number of hypotheses, the greater the chance for error. Also, depending on the granularity of observation, one can continually increase events along the chain to as many elements as one wishes. Referring again to Figure 4.1, might we want to add a measurement of workers' opinions as they observe the behavior of managers? Doing so might help us with measuring short-term change, but do we really believe that aggregating personal belief equates to change in organizational culture? The answer has both theoretical and practical dimensions. The theoretical problem is as stated earlier. Each addition adds a hypothesis that could be wrong. On a practical level, each time an element is added to the causal chain, the cost and complexity of the evaluation increase. Increased cost will require trade-offs that would slight other aspects of the evaluation.

Complexity increases the chance that something will go awry. To continue the previous example, what would be the implications of adding measures of workers' internal psychological states? Instruments would have to be developed and tested. Risk of evaluation resistance might increase. The evaluation would become more intrusive. Costs would increase or resources intended for other aspects of the evaluation would be diverted. Program theory would assert that internal psychological states determine behavior.

Scanning for change is critical, but this too can be problematic. Spending too much time scouting for looming change can cause three difficulties. One problem is simply the time and effort expended. Scouting requires asking stakeholders to make the effort to provide information. Their efforts might also be needed to revise logic models, advocate for evaluation, access data, assist with data interpretation, and myriad other tasks. There is only so much one can ask of those people. The second problem is a consequence of having successfully obtained information. As information accumulates from the scouting exercise, so too will plausible alternate trajectories for how the program and the evaluation may develop. The greater the number of alternate futures that must be considered, the harder the task of making decisions will be. Too much choice is not always a good thing. Finally, success can breed its own destruction. Suppose data were collected and correct decisions were made about how to change the evaluation. Change drives up cost, delays the delivery of findings, and confuses stakeholders' expectations. None of this bodes well for a successful evaluation.

MAXIMIZING CHOICE, MINIMIZING RISK

Many of the tactics for dealing with surprise that I have proposed involve either changing how an evaluation is managed, or how information is obtained, or both. While the outputs of these activities are technical aspects of evaluation, the activities themselves rely on social interaction. For instance, revising logic models requires working with stakeholders. Changing an evaluation's time frame requires negotiation with the sponsors. Adding a new measure may require cooperation from program staff, their managers, or data owners. Scanning for environmental changes may require developing relations with a new group of key informants. All of this activity can be burdensome. What's needed are ways to do this work effectively and efficiently so that as much of it as possible can be done before the negative effects of doing too much set in. Finally, once all the advice is in, evaluators have considerable leeway in how they reconfigure their designs. Wise choices can reduce the negative consequences of too much effort to buffer against surprise.

Working with Stakeholders along the Evaluation Life Cycle

Key to working with stakeholders is the notion that negotiation between stakeholders and evaluators can take place along the whole evaluation life cycle. Most such negotiation takes place early in the evaluation life cycle, but as we have discussed, evaluators can engineer ample opportunity to revisit evaluation plans as their work proceeds. At these times there is low cost and high payoff for explicit discussions of unintended change. The cost is low because careful work with stakeholders is almost always a rich part of the evaluation enterprise. That work will be done whether or not any mention is ever made about preparation for unintended events. The payoff is high because it increases the probability that the evaluation will succeed (i.e., that proper measurement and methodology will take place) and that stakeholders will be satisfied (i.e., that the information they get will match what they thought they would receive).

Early discussions with stakeholders provide an opportunity to establish "redesign points" at specific times, as discussed in Chapter 6 in the section on retooling. Almost all the cases in this book contain examples of how evaluators and stakeholders can interact to change an evaluation. In all those cases, however, the interaction took place to manage a crisis. My argument here is that interaction between stakeholders and evaluators can be regularized and systematized along the evaluation life cycle, thereby decreasing the need for crisis management. Some of that interaction will be with individuals, and some with groups. Interaction with groups provides the most opportunity for efficiency.

Working with Groups

The ability to detect and adapt to evaluation surprise rises with the number of people and groups whose expertise can be integrated into an evaluation process. Unfortunately, managing those interactions can be time consuming, expensive, and difficult. Moreover, the time, expense, and difficulty may increase in more than a linear fashion as numbers and diversity increase. Nonlinear increases may come about because as numbers and diversity increase, so does the challenge of reaching consensus (if consensus is called for), or simply, of choosing among alternative courses of action. Thus it is useful to employ tactics that can deal with groups effectively and thereby increase the amount of diverse opinion that can be dealt with at any given level of resources. Methods to achieve effective and efficient use of advisors fall into two broad categories—group membership and methods of assuring effective group behavior.

Group Membership

With respect to group membership, one needs to differentiate between essential members and members who may add value but are not essential. Essential members are the key stakeholders whose continued involvement is needed to assure an adequate evaluation design, to support the implementation and conduct of the evaluation, and whose attention to findings is needed to meet the requirements of knowledge transfer. Most of this group is identified very early in the evaluation life cycle, when input into logic modeling and related evaluation design decisions are being made. Donald Campbell (1969) suggested including program opponents when scouting for program effects because such people are likely to focus on consequences that program champions may not see, or may not wish to see. It is not only a good idea but a good general principle to identify groups who are opinionated about the program being evaluated and to solicit different points of view about whether the program is a good idea, and if so, what it will achieve.

While most groups who can comment on a program can be identified early, it is entirely possible that as programs develop, other groups of stakeholders will reveal themselves. In fact, it is useful to assume that one of the objectives of a logic model revision exercise is to identify as many new stakeholders as possible. To draw on the example in Figure 5.2, the initial stakeholder group may contain no representative of the company's enterprisewide Six Sigma program or the labor relations department. (I would not have thought to include them.) But any inspection of the revised model would reveal that a need to include representatives of these groups had arisen.

Nonessential members of the group are those who have only weak (or no) claims on the program being evaluated, but who can provide insight on the likely trajectory of the program or advice on what needs to be measured. Who should they be? To get a sense of how difficult this question can be, imagine an evaluation of a program designed to decrease lengths of hospital stays by using the Internet to provide remote home health care and patient monitoring. At first blush an evaluator would naturally consider getting advice from funders and administrators of the program, physicians who could identify health outcome measures, psychologists who knew about assessing quality of life and well-being, and social workers who could identify family stress factors that might result from sicker patients being returned to a home environment. But who else might provide useful information on what the evaluation should measure? If one takes a systems view of the innovation, the field of possibilities expands considerably. There could be business planners and health care economists with insight on the implications for hospitals of shorter lengths of stay. There could be organizational change experts with opinions about the consequences of a new service that changed power relationships among groups in the health care system. Information technologists may have insights on how the health service system's information infrastructure might affect the success of the experiment. People knowledgeable about insurance reimbursement could provide information relevant to the sustainability of the new service over the long term. As soon as a system view is used to look at interfaces between an innovation and its setting, the list of experts who might inform an evaluation can rapidly expand beyond the capacity of an evaluation team to incorporate input. The volume becomes too great. The task of integrating different opinions becomes too great. The list of elements to be added to the evaluation becomes too great.

So, beyond the obvious advisors, who should be chosen? Again, I refer to the thought experiment I proposed earlier.

1. Conduct an exercise to identify possibly useful perspectives.
2. Form an evaluation team consisting of the core members plus some randomly drawn fraction of the remaining candidates.
3. Design the evaluation.
4. Throw the chosen noncore members back into the sampling pool.
5. Repeat steps 1 through 4 many times.

I believe the experiment would yield two results. First, there will be considerable similarity across the designs. Second, each design will account for more potential surprise than would be identified if only the core team were involved. Why would the similarities occur? Because no matter what the precise makeup of the team, the continued presence of the core members will provide consistency with respect to evaluation requirements. Also, no matter who is on the team, each trial in the experiment would take place in a similar context with respect to the nature of the program being evaluated, its innovativeness, its interfaces with other elements of the larger environment, funding requirements, key stakeholders, and all the other drivers of evaluation. Why would the evaluations be better? Because as we discussed earlier, stakeholders tend to be limited with respect to relevant theory, research findings, and experience with similar programs in different settings. Outsiders make a difference. Diversity makes a difference (Page, 2007).

Assuring Effective Group Behavior

An assumption in the above discussion is that the assemblage of people working on the evaluation constitute a well-functioning group. If they did not, their communication would be subject to groupthink, undue influence from high-status members, restricted disagreement in the service of consensus, and all the other problems that afflict group process. To get good advice, evaluators must assure that four conditions are present: (1) diverse opinion is available; (2) each individual's opinion is independent of the opinions of others; (3) contributors are able to draw on unique knowledge; and (4) there is an effective mechanism for aggregating individual opinion into a collective decision (Surowiecki, 2004). All well and good, but how to get and aggregate as much diverse opinion as possible given a fixed set of resources? Five tactics can help. First, large-group facilitation techniques have been developed that succeed in providing the value of small-group deliberations when working with large groups (Dannemiller Tyson Associates, 2000). These techniques involve an alternating set of interactions between one large group and representative subsets of that larger group. The small groups allow classic group process management, while the large-group interaction assures consensus, or at least understanding, at each stage.

Second, a great deal of time and effort is often taken up when having to deal with groups that are characterized by disagreement and disunity. And the greater the diversity of a group, the greater the likelihood of disunity and disagreement. In these cases Delphi techniques are helpful to minimize the disruption that can emanate from fractious groups (Gupta & Chin, 1993; Keeney, Hasson, & McKenna, 2001).

Third, there is advantage to be gained in maintaining loose groups over time. With such an approach an advisory board can be constituted containing diverse stakeholders and experts who meet occasion-

ally to assess the progress of the evaluation, to debate the implications of its findings, and to consider developments that may affect
what needs to be done. Regular meetings assure shared understanding among group members with respect to the evaluation's history,
purpose, and design. Infrequent meetings keep budgets within limits.
The advisory nature of the group provides freedom of action for the
evaluation team. Together, the combination of diversity of viewpoint,
resource practicality, and freedom of action combine to provide an
evaluation with rapid, informed advice whenever unexpected events
need to be dealt with.

Fourth, much group interaction can be done remotely via telecon-
ferences, asynchronously using Internet-based collaboration tools, or
both. The obvious advantage of these methods is cost. But perhaps a
greater advantage is that the lower cost can lead to more frequent interaction, and thus to more (and more timely) information about leading
indicators of surprise.

Finally, it is useful to exploit variation in connectedness among
subsets of the overall group. For instance, an evaluation that measures
both a program's sustainability and its impact might be conceptualized as two separate evaluations, each requiring a different group of
experts. As a contrary example, questions about the choice of comparison groups, the span of time over which data should be collected, and
the method by which members should be allocated to groups are all
inextricably bound. It would be impossible to make a good decision
about any in isolation from the others. In both of these examples something (and perhaps something important) will be lost by not combining
all advisors into a single group. On the other hand, in the first example,
much will be gained by separating the groups by making it possible to
exploit a greater range of expertise in planning an evaluation.

EVALUATION DESIGN

The last suggestion in the previous section plays on one's ability to capi-
talize on variation in the connectedness of subsets of a whole group of
advisors. The theme of "connectedness" can also be invoked as a guideline for choosing among alternate evaluation plans. This is, in fact, the
topic of the "Partition" section in the previous chapter, which dealt
with increasing evaluation agility. Figure 7.1 provides a framework for
understanding why partitioning might be useful. By partitioning the

design, evaluators can weaken linkages among evaluation elements and thereby decrease the "complexity" of the design.

IN SUM

Any tactic that can be invoked to minimize the impact of surprise on an evaluation carries the risk of making things worse. This risk exists because the very same tactics that can minimize surprise or increase adaptability to it might also adversely affect the time needed to implement an evaluation, the complexity of the evaluation, or the resources needed to carry out the evaluation. These adverse behaviors can either directly harm an evaluation's ability to meet stakeholder needs, or can affect those needs through the intermediaries of increased technical and procedural errors or increased opportunity costs. Worse, all these adverse effects can potentiate one another. None of these problems can be eliminated, but they can be minimized. The more they are minimized, the more leeway evaluators have to deal with surprise before their actions generate the perverse effect of making the evaluation more, rather than less, susceptible to surprise. Useful tactics for providing the greatest potential for agility involve working with stakeholders throughout the entire evaluation life cycle, choices of group membership for advisors to the evaluation, group process techniques to maximize information and minimize conflict, and the methods to promote agile evaluation that were discussed in the previous chapter.

| Chapter 8 |

Applying the Examples to Categories of Cases

THE LIFE CYCLE VIEW

The previous chapters drew on particular cases to help illustrate the nature of surprise. This and the next two chapters transition from a focus on principles with cases as illustrations to a focus on the cases. I begin this chapter with observations that come from placing the cases on the life cycle map that was originally presented in Chapter 3. Chapter 9 does the same for the social/organizational map. Chapter 10 considers each case individually.

As the discussion proceeds, it is important to bear in mind that any patterns I identify and the conclusions I draw must be considered tentative and suggestive. The sample is small, and gets smaller still as cases are partitioned into subcategories. My hope is that the suggestions are worth taking seriously, and that over time the sample will grow so that the analysis can be extended and revised.

It is difficult to write about this subject without sounding like a Monday morning quarterback. When analyzing a case it is all too easy to slip into a mode of discourse that implies: "Of course this problem occurred. The evaluation team should have seen it coming. Had they been appropriately vigilant, they would have implemented such-and-such a tactic to prevent the problem." The truth is that when we plan our evaluations we are looking into a future in which multiple causal chains can lead to the same outcome, and in which chance events can change what seemed like a sure thing. When considering events in a complicated future, our vision is dim, our strategic and tactical choices are many, and we are always gambling. We try to identify all the relevant critical choices, but if we are too good at identifying those choices, we end up dealing with so many eventualities that we risk producing an unworkable evaluation. As long as we keep this caution in mind, a critique of the cases will help us sharpen our insight and develop our wisdom with respect to dealing with surprise.

"UNINTENDED CONSEQUENCES":
UNITY ACROSS PROGRAMS AND THEIR EVALUATIONS

A major observation across all cases touched on the meaning of "unintended consequence." At the start of this project my notion of an "unintended consequence" was bound up with the notion of program outcome or impact. I had the idea that a program might be designed to have consequence A, when in fact it had consequence B (or perhaps, A and B). My reason for this belief came from the planning literature, which is rife with examples of unintended consequences.[1] As the cases show, however, only four dealt with this kind of unanticipated event. Most of the surprises arose from implementation issues. Either a program did not get implemented as planned or the evaluation did not get implemented as planned. Either way, the evaluators had to adapt.

The more I thought about the similarity of programs and evaluations with respect to surprise, the more it made sense to me. As I explained briefly in Chapter 1, I pondered the characteristics of any social construction that is subject to unintended consequences. In doing so I realized that programs and evaluations should be the same with respect to susceptibility to surprise. Why? Because both are assemblages of money, people, and relationships that are organized according to a specified plan to achieve specified aims. Both persist over time. Both are systems that sometimes overlap and sometimes are nested within other systems. Both are subject to feedback loops of varying lengths and latencies. From this point of view it is quite understandable why the same dynamics of surprise that affect programs also affect evaluations.

The above explanation, however, does not explain why there were so many more examples of surprise in the evaluations than in the outcomes of the programs being evaluated. Why should this be? I believe the answer lies in the different sets of linkages that exist between a program and its evaluation on the one hand, and between a program and the world in which it is operating on the other. The primary interface for an evaluation is the program being evaluated. That interface is where all the action is—where data collection behavior is molded, where schedules for tasks and deliverables are determined, and where deadlines are set. Moreover, as we shall soon see, the life cycle of evaluations are compressed relative to the life cycles of the innovations being evaluated. The situation with respect to programs is different. There, programs have a wide and varied universe to interact with. Also, the fact of a program's existence, and the longer-term consequences of its actions, exist beyond the termination of the evaluation. The life cycle is longer, and within any given time frame, the number of systems that have a chance to affect program activity are greater. (This statement assumes quite a lot about the frequency over time of activity that can affect both systems. I'm willing to assume an equal rate, but the real value is, of course, an empirical question.) Hence, the findings from my snowball sample. Because I found few cases of long-term evaluation studies, most of the unintended consequences redounded to the operations of the evaluation rather than the operations of the programs being evaluated. In light of this finding, the plan going forward will be first to focus on short-term surprise as indicated in most of the cases, and then to extrapolate the discussion to the longer term by focusing on the few cases that manifested unintended outcomes. (This discussion takes place in Chapter 12.)

INTERPRETING CASES THROUGH A LIFE CYCLE PERSPECTIVE

Distribution of the cases on the life cycle map appears in Figure 8.1. Insight about evaluation surprise comes from two aspects of this distribution: (1) cases across program × evaluation life cycle scenarios (reading vertically down the three scenarios); and (2) cases over the evaluation life cycle (reading across life cycles within each scenario).

Populating Cases across Life Cycle Scenarios

I wish scenario 1 was populated because it represents a continuous improvement (CI) approach to evaluation—frequent, small-scale studies designed for rapid feedback and midcourse corrections. The CI approach seems extremely valuable, especially for settings that emphasize evalu-

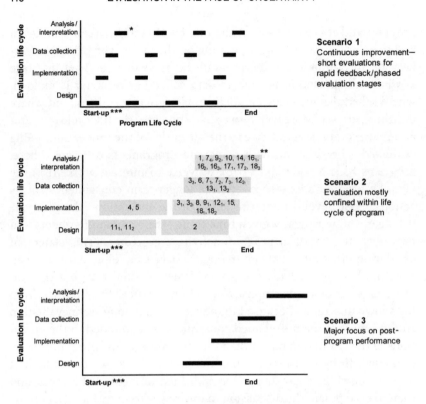

FIGURE 8.1. Placing cases in the evaluation × program life cycle map. *For the sake of simplicity, all life cycle stages are shown as being equal in length. **Cases are aggregated into general categories (e.g., "data collection/mature program"); no effort is made to distinguish finer distinctions within these groups. ***In practice, program stages overlap as well, but for our purposes the evaluation stage overlap is most relevant; including program stage overlap would make the figure overly complicated.

ation as a program monitoring and improvement tool. The value derives from the essential purpose of CI, which is to improve continuously by continually monitoring system behavior, implementing corrective actions, and testing the consequences of the innovation. To this end CI has developed tools and analysis logic that well serve evaluators' needs for agility in the face of unexpected change (Morell, 2000).

If more CI-like evaluation were done, the life cycle approach advocated above might have to be modified because with CI, evaluation life cycles can be so short and recurring that it would be difficult to make clear distinctions between design, data collection, and analysis. In fact, one might argue that CI is *designed* to handle unintended consequences. It is the method that should be chosen when one knows in advance that: (1) there is uncertainty about what will happen, (2) program design allows for rapid midcourse corrections, and (3) determining longer-term program effects are not a priority. I considered eliminating scenario 1 after I saw that it was empty. I decided to keep it because it is a viable form of evaluation, and keeping it illustrates the range of possible relationships between the program and evaluation life cycles. I remain hopeful that, over time, cases will show up to populate this scenario.

All of the cases fall into scenario 2, where evaluation begins somewhere during program start-up or shortly thereafter and ends about the time when the program ends. This timing makes sense because a great deal of evaluation derives from requirements that are built into the funding that established the program and because the program life cycle more or less defines the attention span of many stakeholders who need guidance about what to do next. This attention span also explains the sparse population of scenario 3, which extends evaluation past the end of the program being evaluated. As with scenario 1, I considered eliminating scenario 3, but kept it for the same reasons that I retained scenario 1. In light of what the planning literature tells us about the accrual of unintended consequences over time, there is good reason to advocate for longer-range evaluation.

Populating Cases along the Program and Evaluation Life Cycles

Determining the distribution of the cases along the program and evaluation life cycles required two judgments about boundaries: (1) between "program start-up" and "program maturity" on the program axis, and (2) between "evaluation design" and "evaluation data collection" on the evaluation axis. ("Implementation" does intervene between "design" and "data collection," but the classification problem still hinged on the "design–collection" distinction.)

With respect to the program axis, the classification problem was that because so much evaluation focuses on some sort of innovation, the distinction between the program's start-up phase and the program's mature stage is ambiguous. I based the classification on a judgment about the amount of organizational dislocation that characterized the innovation being evaluated. For instance, imagine an evaluation of an effort to improve an organization's functioning by injecting novel information (e.g., wait time, cost, referral patterns) into routine decision-

making activities that were otherwise left undisturbed. In this scenario there is no effort to change linkages between the innovation and
other aspects of long-established organizational process. Whether such
changes occur constitutes outcome data, but deliberately engineered
changes are not part of program design. Contrast this planning information scenario with an evaluation that began in the early stages of a
new computer-enhanced educational reform, complete with new ways
of teaching, new teacher behaviors, and new ways of organizing classrooms. Here, the core innovation, "computer-enhanced education," is
intimately bound with a host of related changes in the school systems'
operations. This scenario is an example of evaluation of an innovation
that began in a program's start-up phase.

A similar difficulty attended the distinction between evaluation
design and evaluation data collection. The difficulty was that because
lack of data can spoil a design, it can be difficult to determine when
there is a "design" problem and when there is a "data" problem. To illustrate the ambiguity, imagine a situation in which lack of historical data
precluded the use of trend analysis to draw causal inference. Should
this situation be classified as a problem in data access or a challenge to
the evaluation design? In these situations I based my decision on my
estimate of whether the lack of data had a profound effect on the logic
of causal inference. For instance, consider a situation in which a 1-year
time lag was needed to observe pre–post comparisons of the effect of
an innovation. What if preinnovation data collection were delayed 6
months? It is true that the surface problem is one of data access, but
the underlying problem is that the logic of pre–post change cannot be
tested; that is, the design failed. As another example of design change,
consider a case in which differences between groups on a particular
scale defined the critical evaluation question. If that particular scale
could not be used, the logic of the design could not be followed.

Contrast these design change problems with what I judge to be
a data collection problem. Imagine that a questionnaire could not be
deployed, but that similar data could be obtained from interviews, or a
scenario in which children could not be interviewed directly, but their
parents could be asked about their children's behavior. One should
question how the data changes affected the quality of the findings, but
the essential logic of comparison would not have changed.

Because so many cases contained multiple incidents of surprise,
"number of incidents," rather than "number of cases," is the best indicator of where surprise falls on the evaluation life cycle. Figure 8.1 shows

13 incidents taking place early in the evaluation life cycle (in design or implementation), and 19 late in the life cycle (data collection or analysis/interpretation). This result is disturbing because problems should be discovered and fixed during design and implementation, rather than waiting to retool when the evaluation is fully up and running. The fact that so much surprise showed up in later stages speaks to the need for more systematic efforts to anticipate surprise early, to scout for impending surprise as evaluation proceeds, and to use agile designs.

It is insufficient, however, to note how surprise was scattered across the evaluation life cycle. It is also necessary to look at the spread with respect to surprise that caused real problems. These are situations in which the evaluation either: (1) addressed stakeholders' needs for information, but not as well as planned; or (2) ended up addressing a somewhat related but different question than the stakeholders wanted answered. Eight of the 18 cases fell into one or another of these categories. What happened? The answer is summarized in Table 8.1 and explained below.

In three of the eight cases, group comparisons fell apart. In Case 5 (p. 214), lack of statistical power and confounds across groups made it impossible to compare experimental and control groups with respect to the program treatment. In Case 11 (p. 244), participation rates by eligible households combined with alternate routes to receiving the experimental treatment to preclude experimental–control comparisons. Case 18 (p. 281) used a qualitative design that required baseline interviews with service recipients. Those comparisons could not be made because the sponsor misrepresented the timing of the program start to the evaluators.

Another three cases ran into problems because staff resistance prevented the necessary data from being collected. In each of these cases resistance popped up for different reasons, but the effect was the same —the evaluation had trouble addressing the sponsors' original question. In Case 3 (p. 204), staff who were supposed to provide data did not and could not be induced to do so. Case 7 (p. 224) had a similar problem, in this instance founded on resistance to thinking in terms of both costs and benefits. Case 15 (p. 263) is similar to Case 7 in that values were at play. In Case 7 the values dealt with the role of "cost" and resulted in data not being forthcoming. In Case 15 (p. 263) the contentious issue was staff beliefs about trauma in their client population.

Problems in two of the eight cases emanated from the nature of the service that was provided. In Case 1 (p. 197), the sponsor's commit-

**TABLE 8.1. Cases Where Surprise Caused Major Difficulty
for Evaluation**

Case	Page	Title	Nature of surprise
1	197	Grasping at Straws and Discovering a Different Program Theory: An Exercise in Reengineering Analysis Logic in a Child Care Evaluation Setting	Client interest in an outcome with restricted range
3	204	Evaluating Programs Aimed at Promoting Child Well-Being: The Case of Local Social Welfare Agencies in Jerusalem	Staff resistance to providing information
5	214	Quasi-Experimental Strategies When Randomization Fails: Propensity Score Matching and Sensitivity Analysis in Whole-School Reform	Lack of statistical power and experimental–control confounds
6	219	Unexpected Changes in Program Delivery: The Perils of Overlooking Process Data	Change in service delivery schedule
7	224	Evaluating Costs and Benefits of Consumer-Operated Services: Unexpected Resistance, Unanticipated Insights, and Déjà Vu All Over Again	Staff resistance to providing information
11	244	Evaluating the Health Impacts of Central Heating	Low participation rates
15	263	Trauma and Posttraumatic Stress Disorder among Female Clients in Methadone Maintenance Treatment in Israel: From Simple Assessment to Complex Intervention	Staff resistance to providing information
18	281	Evaluation of the Integrated Services Pilot Program from Western Australia	Inability to collect baseline qualitative data

ment to the "caregiver-to-child" ratio as a primary independent variable resulted in a range too restricted to allow analysis. In Case 6 (p. 219), a change in the delivery schedule made it impossible to implement the planned quasi-experimental design.

Taken together, these eight cases contain three distinct reasons for evaluation surprise. Cases 1, 5, and 18 (two quantitative and one qualitative) involve difficulty in establishing or maintaining boundaries among comparison groups. Cases 3, 7, and 15 center on people's beliefs and inclinations. In these cases program staff who were expected to provide data for the evaluation were unwilling to do so. In Cases 1 and

6, reasonable changes in how services were provided challenged how the evaluation could be conducted. Half of the incidents of surprise in these cases took place in either the data collection or analysis phases of the evaluation life cycle. If this percentage holds as more cases are studied (should the opportunity to do so present itself), we will see that evaluators often find themselves in truly difficult situations. Remember that these are not just incidents of surprise. These are the subset of incidents that posed serious threats to the integrity of the evaluation. Because of the relationship between the two life cycles, problems that occur in the data collection or analysis phases of the evaluation cycle are also occurring toward the end of the program life cycle (i.e., at a time when stakeholders' need for information is most pressing), and when their expectations for what they will get from evaluators are firmly set.

The following chapter is a discussion of the cases with respect to the social/organizational framework. Dividing the chapters this way facilitates explanation, and it also recognizes that most of the discussion of cases within the two frameworks can be carried out separately. However, to telegraph what is to come, there are times when understanding surprise is furthered by using both approaches simultaneously. For example, the next chapter illustrates that understanding what kind of adjustments evaluators make to accommodate surprise (a social/organizational issue) is best understood in terms of when the surprise is detected in the evaluation life cycle.

IN SUM

This chapter transitioned from a discussion of general principles to a focus on cases. It did so by placing the cases on a map that related the evaluation life cycle to the program life cycle. An important observation that derived from this exercise was that the same dynamics that explain surprise in programs also explain surprise in evaluation. This commonality exists because programs and evaluations are similar social constructions. They are both assemblages of resources and processes that are brought together to achieve a specific purpose, and they are both embedded in a set of overlapping systems. Relationships between program and evaluation life cycles can be categorized into three broad categories: (1) multiple successive evaluations nested in one long program life cycle, (2) a single evaluation that begins after a program starts and ends about the time the program ends, and (3) evaluations that continue for an extended period after the program ends. Scenarios 1 and 3 represent desirable forms of evaluation, but all the cases collected for this book fell into scenario 2. Although all the incidents of surprise in the cases can be placed on the "evaluation × program" life cycle map, only those incidents of surprise that posed a challenge to the integrity of the evaluation are important for our purposes. Those problematic situations involved three challenges to evaluation: (1) establishing or maintaining boundaries among comparison groups, (2) values and beliefs that thwarted data collection, and (3) changes in how services were provided. These problems are generic to evaluation, and not exclusive to quantitative or qualitative designs.

NOTE

1. See, as a few of many examples, industry sponsorship of university research (Behrens & Gray, 2001); marketing (Fry & Polonsky, 2004); tobacco restrictions (Hoek, 2004); drinking age regulation (DiNardo & Lemieux, 2001); speed and quality relationships in new product development (Lukas & Menon, 2004); welfare (Courtney et al., 2004); national fiscal reform (Kildegaard, 2001); teacher empowerment (Pugh & Zhao, 2003); NGO activity in developing countries (Stiles, 2002); and workplace safety (Kaminski, 2001).

Chapter 9

Applying the Examples to Categories of Cases

THE SOCIAL/ORGANIZATIONAL VIEW

The previous chapters drew on particular cases to help illustrate the nature of surprise with respect to evaluation and program life cycles. This chapter looks at the cases in terms of the social/organizational framework. The same cautions raised in Chapter 8 still apply: (1) the small sample can only provide hints as to what patterns may exist, and (2) we should avoid being smug. I would have acted as the authors of the cases have, and I bet that many of you readers would have, too.

One use of the information discussed here is practical. If we know how surprise is distributed across the social/organizational landscape, we will have some guidance as to where to direct our efforts when searching literature, questioning stakeholders and other experts, and monitoring programs for signs of change. Another use is more theoretical. If we know something about where surprise comes from, we may learn something about how evaluations and programs operate as systems.

NAVIGATING THROUGH THE CASES

What follows is a long journey that will draw on all 18 cases in many different ways to illustrate numerous aspects of evaluation surprise. It will be easy to get lost, but a few guides will help you maintain a sense of place. First, bear in mind that this chapter can be thought of as dealing with three broad topics. The first compares where surprise comes from in terms of the possible sources that are identified on the left column of the social/organizational map shown in Figure 9.2, which can be found on page 136. The second part discusses what evaluators did in order to respond to surprise. The third part presents ideas that emerged from the social/organizational analysis, but which are not reflected in the map. Below are navigational aids to each of these three topics.

Getting Acquainted with the Content of the Cases

Because this chapter draws so heavily on the cases, it is worth revisiting the various ways to read the cases that I laid out in Chapter 1. Whenever I cite a case, I provide a snippet of information about it. If you do not find this information sufficient, either of two approaches might work. One is to read through (or skim) the whole case when I refer to it. Or, you may want to read (or skim) through all the cases now, before descending into the detail that follows.

Navigational Guide to Sources of Surprise

Figure 9.1 is a hierarchical breakdown of sources of surprise. In it, the hierarchy depicts how categories of surprise are nested within one another, while the thick horizontal lines indicate comparisons I will make. For example, surprise emanating from "program operations" is split between surprise that comes from a program's external environment and surprise that comes from the program's internal operations. The number 2 on the thick line between "environment" and "internal" is an index number that I will refer to as the explanation proceeds.

A limitation of Figure 9.1 is that while it shows the hierarchy, it does not identify the cases that make up the hierarchy. This limitation is addressed in Table 9.1. There, rows of the table identify each case by number, page, and name, while columns to the right of the titles are indexed to Figure 9.1.

Navigational Guide to Changes in Evaluation

The right-hand section of the social/organizational map (Figure 9.2) shows three types of responses that evaluators can make to respond to

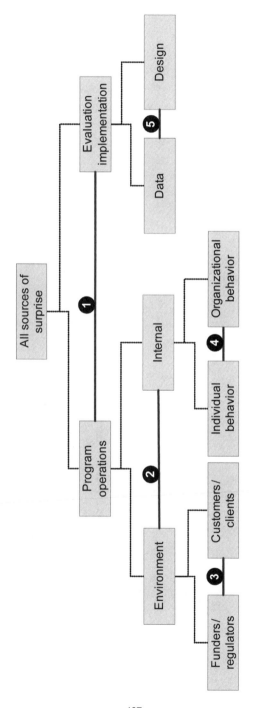

FIGURE 9.1. Hierarchical breakdown of sources of surprise.

TABLE 9.1. Sources of Surprise: Overview of Comparisons

					Index to Figure 9.2		
			1 Program operation ↔ Evaluation implementation	2 Environment ↔ Internal	3 Funders/regulators ↔ Customers/clients	4 Individual behavior ↔ Organizational behavior	5 Data ↔ Design
Case	Page	Title					
1	197	Grasping at Straws and Discovering a Different Program Theory: An Exercise in Reengineering Analysis Logic in a Child Care Evaluation Setting	•	•	•		
2	200	Shifting Sands in a Training Evaluation Context	•	•	•		
3	204	Evaluating Programs Aimed at Promoting Child Well-Being: The Case of Local Social Welfare Agencies in Jerusalem	•	•		•	•
4	210	Assessing the Impact of Providing Laptop Computers to Students	•	•			•
5	214	Quasi-Experimental Strategies When Randomization Fails: Propensity Score Matching and Sensitivity Analysis in Whole-School Reform	•	•		•	•
6	219	Unexpected Changes in Program Delivery: The Perils of Overlooking Process Data When Evaluating HIV Prevention	•	•	•		•
7	224	Evaluating Costs and Benefits of Consumer-Operated Services: Unexpected Resistance, Unanticipated Insights, and Déjà Vu All Over Again	•	•		•	•

129

surprise: (1) design, (2) procedures/logistics, and (3) analysis/interpretation. Table 9.2 indicates which cases use each kind of adjustment. For example, the table shows that Case 9 made adjustments involving both procedures/logistics and analysis/interpretation. Reading down the columns, we see that six cases made changes in design, six in procedures and logistics, and 10 in analysis/interpretation. The nature of these changes, why they occurred, how they relate to the evaluation life cycle, and their implications for the information that could be provided to stakeholders are the subject of much of the discourse to come.

Navigational Guide to Categories Derived from the Social/Organizational Map

Analysis of the cases in social/organizational terms yielded three additional ways to understand where surprise comes from: (1) use of pilot tests and feasibility assessments, (2) resistance to evaluation, and (3) incorrect assumptions made early in the evaluation life cycle. Table 9.3 shows which cases contain each of these types of surprise.

The distinctions shown in Table 9.3 do not fit neatly into the social/organizational map, but they do reveal useful insight. Three categories emerged: (1) use of pilot tests and feasibility assessments, (2) resistance to evaluation, and (3) incorrect assumptions that were made early in the evaluation life cycle. The first two categories popped up infrequently—there were three instances of the use of pilot tests and feasibility assessments and four of resistance to evaluation. Although their occurrence was infrequent, I made the effort to discuss them because they brought up important issues that evaluators should consider.

The third category—incorrect assumptions made early in the evaluation life cycle—was the most common and also the most problematic. It showed up in seven cases. Pilot tests and feasibility assessments are familiar activities, and how to use them is an important part of graduate training in many social science disciplines. Resistance to evaluation is a well-known problem in evaluation and the subject of a lot of writing and discussion in our field. On the other hand, incorrect assumptions early in the evaluation life cycle create an insidious problem that is difficult to anticipate and to deal with. What, for instance, is an evaluator to do when a client issues a request for proposals (RFP) that seems to ask a reasonable question about a program's outcome, but which in fact asks the wrong question?

PLACEMENT OF CASES ON THE SOCIAL/ORGANIZATIONAL MAP

Placement of the cases on the social/organizational map is shown in graphic form in Figure 9.2. The following discussion moves through Figure 9.2 in a vertical fashion, and from left to right. First I consider program-related sources of surprise (top left in Figure 9.2). Then I discuss issues related to evaluation implementation (bottom left in Figure 9.2). Finally, I discuss the adjustments to evaluation that were made (right side of Figure 9.2). As I went through this structure while preparing this book, finer distinctions were revealed within each of these categories. These, too, are discussed. As we work our way through, note that on three occasions the life cycle view is added to provide further insight: (1) direct and indirect routes between program-related change and adjustments to evaluation, (2) design change versus other kinds of adjustments to evaluation, and (3) incorrect assumptions made by evaluators.

Placement of the cases revealed the extent to which changes in evaluation came from the two different paths shown in Figure 9.2. Of the 32 instances of surprise, 12 took a direct route from program-related activity to changes in how evaluation was conducted (see the dotted line in Figure 9.2); 20 of the 32 involved changes in program operations that had consequences for how the evaluation was implemented or conducted, and which in turn required a change in the evaluation plan (the solid line in Figure 9.2). Case 1 (p. 197) is an example of the direct route. In this case, regulations emanating from the stakeholder led to changes in how data were analyzed and interpreted. The problem became manifest during data analysis, but up to that point the implementation and conduct of the evaluation proceeded as planned. Case 4 (p. 210) is an example of the indirect path. Here, delays inherent in the operations of a large organizational system (schools) caused a problem with implementing the evaluation according to plan by limiting the availability of baseline data.

Of the 12 instances where program change led directly to a need to adjust the evaluation, all but one were situations in which surprise was discovered late in the evaluation life cycle—during analysis/interpretation activities. This finding highlights a trap for evaluators. If a program change affects how an evaluation is carried out, the very fact that a problem with evaluation implementation has occurred can serve as a warning of impending difficulty. But if there is no obvious reason to change an evaluation implementation plan, problems can lurk invisibly

TABLE 9.2. Cases Used to Explain Adjustments to Evaluation in Response to Surprise

Case	Page	Title	Design	Procedures/ logistics	Analysis/ interpretation
1	197	Grasping at Straws and Discovering a Different Program Theory: An Exercise in Reengineering Analysis Logic in a Child Care Evaluation Setting			•
2	200	Shifting Sands in a Training Evaluation Context	•		
3	204	Evaluating Programs Aimed at Promoting Child Well-Being: The Case of Local Social Welfare Agencies in Jerusalem	•	•	•
4	210	Assessing the Impact of Providing Laptop Computers to Students			•
5	214	Quasi-Experimental Strategies When Randomization Fails: Propensity Score Matching and Sensitivity Analysis in Whole-School Reform			•
6	219	Unexpected Changes in Program Delivery: The Perils of Overlooking Process Data When Evaluating HIV Prevention			•
7	224	Evaluating Costs and Benefits of Consumer-Operated Services: Unexpected Resistance, Unanticipated Insights, and Déjà Vu All Over Again		•	•
8	231	Keep Up with the Program!: Adapting the Evaluation Focus to Align with a College Access Program's Changing Goals	•		
9	235	Assumptions about School Staff's Competencies and Likely Program Impacts		•	•

TABLE 9.3. Sources of Surprise That Emerged from Analysis of the Social/Organizational Map

Case	Page	Title	Pilot tests/feasibility assessments	Resistance to evaluation	Incorrect assumptions early in the evaluation life cycle
1	197	Grasping at Straws and Discovering a Different Program Theory: An Exercise in Reengineering Analysis Logic in a Child Care Evaluation Setting			
2	200	Shifting Sands in a Training Evaluation Context			
3	204	Evaluating Programs Aimed at Promoting Child Well-Being: The Case of Local Social Welfare Agencies in Jerusalem			•
4	210	Assessing the Impact of Providing Laptop Computers to Students		•	•
5	214	Quasi-Experimental Strategies When Randomization Fails: Propensity Score Matching and Sensitivity Analysis in Whole-School Reform			
6	219	Unexpected Changes in Program Delivery: The Perils of Overlooking Process Data When Evaluating HIV Prevention			
7	224	Evaluating Costs and Benefits of Consumer-Operated Services: Unexpected Resistance, Unanticipated Insights, and Déjà Vu All Over Again		•	•
8	231	Keep Up with the Program!: Adapting the Evaluation Focus to Align with a College Access Program's Changing Goals			•
9	235	Assumptions about School Staff's Competencies and Likely Program Impacts	•		

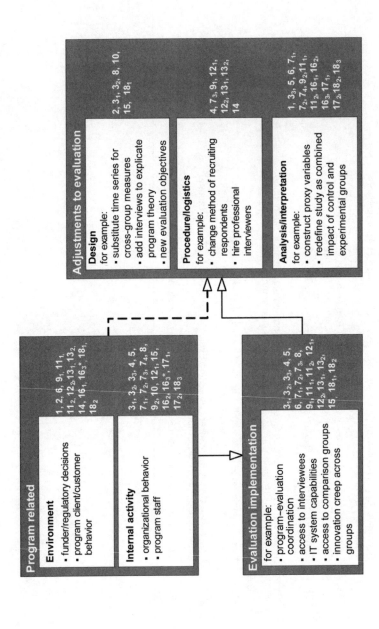

FIGURE 9.2. Placement of cases on the social/organizational map. *16_3 was a tight interaction between the behavior of service recipients and program staff.

for long stretches of the evaluation life cycle. This possibility of hidden problems is one reason why program monitoring and, as we shall see later in this chapter, why assumption testing is so important.

Program-Related Surprise

Looking within the broad category of program-related surprise, 13 instances are environmental and 18 are internal (line 2 in Figure 9.1). (There is one double count because of the tight relationship between an environmental and internal component.) To illustrate an environmental source of surprise, consider Case 14 (p. 258). This case was a test of using service-related information to help agencies improve their operations. A change in reporting requirements by state officials led to an artifact of reporting that cast participating agencies in a negative light. To illustrate an internal source of surprise, consider Case 16 (p. 270). There, patients' drug hoarding resulted in unexpected program behavior.

Within the environmental category, 13 instances of surprise split about evenly between those coming from changes imposed by funders or regulators and those coming from clients or customers (line 3 in Figure 9.1). A summary of what happened in these cases is presented in Table 9.4.

The high proportion of change coming from outside the boundaries of the program implies a level of difficulty I had not anticipated. As an evaluator, I am pretty good at staying in touch with activity that resides within the programs I am evaluating. I have always found it harder to attend to activity outside the program because I am not as familiar with the situation or the players. They, in turn, are not as familiar with me. The distribution of surprise across "environment" and "internal activity" has heightened my feelings about the importance of the environmental scanning tactics that I discussed in Chapter 5.

With respect to surprise due to clients or customers, most of the difficulty stems from clients' engagement with the services they received. As an example, in Case 6 (p. 219) client needs dictated a change in the service delivery schedule, which in turn had consequences for the evaluation's quasi-experimental design. Only one scenario involved a direct relationship between service recipients and the evaluation. In Case 12 (p. 249), service recipients were reluctant to provide follow-up data for the evaluation.

With respect to internal program change, what stands out is the

TABLE 9.4. Sources of Surprise: Funder/Regulator versus Client/Customer

Case/ incident	Page	Funder/regulator	Client/customer
1	197	Funder's emphasis on a restricted range for primary outcome measure precluded addressing evaluation question.	
2	200	Nature of evaluation was unclear even after funder commitment to it. Discussion and negotiation was needed to define scope.	
6	219		Three-session intervention was changed to a single session due to client preferences.
9_1	235		Baseline knowledge of participants in a training program was overestimated.
11_1	244		Size of potential control group and desirability of service provided, precluded experimental–control comparisons.
11_2	244		See 11_1.
12_2	249		Low response rate to posttreatment follow-up survey.
13_1	253	Regulatory changes precluded employing interviewers with criminal records.	
13_2	253	Regulatory changes removed need for clinical follow-up that also provided evaluation data.	
14	258	Artifact in new state-mandated reporting requirements threatened agencies with false rating of poor performance.	
16_1	270		Patients hoarded medicine from prenatal services because of belief that supply would end.
16_3	270	Hoarding behavior by patients combined with staff efforts to check the hoarding behavior resulted in a decrease in both customer and staff satisfaction.	
18_1	281		Ethnic composition of refugees was less diverse than had been assumed.
18_2	281	Despite assurances by funder about dates, program start precluded collecting baseline interview data.	

distinction between settings where surprise can be understood in terms of the behavior of individuals versus the behavior of organizations (line 4 in Figure 9.1). Table 9.5 displays this information.

To illustrate the classification rule, contrast Case 8 (p. 231) with Case 15 (p. 263). In Case 8, the evaluators discovered that, contrary to the funder's assumptions, participating organizations did not have information systems that could support the evaluation they originally wanted. In Case 15, evaluators experienced resistance from clinic staff to asking clients about traumatic events in their lives. Of course, the individuals' actions were ultimately behind all of the difficulties the evaluators faced in both of these cases. But in Case 8, a search for the immediate cause of the problem would reveal an organizational issue (i.e., the IT infrastructure), while in Case 15, a similar search would reveal the personal values of staff members (i.e., a person-centric factor). Eight of the cases can be traced to individual behavior, while 10 can be traced to organizational behavior. (There was one double count.) Considering the 5:4 ratio, it seems reasonable to assume that about equal effort is needed to assess the likely reactions that people will have to the evaluation and to the way organizations will interact with evaluation processes. In my experience, identifying issues at the individual level is easier because only two questions frame most of the individual-level issues: (1) How might the evaluation challenge people's self-interest? and (2) How might the evaluation challenge people's beliefs and values? I do not mean to imply that these are easy questions to answer, only that they are useful for framing an investigation that will reveal most of what needs to be discovered.

Organizational issues are much more diverse. To get a sense of the extent of the diversity, look down the organizational column of Table 9.5, where you will find: change management capability, incentives for organizations to participate in an experiment, unused resources, IT infrastructure, decision making invested in organizational roles, reward systems, organizational learning, and the ethnic composition of service recipients.

Evaluation Implementation

Surprise touching on evaluation implementation can be thought of in terms of issues that touch on either data availability or design change (line 5 in Figure 9.1). In the former, the logic of comparison remains undisturbed even if some data are missing or if one data source is sub-

TABLE 9.5. Sources of Surprise: Individual versus Organizational Behavior

Case/incident	Page	Individual	Organizational
3_1	204	Staff were unable to identify clear and measurable goals for client outcome.	
3_2	204	Staff did not actively partner with evaluators in an effort to identify relevant variables and measurement tools.	
3_3	204	Staff did not provide evaluation data. Low response rate.	
4	210		Difficulty of managing change led to resistance to the evaluation and delay in implementation.
5	214		Difficulty in recruiting schools into a school reform evaluation combined with a smaller-than-expected number of eligible schools to force a change in the evaluation purpose and design.
7_1	224	Staff and service recipients had difficulty understanding distinctions between "costs" and "benefits."	
7_2	224	Staff resistance to measuring cost of service.	
7_3	224	Staff resistance to monetizing the value of volunteer and donated services.	
7_4	224		Unused capacity led to high per-client cost in a manner that challenged value of assessing costs and benefits.
8	231		Participating organizations did not have IT systems that could support the evaluation's data needs.
9_2	235		Program impact was unexpectedly different for math and reading scores.

140

10	241	Participants expressed unexpected negative feelings about the service they were receiving.
12_1	249	An incorrect assumption was made about which roles made decisions about organizational participation in an innovative program.
15	263	Clinic staff objected to questions they thought their clients would find upsetting.
16_2	270	Health care workers integrated a parallel system of fees into a system where patients paid individually for every part of the services they received. Abolition of fees perturbed the informal system.
16_3	270	Hoarding behavior by patients combined with staff efforts to check the behavior resulted in a decrease in both customer and staff satisfaction.
17_1	277	As experience was gained using a new case management database, new ways to measure client services evolved.
17_2	277	As experience was gained using a new case management database, new ways to improve service delivery and organizational capability evolved.
18_3	281	Unintended outcomes resulted from an innovative program to integrate services for refugees: less pressure on existing services, better outreach capability, new needs met, and higher workload on staff.

stituted for another. In the latter, there is a need to change the logic of analysis because either the desired comparisons cannot be supported by the evaluation plan or because changing needs of the program required that new questions be asked.

About twice as many implementation issues dealt with design (13), as with data availability (7). Table 9.6 summarizes these cases.

The nature of the data availability problem is illustrated in Case 15 (p. 263). In that case, concern for clients' well-being led a clinic's staff to resist evaluators' plans to collect patient data concerning posttraumatic stress. An example of problems with methodology execution is Case 5 (p. 214). Here, evaluation of a school reform could not recruit the requisite number of participating schools, thus requiring both a change in the design and a shift in emphasis from evaluation of an innovation to research on education.

The implication of the design:data ratio (assuming it holds as more cases are collected) is that if an evaluation plan is perturbed, the likelihood is that hard work and clever work-arounds to get data will not be sufficient to maintain the ability of the evaluation to achieve its original purpose. This speculation is reflected in the distribution of incidents in the adjustments to evaluation section in Figure 9.2 (right-hand column). There, only eight of the problems with evaluation implementation could be addressed by changes in procedures/logistics. The rest fall into either the design or analysis/interpretation categories.

Adjustments to Evaluation

Three types of change in evaluation are identified in the social/organizational model: (1) design change, (2) procedures/logistics, and (3) analysis/interpretation. Allocating cases to these categories required a careful judgment to distinguish design from logistics. To illustrate the kind of judgments that were necessary, contrast two circumstances in which a questionnaire might have to be added to an evaluation. In the first scenario the original plan was to interview clients 6 months after they received a service. When cost and time considerations made personal interviewing impractical, the questionnaire was substituted. One could (and should) argue the relative merits of using questionnaires and interviews, but the logic of a 6-month posttreatment follow-up remains constant. Here, the use of the questionnaire would be considered a change in procedures/logistics.

TABLE 9.6. Sources of Surprise: Data versus Design

Case/incident	Page	Data	Design
3_1	204		Staff's inability to identify goals for treatment led to a new objective for the evaluation.
3_2	204		Inability to agree on measures of child well-being required an additional component in the evaluation to develop those measures. Instrument development was never viewed as an original intent of the evaluation.
3_3	204	Low response rate from clinicians about service outcome made it difficult to interpret the evaluation findings.	
4	210	Difficulties with implementation made it difficult for school personnel to provide data per the original plan.	
5	214		Data availability problems required a redefinition of the evaluation from an evaluation of a school reform effort to research on change in school systems.
6	219		A change in the service delivery schedule affected data collection in a manner that made it impossible to execute the planned quasi-experimental design.
7_1	224		*Confusion over the meaning of "cost" and "benefit"* made it impossible to collect enough data from enough sites to adequately address the evaluation question as it was originally posed.
7_2	224		*Resistance to measuring "cost"* made it impossible to collect enough data from enough sites to adequately address the evaluation question as it was originally posed.

(continued)

143

TABLE 9.6. (*continued*)

Case/incident	Page	Data	Design
7₃	224		Resistance to monetizing the value of donated and volunteer resources made it impossible to collect enough data from enough sites to adequately address the evaluation question as it was originally posed.
8	231		An objective of the evaluation had to be changed because agencies providing college access assistance did not have information systems that could provide the needed data on transition to postsecondary education.
9₁	235	In a test of school personnel's ability to use data to make decisions about students' educational needs, participants did not have the assumed baseline level of skills. Adding training allowed people to participate.	
11₁	244		Desirability of the central heating assistance services being evaluated precluded finding enough households to remain in a control group.
11₂	244		Control–experimental comparisons were further complicated because not all eligible households received the central heating service, while some in the control group acquired central heating by other means.
12₁	249		Feasibility test of physicians' willingness to participate in a substance abuse treatment intervention did not predict the actual (low) level of enrollment.

12_2	249	Low response rate by patients to a follow-up survey required adding an incentive for cooperation.
13_1	253	Data from a clinical information system had to be substituted for interviews when a mandated requirement for a 12-month follow-up of patients in substance abuse treatment was eliminated.
13_2	253	Training for a new set of interviewers was needed when experienced interviewers in a substance abuse treatment program could no longer be employed because they had criminal records.
15	263	Evaluation questions had to be changed when clinical staff resisted evaluators' efforts to question clients about posttraumatic stress disorder (PTSD) and traumatic experiences.
18_1	281	Evaluation question about differential impact of refugee services on people of different ethnic groups was eliminated because of lack of expected ethnic diversity in the service population.
18_2	281	Unexpected change in date of program start eliminated the collection of baseline interview data.

In the second scenario, interim data analysis raises a suspicion that the program theory as originally articulated by stakeholders is incorrect. A questionnaire is employed as part of a previously unplanned effort to check on the accuracy of the program theory. Here, the logic in the original evaluation plan did not call for an ongoing assessment of program theory. (Maybe it should have, but it did not.) In this case the questionnaire represents a new design element to the evaluation.

Two of the seven instances of design change were situations in which circumstances forced the evaluators to lower the quality of the answers their funders sought. In one situation (Case 3; p. 204) staff resistance moved the focus of the evaluation away from the intended purpose. In the other instance (Case 18; p. 281) a timing problem prevented baseline data from being collected, thus turning a qualitative pre–post design into a post-only design. In contrast to these undesirable events, five of the seven instances of design change highlight precisely the kind of interaction we would like to see between evaluators and their funders. In these cases, discussions between evaluators and funders early in the evaluation life cycle led to information that caused funders to rethink their needs.

In contrast to the constructive interaction that emerged from surprise during early phases of the evaluation life cycle, most of the outcomes involving changes during the analysis/interpretation phase of the evaluation life cycle were less sanguine. One of two situations occurred. In one situation the evaluators were able to address their funders' evaluation questions, but not as well as they originally planned. The elimination of baseline data in Case 18 (p. 281) is an example. In the other situation evaluators were forced to engage in "retrospective design changes," that is, exercises in which evaluators had to analyze their data *as if* a different question had been asked. Retrospective design was done, for instance, in Case 1 (p. 197), where the restricted range of an important outcome variable forced a change from a focus on the ratio of caregivers to children in groups to a focus on the number of children alone.

Comparing what happened in the design and analysis scenarios shows a stark difference in the quality of service that evaluators were able to render to their customers. Surprise in the design or implementation stages revealed useful new information that led funders to rethink issues that mattered. Surprise in the analysis stage of the evaluation life cycle tended to confront evaluators with the need to make the best of a bad situation. In one sense it is obvious that detecting problems early is a good idea. It is sobering, however, to see the actual differences between early and late detection in real evaluations that have been executed in the field.

CATEGORIZATIONS DERIVED FROM THE DATA

The discussion so far has been guided by the life cycle and social/organizational frameworks that were introduced earlier in Chapter 3 and expanded on in subsequent chapters. Those frameworks were largely developed a priori, before I began to inspect the cases. That inspection revealed three other ways to classify the cases that would illuminate how evaluators might prepare for and deal with surprise: (1) use of pilot tests and feasibility assessments, (2) resistance to evaluation, and (3) incorrect assumptions made early in the evaluation life cycle.

Use of Pilot Tests and Feasibility Assessments

Use of pilots and feasibility assessments early in an evaluation strike me as the essence of good practice. And in fact, they worked in Cases 9 (p. 235) and 10 (p. 241). In Case 9 early understanding of people's relatively low baseline knowledge resulted in a timely training program to increase their knowledge, thus allowing an evaluation of whether high levels of skill in using data to inform educational decisions would be beneficial. In Case 10, timely discovery of a potentially negative effect of support to community organizations allowed the evaluators to include an assessment of whether the issue was, in fact, serious and widespread. But an early test did not work in Case 12 (p. 249), where physicians' responses to a survey about willingness to participate in a substance abuse education program misled the evaluators as to the real extent (low) that physicians could be recruited into the program.

What might account for the difference between success in Cases 9 and 10, and failure in Case 12? I believe the answer lies in the unit of analysis in each case. Cases 9 and 10 dealt with individuals. Could individual school staff (teachers and principals) make better decisions? Did people working in nonprofit community agencies feel patronized by their interactions with a support organization? Case 12 also focused on individuals (physicians), but for reasons rooted in organizational behavior, it focused on the wrong individuals. Put another way, the challenge to the evaluators in Case 12 was not to determine what people were willing to do, but to determine whether an entire practice would change its procedures. To know that, it was important to know which individuals were in a position to commit the practice to a change. It ultimately came down to identifying individuals (non-physician practice managers), but knowing that the practice managers were the appropriate champions hinged on knowledge of how the organizations (physician practices) functioned. That level of knowledge was not an issue for Cases 9 and 10.

The explanation offered above about the differences among Cases 9, 10, and 12 touches on a theme that has been lurking in much of the discourse in this chapter, namely the distinction between individual and organizational units of analysis. This theme is also manifest in the discussion of Table 9.5. A lesson can be drawn, namely that understanding surprise in evaluation requires two separate analytical lenses: one that helps us understand how people behave, and one that helps us understand how organizations behave.

Resistance to Evaluation

Resistance to evaluation was manifest in Cases 4 (p. 210), 7 (p. 224), 14 (p. 258), and 15 (p. 263). Two (often commingled) reasons for resistance can be discerned in these cases. One reason is based on professional belief and clinical judgment. The second is self-interest. In Case 4, cooperation with evaluation required time-consuming activities that would disrupt both routine educational activities and efforts to implement a complicated change. Professional beliefs undoubtedly favored educational objectives over evaluation objectives, while self-interest favored keeping individual workload and organizational disruption to a minimum. In Case 7, there was a belief that only benefits were important in a mental health service setting and that costs should not be included in measures of mental health service quality. In Case 14, service agencies resisted an innovative reporting system out of concern that an artifact of the new process would overestimate the proportion of their cases that were incomplete. In Case 15, social workers objected to an evaluation that included an exercise to determine whether their service population suffered from posttraumatic stress disorder (PTSD) by asking clients about traumatic events in their lives. The social workers saw no need for this assessment because they were convinced that all their clients suffered from PTSD and that asking them about past experience served no purpose other than to revive painful memories.

Resistance to evaluation is a common problem in our business, but what is the connection to dealing with surprise? To show this connection, imagine an evaluation scenario that does not begin with any resistance at all to the evaluation. Might resistance pop up unexpectedly? Of course! Evaluation is dynamic. Funder priorities change. Program environments change. Program staff change. Program operations change. Evaluation staff change. Evaluation designs morph over time. Any or all of these changes can spawn resistance to evaluation. (This is precisely what happened in Case 14.)

As with any surprise, the more lead time the evaluator has to take corrective action, the better. Lead time is particularly important in the case of resistance to evaluation because resistance is the kind of problem that can start small and grow through social contagion effects. As such, it is the kind of problem that high-reliability organizations have learned to detect early and to address with a disproportionately large response—that is, they have learned to take these kinds of small problems seriously (Weick & Sutcliffe, 2001). As evaluators exercise their monitoring activity, they are well advised to include incipient resistance to evaluation as one of the parameters to consider.

Incorrect Assumptions Early in the Evaluation Life Cycle

A great deal of surprise came about because of assurances provided to evaluators very early in the design phase of the evaluation life cycle. Sometimes these assurances were explicit and sometimes they were implicit. But in all cases, either the evaluation's funders or an important constituency made representations to the evaluators that turned out to be incorrect. Not all of these surprises were problematic, but some had a major impact on the conduct of the evaluation. These problematic scenarios manifested two intersecting themes. They tended to deal with beliefs about data availability and about program behavior, and they tended to involve decisions that were made very early in the evaluation life cycle. Table 9.7 summarizes these early life cycle assurances that misled evaluators.

Evaluators usually have little room to maneuver when confronting these problems because they are often rooted in decisions that are embedded in requests for proposals, and then solidified in contractual agreements. In other words, the problems arise very early in the evaluation life cycle. But scant wiggle room is different from no wiggle room. There are actions evaluators can take.

TABLE 9.7. Incorrect Assumptions as Sources of Surprise

Case	Page	Assumption
1	197	The sponsor believed that differences in measures of child development in day care settings would be detectable under a narrow range of staff-to-child ratios. They also believed that the ratio was an important independent variable in explaining the quality of service. In fact, the range was too narrow to detect any effects that may have been present. The evaluation had to be recast as a study of the number of children in groups, rather than the ratio of caregiver to children.
3	204	A government funder of community support programs to improve child well-being wanted to know whether the many agencies they were funding were making progress in achieving their goals. The funder assumed that program staff would be able to articulate those goals in well-defined, measurable terms.
4	210	This was an evaluation of the educational impact of introducing laptop computers into schools. The organization funding the evaluation was the same organization that funded acquisition of the computers. Furthermore, a requirement for obtaining the equipment funding was an agreement to participate in the evaluation. Thus it seemed reasonable to believe that cooperation and data would be forthcoming. Despite this tight connection between the evaluation and the program at the level of the funder, resistance to the evaluation developed at some participating schools and school districts. The root of the problem was that while the funder could extract promises from the schools, the funder had no contractual authority over those schools.
7	224	This was a test of adding consumer-provided services to traditional mental health service settings. Proposals were submitted by organizations representing the settings in which the evaluation would take place. The submitters of the proposal, however, did not account for the fact that staff in the agencies they represented would object to providing cost-related information.
8	231	This was an evaluation of a statewide network designed to support local college access support programs in Ohio. One major goal of the evaluation was to determine the effectiveness of the network on improving college access. To evaluate whether this goal was achieved, it was necessary to track service recipients in many different college access programs, from high school through the postsecondary system. The funder incorrectly assumed that the organizations participating in the network had the necessary data systems, that is, systems that did the appropriate tracking and could provide data that could be aggregated across systems.
11	244	This evaluation was designed to test the health impacts of providing central heating assistance to households in Scotland. The assumption at the beginning of the program was that it would be possible to recruit a comparison group of households that did not have central heating. This assumption proved incorrect because of the small number of households that did not have central heating, and because the attractive nature of the program made it unlikely that eligible households would not apply for assistance.

TABLE 9.7. (*continued*)

Case	Page	Assumption
15	263	An important part of this evaluation was an assessment of the extent to which patients in methadone maintenance clinics had service needs related to PTSD and physical or sexual abuse. The early assumption was that such needs existed for a proportion of the clients, and that because the data could lead to better treatment, clinic staff would support the data collection. Staff, however, had other views. Their dominant opinion was that *all* their clients suffered from PTSD, hence making the needs assessment unnecessary. Moreover, they believed that any data collection that asked women about their traumatic experiences would be detrimental to their mental health. The upshot of these beliefs was strong opposition from clinic staff to the execution of the evaluation.
18	281	This was an evaluation of a project designed to integrate diverse services for refugees. The design was a qualitative pre–post assessment. The evaluators assumed that they and the sponsor had a common understanding of what "baseline data" meant. However, they did not, and it turned out that the program had been in operation for several months before the evaluation started, thus making baseline comparison impossible.

Cases 3 (p. 204), 7 (p. 224), 8 (p. 231), 15 (p. 263), and 18 (p. 281) all ran into unexpected problems because assurances about access to data proved to be incorrect. What evaluators need is a way to assess those assurances. Making such a determination is not easy because sponsors may honestly not know that the data they offer will be hard to come by, or not available at all. Still, it will help evaluation planning if evaluators ask themselves two questions: "Given the organization where the evaluation will take place, *can* they deliver?" And, "If they can, *will* they?"

As to the question of whether they *can* deliver, the problem is either that the organization does not have the information in question or that it cannot get the information from those who do. Case 8 (p. 231) is a good example of an organization not having the information. Contrary to assumptions made by the evaluation's funder, organizations providing college access assistance did not have information systems that could produce data on their clients' transition from high school to college. As for not being able to deliver information that does exist, a good example comes from my own experience. I was hired to evaluate the organizational impact of a new IT-driven business system at the Defense Logistics Agency (Morell, 2004). My sponsors were the people who built the system and who wanted to demonstrate its value. The data needed for the evaluation, however, were owned by the users of the system. The builders and users were different organizations with very different environments and organizational incentives. These differences, combined with the sensitivity of the data, made it impossible for my highly motivated sponsor to get me the data I needed.

As to whether an organization *will* provide information, one aspect of the problem is the extent to which providing evaluation information will perturb standard operating procedures. For instance, imagine the disruption involved if providing information would alter well-established routine or impinge on the effective delivery of services. This kind of disruption was certainly manifest in Case 4 (p. 210), where providing evaluation information was yet one more task added to the already hectic effort of introducing new laptop computers (along with instructional support and professional development for teachers) into schools. In such cases it is not a stretch to conclude that the level of disruption would keep the organization from providing the information, no matter how much money and help they were given, or how motivated individuals within the system were to assist.

A second aspect of the problem is whether asking for information is tantamount to asking people to violate their ideology or self-interest. Mental health service providers in Case 7 (p. 224) were not irrational to worry about the consequences to their clinics of providing information on cost. The social workers in Case 15 (p. 263) really felt that it would be detrimental to their clients to answer the evaluators' questions.

If the answers to the questions "Can they deliver?" and "Will they deliver?" raise caution flags, there are tactics evaluators can use to affect the outcome. One set of possibilities touches on relationships between the evaluators and the program being evaluated. A second set of possibilities deals with the evaluation design that is being implemented. (These categories are related, of course, because design affects what evaluators ask of the organizations they deal with. But for the sake of explanation it helps to think of relationships between evaluator and organization differently from the evaluation design itself.)

With respect to relationships between the evaluator and the organization being evaluated, one approach is to offer technical support to make it possible to obtain data. For instance, evaluators may offer consulting on database construction or system interoperability in order to make it possible for an organization's reporting systems to provide the needed data. They may offer resources, for example, reimbursement for staff time or training to support data collection. The success of a technical support approach is illustrated in Case 13 (p. 253), where evaluators worked with clinics to ensure that information systems contained data on service encounters for clients.

In addition to offering technical support, another aspect of the evaluation–program relationship is the level of understanding between the parties. For instance, evaluators might put more effort into understanding the legitimacy of resistance to evaluation. In the spirit of mutual understanding, evaluators might also work to develop better explanations as to why the evaluation they want to carry out is a good idea. An illustration of how this might work comes from an evaluation I am doing that involves a large number of related stakeholder groups, all of whom depend on each other in a variety of formal and informal ways. Only one of these groups is implementing the innovation being evaluated, and that is the only group that needs to provide data for the evaluation. From their narrow point of view, providing the sensitive data I need is difficult and risky. Given the relationships involved, the stakeholders who are implementing the innovation fully realize that they are not alone. They know that others have a legitimate stake in the evaluation. They also know (although it helps to reinforce this point), that their own self-interest is tied to the evaluation needs of the other stakeholders. Given these understandings and relationships, good explanations of the evaluation methodology are proving to be a useful tactic in obtaining the needed data. (Unfortunately, the "explanation" tactic only seems to work in narrow circumstances. I have to admit that it did not seem to work very well in the cases I have been discussing or in a lot of other evaluation that I have done.)

In addition to various tactics for better data access, there is also the possibility of improving data access by changing the evaluation design. There is always the tried-and-true tactic of using multiple data sources to buffer against the loss of any one. For instance, one might survey an entire population and interview a sample, or one might use both clinical records and self-reports. Evaluators also have considerable latitude to invoke designs that buffer against the problem of data not showing up when it is supposed to. To illustrate, consider a design I planned that involved testing an innovation in four companies. Within each company the plan was to compare long-term trend data for departments that received the innovation with a control group of departments that did not receive the innovation. This was a powerful design (or so I like to think), because it combined time series with experimental–control comparisons across multiple organizations. As it turned out (despite the expectations of my sponsor), at least one company was willing to provide the data for the experimental group but not for the control group.[1] I'd rather have all the data, but because of the nature of the evaluation design, reasonably good analysis (based on trends but not cross-group comparisons) will be possible despite the fact that a good deal of the data that were supposed to show up probably will not.

All of these suggestions carry the risk of making the evaluation more complicated, and as we saw in Chapter 7, anything that makes an evaluation more complicated carries its own considerable risks. There are additional problems, however, because the difficulties I have been discussing take root very early in the evaluation life cycle, when funders are first formulating requirements for requests for proposals, or when evaluators are consumed with writing proposals that conform to the RFP's requirements (no matter how misguided they may be), which will be competitively priced and which will manifest methodological integrity.

How might evaluators navigate these straits? One possibility is to propose that the sponsor allow alternate measures in addition to those originally requested. Depending on the situation, this idea can be pitched as a low-cost way of giving the sponsor some insurance that something worthwhile will emerge from the evaluation. A second possibility is to include a task in the evaluation plan to identify and vet the explicit and implicit assumptions that are built into the sponsor's stated description of the evaluation task. This kind of assumption testing is highly compatible with logic model building, so any plan that can include the development of a logic model can include assumption testing at relatively low cost. Finally, it can be useful for the evaluators to use their experience to identify critical assumptions and to include those assumptions in the proposals they write. Doing so would educate the funder, justify tasks designed to test those assumptions, and justify costs for redundant data collection methods or designs.

IN SUM

This chapter inspected all the evaluation surprises found in the 18 cases that appear at the end of this book. Thirty-two instances of surprise were found within these cases. These were placed into a social/organizational framework that shows where surprise comes from and how it affects evaluation (Figure 9.2). The social/organizational view begins with a program's operations as the source of evaluation surprise and traces surprise to adjustments in three aspects of evaluation: design, logistical procedures, or analysis/interpretation. One path in the framework goes directly from program change to evaluation change. A second path is routed from program change to problems with the implementation of evaluation, which then drives change in design, logistics, or analysis/interpretation. (Examples of implementation problems are changes in treatment schedules that remove opportunities for data collection or organizational changes that prevent access to control groups.)

Twelve instances of surprise took the direct route, while 20 moved through evaluation implementation. Changes that were routed through evaluation implementation resulted in adjustments to evaluation that occurred early in the evaluation life cycle, and thus allowed the evaluation to respond to stakeholders' needs. Changes that went directly from program change to evaluation change showed surprises that took place late in the evaluation life cycle, and thus were limited in their ability to respond to stakeholders' needs.

Changes in program operations came about either because of internal organizational behavior or because of outside forces acting on the program. Fourteen instances of surprise were attributable to outside forces. (Half came from funders or regulators and half from clients or customers.) The high proportion of change forced from the outside poses a difficulty for evaluators because it is harder to monitor outside changes than to detect incipient changes emanating from within the program itself. Surprises residing in internal program change divided into those that could be understood in terms of individual behavior (eight instances) and those where change had to be understood in organizational terms (10 cases.)

With respect to evaluation implementation, there is an important distinction between implementation issues that dealt with data availability and issues that touched on evaluation design. Seven instances of changes in evaluation design revealed two that resulted in a diminished ability of evaluators to meet stakeholders' needs and five in which adjustment successfully maneuvered the evaluation into a position that was able to meet stakeholder needs. These five successful changes all took place early in the evaluation life cycle, while the problematic changes took place in late stages of the life cycle.

As a result of working through the cases, three topics that were not originally envisioned became evident: (1) pilot tests and feasibility assessment, (2) resistance to evaluation, and (3) incorrect assumptions made by evaluators. *Pilot and feasibility* tests seem to work as a technique for detecting surprise when the analysis works at the level of individual behavior and examines how people interact with an evaluation. Pilot tests are less successful when evaluation surprise is manifest in organizational behavior. *Resistance to evaluation* is an important issue with respect to surprise because resistance can emerge and spread quickly. *Incorrect assumptions* tended to be about either the availability of data or the behavior of the program being evaluated. Also, they tended to involve issues that were locked in very early in the evaluation life cycle, often at the time when RFPs were composed by sponsors or responded to by evaluators. The key to anticipating these kinds of surprises is for evaluators to ask themselves two questions about sponsors and stakeholders with respect to cooperation in the evaluation process: Can they deliver? If so, will they?

NOTE

1. As of this writing, the situation is in flux, but this description is a reasonable portrayal of how things will probably work out.

Chapter 10

Lessons from Individual Cases

TACTICS FOR ANTICIPATING SURPRISE

So far I have discussed the cases as belonging to various categories. This is the first of two chapters that shift the focus to individual cases. This chapter deals with cases in which surprise resided at the "foreseeable" end of the "foreseeable ↔ unforeseeable" continuum. The next chapter edges into the gray zone in the middle of the continuum and continues into the territory where agile evaluation strategies are most needed. Of course it is hard to place messy, real-world cases on precise points along the continuum. In rough measure, though, a general placement does direct attention to what emphasis should be placed on tactics to anticipate surprise versus those needed to respond to surprise. Others may disagree with my placement. I hope they do. It will spark enlightening conversation.

Because there is about to be so much discussion of specific cases relative to different types of surprise, it may be useful to scan Table 10.1, which shows which cases I invoke for discussion of surprise in different regions on the "foreseeable ↔ unforeseeable" continuum.

In addition to its value in helping with place holding, Table 10.1 reveals a worthwhile surmise about evaluation surprise. Leaving out the difficulty I had that forced me to waffle on Cases 6 and 12, nearly 70% (11/16) of the cases fell into the region where the surprises that cropped up might (if only dimly) have been anticipated. If the pattern were to hold with a larger sample, there is an important lesson here for how we conduct our business.

**TABLE 10.1. Case Location to Illustrate Surprise
on the "Foreseeable ↔ Unforeseeable" Continuum**

		Region		
Case	Page	Close to "foreseeable"	Gray zone	Close to "unforeseeable"
1	197	•		
2	200	•		
3	204	•		
4	210	•		
5	214	•		
6	219		•	
7	224	•		
8	231	•		
9	235			•
10	241			•
11	244	•		
12	249		•	
13	253			•
14	258			•
15	263	•		
16	270	•		
17	277			•
18	281	•		

Cases 1, 2, 3, 4, 5, 7, 8, 11, 15, 16, and 18 are situations in which some combination of the application of theory, past experience, cross-functional teams, and planning methods *might* have combined to reveal the problems that eventually developed. (Others might reach different conclusions, but to my mind these methods would have yielded a reasonable chance of succeeding.)

Case 1 (p. 197) is a situation in which regulations for minimum requirements for caregiver-to-child ratios resulted in a restricted range for a major independent variable. Program theory, as expressed by the sponsor, held that the range varied enough that differences could be detected. Counterbalancing this program theory is measurement theory that suggests that any time the range of a variable is restricted, the possibility of finding statistically significant results is diminished. Furthermore, the expectation of significant results across a restricted range implies a nonlinear pattern with an inflection point at which a small change in an independent variable produces a disproportionate change in a dependent variable. While nonlinear change certainly occurs, identifying the location of the inflection point within a small range implies a very high level of empirical and/or theoretical understanding that is hard to come by in most of the situations we deal with.

While knowledge of measurement theory and patterns of change seem like obvious lenses that would have revealed later problems, the previous discussion glossed over two difficulties. First, it skirted the question of what a "restricted range" means. Depending on the phenomenon, what appears to be a small range may in fact comprise large variation in a system's behavior. (Likewise, the largest and smallest values in what appears to be a wide range may include only a small part of a system's variation.) Still, given our intuitive understanding of social phenomena in general, and child care in particular, it seems reasonable to question whether the caregiver-to-child ratio in this evaluation was sufficiently large to detect effects.

The second difficulty was that, measurement theory notwithstanding, the sponsor believed that the range was sufficient to detect change, and as a result committed to a test of that proposition. Customers are allowed to be wrong, be it about the range of an outcome variable or an entire program theory. Sometimes we can help correct these errors when we take on the role of planner or management consultant. But as evaluators, we can only report the consequences of their errors.

While Case 1 (p. 197) is an example of change in analysis/interpretation, it can also be seen as a case of an agile "virtual" design change. It is not a "real" design change because there was no alteration in design elements such as instruments, groups from whom data were collected, or alteration of historical or cross-group comparisons. None of these were changed to address an evaluation question that was not anticipated at the beginning of the work. Rather, the change was retrospective—the data were analyzed and interpreted *as if* the study started out to answer a different question. The analysis acted as if the evaluation question dealt with the overall number of children in groups, rather than the ratio. This adjustment was required because the initial program theory was wrong. The theory implied that the existing caregiver-to-child ratio was sufficient to make a difference in outcome. This theory turned out to be incorrect. After a great deal of creative thought and inspection of the data, the evaluation was able to address an important question about child care, but it was *not* the question that the sponsor wanted addressed when the evaluation was commissioned.

Case 2 (p. 200) shows a highly politicized situation in which some stakeholders did not want the evaluation, there was disagreement among other stakeholders as to whether and how to do the evaluation, and the sponsor had a new business opportunity riding on a positive outcome. While the specifics of what problems might occur could not have been predicted, the likelihood of such problems could certainly have been expected. And in fact they were expected, as evidenced by the evaluators' careful attention to stakeholders' positions early in the evaluation design phase and their negotiations over the nature of the evaluation.

Evaluators like to chant the mantra, "The earlier we are involved the better." This mantra is usually true, but this case shows that advantage can be gained by getting involved later, when the program is mature. Later involvement loses many opportunities for collecting baseline data, but it has the advantage of giving the evaluator ample opportunity to determine what the program really is (and is likely to remain) and give the sponsors ample opportunity to realistically consider what impacts their program may be having.

Another feature of Case 2 was the opportunity for the evaluators to negotiate with their sponsors over the evaluation design and outcomes to be measured. In many cases bad timing or lack of power lead to evaluators' having to accept designs or measurements imposed by their sponsors. Here, evaluators had the ability to negotiate and the skills to do so in a way that led to an evaluation that was acceptable to both evaluator and sponsor.

Case 3 (p. 204) began by relying on two (to my mind at least) very reasonable assumptions. The first was that program staff who are deeply involved with providing services would be able to articulate goals for their programs and clients. The second was that by nurturing involvement of program staff in the evaluation (e.g., by their having a say in selection of metrics), that staff would engage the evaluation process and provide information to evaluators. Neither of these assumptions proved correct.

Case 3 strikes me as an object lesson in always applying an important planning principle. Never fail to ask two questions: (1) What assumptions must hold true in order for this evaluation to be implemented successfully? (2) Representatives of what groups are needed to get a good answer to the first question? I can imagine how considering the assumption about how well staff can identify goals might have revealed their inability to do so. (I would have bet that they would be able to identify goals, and I would have lost.) Testing the assumption about nurturing involvement is more problematic because it deals with people's reactions to an ongoing process. It assumes that involvement with evaluation over time will translate into support. Such support is reasonable to expect, but not certain, and it is only testable as the evaluation unfolds. Thus Case 3 highlights two aspects of testing assumptions early in an evaluation's life cycle: (1) that doing so might keep evaluators out of trouble, and (2) that even if identified, not all assumptions are equally testable. Some are easy to check. Others will require activating the top row of Figure 7.1, with the attendant downside of extending an evaluation's time line, complexity, and cost. In this case, monitoring ongoing support for the evaluation would entail added resources for interviewing clinic staff. Complexity may also come into play because the extra interviewing itself may cause a reaction among the staff, which would in turn require still other evaluation elements to monitor and minimize any difficulties that may arise.

Case 4 (p. 210) involves providing computers to students, integrating computer use into teaching, and having teachers both observe and record student behavior. An important assumption in this evaluation was that a lot of novelty and change in standard operating procedure could be successfully integrated into the schools' routine activities. A few different perspectives can be used to show that this assumption could easily break. Experienced school-based researchers and evaluators could speak to the practical risk of succeeding in such efforts. From the perspective of system theory, the evaluation was risky because it required a high level of coordination among many tightly linked interacting elements, each of which was operating with few slack resources. A more economic-centered lens would reveal that high transaction and opportunity costs would be incurred because teachers had to change their normal operating procedures, take time to learn the new methods, and find time to do student observations. The evaluators' response to the problem engaged the "resources" aspect of Figure 7.1. Solutions included bringing in external observers, a communications campaign, and the development of templates to increase the efficiency of conducting surveys, making observations, and submitting data.

Case 5 (p. 214) involves evaluation of a major intervention in a school system. At first blush one would think that participation in the study would appeal to schools. The intervention did not interfere with instructional time. Schools did planning anyway, and the intervention provided a structure that could add clarity and economy to the planning process. It also held the promise of better (data-based) planning that would lead to greater student achievement.

Despite these appealing features, however, participation in the evaluation entailed three components that might give a school pause before deciding to participate. First, a survey of students was required. Although the school may not have had much of a burden in administering the survey, the survey did represent yet another of many requests that were being made of families in the school community. Second, implementing the new planning process required changes in standard operating procedures for planning, with a move toward a more structured approach. Imposing more structure on any process requires a learning curve, an adjustment to change, and an acceptance of new constraints. Finally, participation required a school employee at each site to take on a considerable data collection burden. Any one of these requests may be manageable, and it is easy to imagine why considerable benefits of participation would move schools to participate. But depending on local circumstances at any candidate school, it is also easy to imagine that any one of those requirements for participation would inhibit agreement and that their cumulative effect would make it difficult for the evaluators to get the necessary agreements in the short time available to ramp up the evaluation.

The evaluation assumed that the reasons to participate would outweigh the reasons not to in enough schools that a sufficient sample could be recruited. This is not an unreasonable assumption, but it is a far cry from a sure bet. I have not a shred of doubt that the evaluators understood these issues intuitively and did the best they could to devise a powerful implementation plan. (I'm sure they did a better job than I would have.) Still, one can't help but wonder what design decisions would have been made, or negotiation with sponsors conducted, had the assumptions been specified and probed in advance.

Case 7 (p. 224) made two assumptions—first, that staff in participating mental health clinics would be able and willing to think in technical terms about costs and benefits, and second, that the staff would accept the notion of casting their work in cost:benefit terms. These seemed like reasonable assumptions because agreement to provide the data was explicitly stated in the request for proposals to which all participating clinics agreed. Furthermore, each participating clinic (or group of clinics) submitted its own application to the federal government. It certainly seemed reasonable for the evaluators to believe that participating clinics had agreed to terms that would allow the evaluation to go forward. What happened? Two factors seem to have converged. First, as the project unfolded, the consequences of participation revealed themselves to the participating clinics. At that point the second factor came into play. The project's governance structure allowed the clinics to act on their newfound understanding. That structure was composed of two kinds of entities—participating clinics, and a coordinating center that served as a centralized data collection point and as the keeper of the evaluation's methodology. An equal number of votes was distributed across all the participating organizations. Because of this distribution, the coordinating center could be easily outvoted. One can argue the pros and cons of this governance structure, but it is certainly true that such a system could make it hard to maintain the integrity of an evaluation design. As the evaluation began in earnest, service providers realized that the data expected of them challenged their ideological commitments and their self-interest. The governance structure allowed them to act on their beliefs.

Might the service agencies' concerns have been detected before they became full-blown challenges to the evaluation? Perhaps. Would detection have led to amelioration of those problems? Perhaps. The evaluators might have conducted introductory discussions with some of the clinics, explaining exactly what they needed, and used the experience to judge reactions to the request for information. Considering the resistance encountered, and the extent to which data collection had to be scaled back, it is not clear that earlier detection would have made much difference. But one never knows. Maybe those discussions would have revealed a few evaluation champions among clinic personnel whose influence might have made a difference. Maybe successful examples of cost–benefit analysis in mental health could have been found to persuade clinics to participate. Perhaps discussions with the Substance Abuse and Mental Health Services Administration project officer might have led to some education or pressure that would have made a difference. We don't know what might have been, but we do know that the problem of resistance to the evaluation did not become evident until data collection efforts were underway (i.e., when unpleasant demands started to be made on participating clinics). It seems reasonable to think that resistance *might* have been ameliorated had the problem been known before the reaction set in.

As an aside, this case is an object lesson in why it is difficult to place cases on the "foreseeable ↔ unforeseeable" continuum. Much of what I just talked about dealt with what the evaluators could have done early in the evaluation life cycle. But I also fudged a lot by admitting how difficult that determination would have been and how scouting for developing problems would have helped. Anyone who insisted in placing this case in the next chapter would not get too much of an argument from me.

Case 8 (p. 231) dealt with community-based college access programs. Funders and evaluators made the assumption that comparable success data would be available across many independent programs. This assumption might have been suspect because the various programs developed independently of each other, historically had minimal requirements to maintain data on success, and had no history of standard reporting. Data systems develop to meet the idiosyncratic business needs of the organizations in which they dwell. To say that data can be aggregated across organizations is to say that there are common business processes that unite the disparate organizations. Common business processes can happen for a variety of reasons. For instance, there may be data reporting requirements imposed from an external source, or there may be a cross-organizational agreement to work together for a common purpose, or there may be a third party that acquires different organizations and brings them under the same corporate umbrella. But absent circumstances such as these, organizations have no incentive to confront the organizational, technical, and financial costs of common reporting. In organizational terms, common (or at least interoperable) reporting systems can require change in organizational structure, process, and job content. From a technical point of view, there may be a need to acquire hardware or software or to redesign existing systems. None of this is easy or cheap.

It is true that in Case 8 (p. 231) the existence of inadequate systems, and their implications for evaluation, were caught in time. But the method of discovery is worrisome. As the authors put it: "While discussing the draft strategic plan and an unrelated topic of challenges in developing a database for college access programs to track student service recipients from high school through the postsecondary system, it became clear to the program officer and evaluator that OCAN member college access programs did not have a consistent way to track participant outcomes, and thereby it would be a challenge to address the second goal of the evaluation, which centered around outcomes for OCAN member programs." In other words, the problem was caught by chance.

Two points emerge from this story. First, a systematic effort to test assumptions may have detected the difficulty earlier. Second, the problem was detected because the evaluation process included a rich web of communication between the parties. Even without targeting specific topics (e.g., underlying assumptions), a lot of important information can be caught in these kinds of webs. So in addition to all the other good reasons to interact with stakeholders, we can add the likelihood that communication will stray from predicted paths, and in so doing, to reveal problems earlier than they would otherwise be detected.

Case 11 (p. 244) dealt with outcomes that might come from helping people obtain a desirable resource, in this case central heating. The design called for an experimental and a control group. Those groups could not be established or maintained. One impediment was the small number of households that did not have central heating and also were not involved in the program being evaluated. A related difficulty was that some intended clients in the experimental sample did not receive the intervention, while others acquired central heating in other ways. Under the circumstances, it seems clear that these problems (or ones very like them) would occur. The numbers of eligible enrollees was small. The program was voluntary and desirable. Other means of obtaining central heating were available. In fact, the difficulties *were* anticipated during the planning stage of the evaluation life cycle. This discovery led to a deliberate set of design decisions that changed the original plan. Rather than the intended experimental–control design, comparisons focused on households whose central heating status could be expected to remain stable over the study period, and then took an "intention to treat" approach to comparison.

A noteworthy aspect of this case is that the problem was detected very early in the evaluation life cycle, thus allowing change at a pace that met the needs of careful planning with respect to both the evaluation itself and the needs of the sponsors. This situation is similar to Case 5 (p. 214). There, too, a design surprise was detected early, thus allowing a change in methodology and in focus that satisfied both technical requirements and the sponsor's needs. (But note that in both cases, there had to be a shift of emphasis from an evaluation of program outcome to research on an important social issue.) Contrast these cases with Cases 1 (p. 197) and 7 (p. 224), both of which encountered problems late in the evaluation life cycle. Neither of these cases had the opportunity to revise methodologies or negotiate with sponsors.

Case 15 (p. 263) assumed that program staff would accept the need for evaluation. Here, the assumption did not hold because of social workers' strongly held professional judgment that all women who go through multiple traumatic experience suffer from PTSD. Given this belief, it was pointless to do an evaluation to determine *whether* women suffered from PTSD. Research supporting the evaluators' point of view had no persuasive power, thus highlighting the difficulty of implementing an evaluation that is based on empirical research findings when those findings contradict strongly held beliefs. The second assumption in Case 15 was that interviewing the clinic's clients as part of the evaluation would not in itself cause them discomfort by leading them to relive their trauma. In terms of resistance to the evaluation, these two assumptions reinforced each other. If, in fact, all the clients suffered from PTSD, it was particularly inappropriate to ask them questions that would induce them to relive their experiences.

I have spent a good deal of effort in this book trying to make the case that research findings should be included when evaluation plans are laid. I do believe that we should attend to research findings, but this case is a good example of why trying to use past research can be difficult. It is one thing to think of outside information as adding to stakeholders' perspectives. It is quite something else to deal with situations where stakeholders' views and research findings conflict.

Case 16 (p. 270) is the story of what can happen when a social system is perturbed. A seemingly simple innovation sought to provide free prenatal care and delivery services to mothers and to compensate health care workers for any loss of income that derived from the innovation. What actually happened was an interaction between clients' experience with similar programs in the past and service providers' beliefs about adequate compensation. Past experience led patients to hoard medicines and service providers to find ways to impose fees where none should have been. In this case two observations are noteworthy with respect to surprise. First, because of the qualitative design used, the evaluators were perfectly capable of detecting and reporting on the situation. Second, the findings may have been unexpected by the project's sponsor but were not unexpected to the evaluators. Their work in other settings and knowledge of the research literature made their observations perfectly sensible and reasonable. Unfortunately, the evaluators arrived on the scene too late for their knowledge to do any good.

Case 18 (p. 281) is an evaluation of a refugee resettlement program. Because of the jarring nature of refugee resettlement, and the amount of adjustment that people undergo when they first move, baseline interviews are important for capturing service recipients' ephemeral initial impressions and attitudes. The funder appreciated this need and led the evaluators to believe that the requisite interviews could be conducted. Unfortunately, the funder lacked a proper understanding about what constituted a baseline methodology. Because of this misunderstanding, the evaluators were appointed only after the program had been operating for 3 months, thus making collection of a true baseline impossible. As a result, what was conceived of as a pre–post qualitative design was transformed into a design that collected data several times while the program was in operation, but which could not speak to critical change during early phases of resettlement. Fortunately, the problem was discovered during discussions with the sponsor that occurred soon after the project was funded. As a result, the funder was aware early on of what could and could not be expected from the evaluation. In this sense, Case 18 is similar to Case 8 (p. 231), where open-ended discussions with the sponsor unearthed the surprise that, contrary to expectations, participating organizations did not have the data systems needed to support the evaluation. The lesson is the same.

In both Cases 8 and 18, discovery of the unexpected did not come from a focused conversation that had an agenda item to question assumptions. Rather, the discovery was made because there was a web of communication that allowed discussion to segue from one topic to another. The specific content of any one conversation may be a matter of chance, but the likelihood that something useful and unexpected will emerge is a function of the overall amount of discussion that takes place. In Cases 8 and 18 the conversations were with sponsors, but it is prudent to assume that conversations with other stakeholders might also provide unexpected and important information, and that useful discoveries can take place throughout the course of an evaluation.

The second surprise in Case 18 was the ethnic makeup of the refugee population. Past experience led the funders to believe that refugees from many different locations would receive the service that was being evaluated. Thus the evaluators expected to be able to enlighten the sponsor on the differential value of the program for different ethnic groups. The sponsor was not aware that a combination of a recent influx of Africans, combined with people's desire to settle near their compatriots, resulted in a homogeneous population of service recipients. In theory, the evaluators could have checked on the population makeup prior to developing their plans for group comparisons. On the other hand, why should they? There was a historical pattern that was known to both the evaluators and the project sponsor. If the pattern did not hold, I certainly would have expected the people funding the refugee program to know about it. The situation in Case 18 parallels the situation in Case 5 (p. 214), where historical data on school performance did not reflect the situation for the time when a sample of schools had to be chosen. The lesson is the same. It is sound practice to rely on the best historical data available, but it is also a good idea to test that data as early as possible in an evaluation's life cycle.

IN SUM

This was the first of two chapters that combined principles from the previous chapters with details of the cases in order to heighten our understanding of surprise in evaluation. The focus was on cases whose surprise fell roughly into the "foreseeable" region. Of the 18 cases in the book, nearly 70% (not counting two ambiguous cases) fell into this region. There was discussion about how evaluators successfully dealt with surprise and suggestions as to how they might have dealt with surprise in more powerful ways. Those suggestions were included to prod the reader's thinking about possibilities, not to prescribe action. What any of us might do in similar circumstances would be highly dependent on time and context. Furthermore, no matter what tactics we might think to invoke, we would also have to consider the potential negative consequences of whatever action we contemplated.

Chapter 11

Lessons from Individual Cases

Responding to Surprise

The previous chapter applied tactics for anticipating surprise to individual cases. This chapter continues the discussion of cases, but with the focus shifted to the "unforeseeable" region in the "foreseeable ↔ unforeseeable" continuum. (To see where each of the 18 cases fall on the continuum, see Table 10.1.)

THE MIDDLE

I placed only two cases in the middle of the continuum. These were the cases in which I felt that some impending surprise might have been anticipated, but only in particularly vague and uncertain ways. These are the cases where an emphasis on agile evaluation should begin to come into play.

Case 6 (p. 219) is an evaluation design that was very tightly linked to a specific treatment schedule. It fell victim to schedule changes that were needed to improve the quality of service. A single treatment schedule became three treatment schedules with different dosages, with no attendant increase in the size of the study, and with no control over the assignment of subjects to conditions. This change led to a change in analysis strategy which involved checking for differences among clients in the different groups with respect to basic demographics, and then checking on whether those differences affected outcomes. Based on that

169

analysis, groups were combined and an overall impact was determined. Given the realities of clients' reactions to the original program, changing the treatment schedule was an eminently reasonable action. Also, given the need for assessing change, the original design was equally reasonable. The problem was the tight linkage between the treatment schedule and the evaluation design, *combined with* lack of data on three topics, each of which might have helped to rescue the design: (1) data on whether the various treatment schedules differed in terms of what was provided to clients, (2) client satisfaction, and (3) client characteristics that might have affected treatment.

I can imagine how various planning techniques might have been useful. Using these techniques, the evaluators could have addressed questions such as: "What assumptions about the treatment need to hold for the evaluation to be successful?" Or, "Based on the experience of others who have worked in similar settings, what alternate scenarios might develop for how this program evolves over time?" Obviously, there is no guarantee that asking these questions would reveal precisely the problem that occurred. But it seems reasonable that such an exercise might have revealed a set of likely futures that would highlight the need for a richer understanding of program behavior and client characteristics. In that sense Case 6 is in the gray zone between surprise that can and cannot be anticipated. The fragility of the evaluation design could have been predicted. It might also have been possible to make a decent guess concerning what information about clients would be useful, should the design break. But beyond these general notions, actionable knowledge about likely surprise would be impossible to discern in advance. We could not know how clients would react to the service offered, what adjustments the service provider would make, the number of people receiving service, or the timing of the service, to name just a few of the factors that would affect how the evaluation would have to adjust.

Case 12 (p. 249) used a pilot study to assess physicians' interest in participating in a program that would improve their substance abuse assessment and management skills. A 65% positive response gave the evaluators confidence that they would have enough participation to go ahead with full-scale implementation of the innovative program. But despite the assurance provided by the survey findings, physicians did not sign up in the expected numbers. The solution was to convene a focus group to explore why the initial findings led the evaluators astray. The use of the focus group was an agile response to an unanticipated event. The evaluators were attempting to implement a process change in health service practices and assumed that the physicians spoke for their practices. But the evaluators did not realize that many activities in physicians' practices are determined by their practice managers rather than by the physicians. This reality is far from obvious. (At least, it was far from obvious to me.)

Case 12 illustrates the subtle kinds of mistakes that can end up making a big difference. Because of an eminently reasonable assumption about decision making, the evaluators asked the physicians directly whether they would participate in the substance abuse education program. What might have happened if the question were asked differently? Suppose the evaluators began by asking themselves: "How can we find out whether physicians working in a practice will participate in our substance abuse education program?" Starting with this question challenges the underlying (and to me perfectly reasonable) assumption about how decisions are actually made in physicians' practices. Posing the question in its more general form would lead to a different type of inquiry to determine likely participation. Of course, it is all too easy to look at this particular case and identify an alternate form of a question. The principle, however, holds across setting and topic. All else being equal, ask questions in a form that recognizes context and directs inquiry along multiple paths.

Case 12 is in the gray zone because from a practical point of view there are limits on what could have been discovered about how physicians' practices commit to action. It might have been possible to realize that physicians' personal agreements might not be the best path to organizational commitment. What then? Would an unambiguous alternate solution have been discovered? We already know the solution—to work through practice managers. We also know that the evaluators discovered this solution in a fairly simple fashion—by convening a focus group of nurses who were already involved in the research project. But is it so obvious that the tactic of discovery that was so easily available to the evaluators would have worked? Also, what would have happened if those nurses were not available to the research team? The research team would have been confronted with a need to conduct an organizational analysis, complete with choices about breadth versus depth of sampling, concerns about representativeness of sampling, data collection methods, and the specific content of any questions that were asked. There is also the matter of specificity. Just because the general nature of decision making in physicians' practices was known, there would still be a question as to whether the findings applied to the kind of decision the researchers were seeking. Furthermore, it is entirely possible that several different paths would be discovered that would lead to a commitment by the practices. Only in retrospect do we know that none of these complications were present. As a practical matter, when making an a priori decision as to how to proceed, the best we could hope for is a methodology that would tell us that physician agreement alone might not suffice and highlight a path or two that might lead to a good answer about various routes to participation.

LEADING INDICATORS AND AGILE EVALUATION

The previous sections were based on the notion that surprise might be anticipated if only the right methods were applied. For truly unforeseeable change, however, it is *only* in retrospect that one can identify the assumptions that, had they been anticipated, would have kept an evaluation out of trouble. For these kinds of situations, minimizing trouble requires early detection and quick response. The need for early detection and quick response shows up in Cases 5, 10, 13, 14, and 17. Let's see what the cases did and speculate a bit on what they might have done. As we do, remember the caution I outlined above. It is easy to critique in retrospect. We have to look at this discussion as an effort to raise our consciousness, not to find fault. We were not there, and if we were, I bet we would not have acted much differently. At least, I would not have acted differently.

Case 5 (p. 214) assumed that historical information on school performance would hold for the school year in which the evaluation was scheduled to be performed. Knowledge of school performance was critical to the evaluation because it was key to determining the size of experimental and control groups. Here is a case of true surprise. The evaluators were very experienced in doing research in school systems. They knew they were basing their initial calculations on dated information. They used that information to make an initial best guess at an early stage in the evaluation life cycle, a time when some estimate had to be made, and when no other information was available. Theirs was an eminently reasonable way to proceed, and far better than making no early attempt to estimate group size. Knowing the historical vagaries of school performance, the evaluators deliberately planned a recalculation using the newest data they could find when the evaluation began. What could be better? They used the best information available for early planning and built in a task to use more current information as soon as they could.

The assumption they made was subtle—that the difference between the new and old data would allow them to fine-tune their group sizes, but that the size of the difference would be small enough that they could accommodate the adjustment. They were wrong. The most current data turned out to be quite different from the historical data. The adjustment required a change in sampling and a related change in analysis. The original design required a sample of officially designated "No Recognition Schools." When it became impossible to get enough of these schools, the evaluation plan shifted to including other (seemingly similar) schools and invoked a propensity score-matching approach to control–experimental comparisons. In terms of the social/ organizational typology this change had two dimensions. First, it involved a change in logistics and procedures as the evaluators committed to recruiting a group of schools they had not originally intended to include. This change in recruiting methods required a change in the nature of experimental–control comparisons, which was reflected in a change in analysis strategy that shifted the project from an evaluation of an educational program toward a research project on education.

Case 10 (p. 241) is an example of sequential as opposed to simultaneous interaction with stakeholders. The initial evaluation was developed based on discussions between the evaluators and the funders of SHATIL, a program that provided technical assistance to community-based organizations. Those discussions yielded a reasonable list of evaluation objectives: (1) map characteristics of applicant organizations, (2) map services provided to those organizations, (3) assess contribution of the program to applicant organizations, and (4) evaluate satisfaction with the services provided. Full data collection was a structured questionnaire distributed to the several hundred organizations who received services. Interspersed between consultation with the funder and full-blown data collection was another round of discussions with another group of stakeholders, this time the service recipient organizations themselves. The main purpose of this round of interaction was instrument development; that is, it was an effort to ensure that the contents of the questionnaire touched on relevant issues of concern to the client organizations. It seemed like a routine instrument development

exercise designed to make sure that the funder got what it needed—
information on client satisfaction and guidance for what to do in the
future. As it turned out, this stage of the evaluation uncovered an aspect
of "client satisfaction" that was wholly unanticipated and which ended
up driving a modification in the evaluation design. The focus groups
led the evaluators to believe that not only was satisfaction low in some
cases, but that SHATIL's actions might have perverse effects, in this case
making recipient organizations feel patronized rather than helped. If,
in fact, SHATIL was affecting its clients negatively, knowing the details
would be important, far more so than simply understanding how to
boost a satisfaction score from neutral to good, or good to excellent.

To assess the situation, a series of questions were added that would
never have been considered under normal circumstances. In one sense
we might claim that nothing untoward occurred. The evaluation design
assumed that relevant topics could not be known without some kind of
pilot study, and in fact such a study revealed the topics that needed to
be investigated. On the other hand, SHATIL and the evaluators saw the
pilot study as a way to refine topics they felt they already understood
and did not foresee a need to investigate perverse effects. The important
point here was that the evaluation contained a systematic structured
activity that by its nature had the capacity to detect a very wide range
of issues that were unlikely to have been foreseen had SHATIL staff and
the evaluators simply brainstormed a list of likely issues. One way to
look at the SHATIL evaluation is to regard the interviewees and members of the focus groups as close observers of SHATIL's work who were
asked an open question: "Given what SHATIL does, what do you think
its managers need to know to improve the organization's services?" The
system worked because it included a structured process for discovering
this unstructured knowledge.

Cases 13 and 14 endured similar shocks, but reacted to them very
differently. In Case 13 (p. 253), changes in regulations and requirements made it impossible to accomplish two tasks that were important to the evaluation design: (1) collect scheduled follow-up data, and
(2) continue using experienced staff (who had criminal histories) as
interviewers. The solution left the design intact. Archival data was
substituted for follow-up data, and eligible staff were trained to do the
necessary evaluations. These changes could be made because three
conditions were present. First, the evaluators and the staff had a good
working relationship, thus making it possible to build redundancy by

using the clinic's IT systems. Second, the evaluators had the foresight (and resources) to design the redundancy into their evaluation system. Third, the adjustments the evaluators made to the evaluation did not intrude into normal program operations, thus giving the evaluators free reign to solve problems as they saw fit.

Case 14 (p. 258) is an evaluation of how county-level health services could make use of tailored information about outcomes and severity in order to improve their services. As in Case 13, the evaluation suffered an environmental shock when the state expanded the information to be included. In one sense the change was an acknowledgment of the success of the first phase of the test. But an artifact of the shift from one set of information to the other was the illusion of counties' having a large number of incomplete cases. Indicating a large number of incomplete cases, if true, would cast the service providers in a very negative light. In this case there were two layers of surprise that could not be anticipated—first, that the state would decide to change the information flow; and second, that the nature of the change would require a transition that made it appear as if counties were not serving clients.

I don't see any way the evaluators in Case 13 could have known that regulations would arise that would make it impossible to use their intended interviewers. Similarly in Case 14, I don't see how the evaluators could have developed an inkling of what success the program would have, what the regulatory and political environment would be at the time the program demonstrated success, or how officials would interpret that success in the light of current events. The big difference between the cases is that in Case 13 the evaluators had the opportunity and the resources to build a general buffer against data collection problems by making sure the IT system could be used for evaluation purposes. I suppose that this difference provides a glimmer of insight about buffers against surprise. In Case 13 the evaluators' precautions dealt only with data availability, not with core performance issues related to the organization being evaluated. Case 14, however (and also Case 7, for that matter), did challenge core organizational values. We might want to generalize and claim that buffers against technical surprise are easier to build than buffers against organizational surprise.

Case 17 (p. 277) is an example of how using a database can affect an organization's functioning, and in turn, how evaluation needs to adjust to those changes. Katrina Aid Today (KAT), a national case management consortium, used a database to coordinate case management services for households that were displaced or otherwise affected by Hurricane Katrina. One of KAT's activities was the use of a database to support case management coordination and service provision. Evaluation of the participating providers evolved as a result of two developments related to the database. The first change resulted from a realization (based on experience with the data), that what started merely as a case tracking mechanism could be used for other evaluation purposes. The second change resulted from analyses done by KAT's coordinating organization. Those analyses led to reports that went back to the participating agencies, and which had the effect of giving those agencies new insights into their clients' needs. One consequence of these (originally unplanned) uses of the database was that service providers ended up monitoring and evaluating activities that KAT did not account for in its original evaluation design. To complement this new understanding of its clients' services, KAT deployed other evaluative methods, including client and case manager surveys. In other words, the impact of the innovation being evaluated was incremental and evolutionary. It was incremental because experience with the database accumulated over time. It was evolutionary because each incremental change came from an interaction between use of the information that was available and local needs that were felt by users at particular points in time.

IN SUM

This chapter extended the discussion of surprise into those regions of the "foreseeable ↔ unforeseeable" continuum where tactics to design for agility overtake tactics for anticipating surprise. Two cases fell into the middle of the continuum—that place where foresight dims and quick response begins to be important. Five cases were placed into the "unforeseeable" region. In those cases efforts to anticipate surprise lose their potency and tactics to increase the agility of evaluation design become paramount.

Chapter 12

Unanticipated Program Outcomes

Earlier in this book I discussed the unexpected (to me) finding that most of the surprises in the cases dealt with the evaluation of programs, rather than with the programs themselves. The reasons have to do with the relative lengths of program and evaluation life cycles, and with the linkages between a program and its evaluation on the one hand and a program and its environment on the other. (See Chapter 8 for elaboration.) But even though it is rare that evaluators address truly unexpected program outcomes, there are technical and ethical reasons for being prepared to do so. From a technical standpoint, programs do change in strange ways, and we are paid to detect and explain program behavior. There is no telling how quickly or when unexpected outcomes might pop up, and we should be able to deal with them when they do. From an ethical point of view, we have obligations as citizens and taxpayers to look beyond the narrow confines of predetermined outcomes. So what can we learn from the cases that showed unexpected outcomes in the sense that I had originally envisioned the term?

CASE DESCRIPTIONS

Four of the 18 cases showed unexpected outcomes. This section presents the elements of each that are salient to understanding the evaluation of unexpected outcomes.

Shifting Sands in a Training Evaluation Context (Case 2)

This evaluation (p. 200) involved assessment of a training program to enable field engineers to provide service for a major new computer system developed by the corporation and sold throughout the world. The original scope of the evaluation was unclear, as were the expectations of various stakeholders. Defining the scope took considerable, and nimble, negotiations. Once the evaluation scope was agreed to, results flowed in a straightforward manner from the data collection, and in fact had a major impact on the company whose employees were being trained. The company took the expensive step of adding a day to a training program that involved 12, trainees and which required bringing them to a training center from worldwide locations. While this change was dramatic, it nonetheless constituted a direct link between the purpose of the evaluation and the use of the findings. Three other changes that flowed from the company–evaluator interaction were less expected. None involved decisions about the training program. All involved the adoption of evaluation.

1. The evaluation form developed for the evaluation was adopted by the company for other types of training.
2. The company established a new evaluation position. While this evaluation alone was not responsible for this act, it was an important contributing factor.
3. There seemed to be a subtle shift in the corporate culture toward greater receptivity to evaluation.

From Unintended to Undesirable Effects of Health Intervention: The Case of User Fees Abolition in Niger, West Africa (Case 16)

In many African countries user fees are a significant impediment to people's use of essential health services. This evaluation (p. 270) was an effort to determine the effects of abolishing such fees for deliveries and prenatal consultations. The evaluation design was qualitative, with an anthropological perspective. All data collection took place while the innovative program was in operation. Expectations for program outcome (and hence for the evaluation) were straightforward. Abolition of fees would increase access, which would in turn improve health. Three unexpected outcomes occurred, all due to characteristics of the social system into which this health care innovation was inserted.

1. The program came on the heels of a previous program that distributed food in the same area for the purposes of alleviating hunger during a food crisis. The population correctly saw the food distribution as temporary. Part of the user fee abolition innovation included the distribution of medicine. Because of previous history with food, people saw the medicine distribution also as a temporary measure, which led to hoarding. Hoarding behavior stressed clinic operations because to obtain medicine it was necessary to visit the clinic and present (real or feigned) symptoms.

2. The health care workers in the clinics had always drawn on two sources of income. The first was their normal salaries. The second was the imposition of user fees on everything provided to the patients. The NGO funding the program understood this two-tier system and built in bonuses to the health care workers to compensate for their lost income. The NGO did not, however, count on an adaptation by the health care workers to increase their income further. They lobbied the NGO for still additional compensation for working in the free system, justifying their request by citing increased workload. To complicate matters, there was a grain of truth in these complaints because the hoarding behavior described above did increase workload.

3. Health care workers were able to game the system in ways that allowed them to reimpose various fees. For instance, they redirected drugs to other fee-for-service systems, thus creating artificial shortages in the prenatal care program, or began to impose previously unknown fees, for example, the lamination of health record books carried by patients.

Unintended Consequences and Adapting Evaluation: Katrina Aid Today National Case Management Consortium (Case 17)

Katrina Aid Today (KAT) employed a database to coordinate case management services for households that were displaced or otherwise affected by Hurricane Katrina (p. 277). An important aspect of the database's use was submission of brief summary reports to the national partners for each of their agencies and the expansion of those reports for use by program managers for agency-level information sharing during site visits. The reports contained information on cases that were open and closed, cases that had a recovery plan achieved, the reasons for closing a case, and the value of services that were leveraged by external agencies and community organizations. Another dimension of reporting included macro-level information on what services were provided, how the services compared to identified needs, and how services differed by the client's location. The availability of this information gave agencies insights into their operations that they had by no other means. As a result, they evolved in how they monitored their operations and what evaluations they carried out internally. The database began as an aid to case management and a tracking tool whose primary intended outcome was to help coordinate services. In fact, the availability of the information had a much wider range of consequences for how programs operated. Evaluation of the effect that the database had was carried out by means of ongoing monitoring and observation.

Evaluation of the Integrated Services Pilot Program from Western Australia (Case 18)

Australia has been implementing programs to provide humanitarian assistance to its refugees. This evaluation dealt with one such effort, a pilot project to co-locate government and nongovernment services near concentrations of newly arrived refugees (p. 281). The original evaluation design employed a qualitative program assessment to collect data at the beginning and end of the program. The design changed when the baseline data collection moved from program start to 3 months after program start. The intent of the evaluation was to evaluate the official project objectives: (1) improve delivery of critical services to humanitarian entrants, (2) relieve pressure on mainstream services, (3) adopt a whole-of-government approach to improve coordination, (4) provide a holistic service, and (5) promote partnerships and links between relevant government and nongovernment agencies.

In addition to these stated objectives, four unintended outcomes were observed. The first two unintended consequences were unambiguously positive. First, the innovative service eased pressure on mainstream refugee services. Second, improvements in the new service's outreach ability resulted in providing services over an extended area. The third unintended consequence was unambiguously undesirable. The project placed an unrealistically high workload on staff, thus further challenging the goals of organizational maintenance. The value of the fourth unintended consequence depends on whether one took a short- or a long-range point of view. The service was able to meet new needs that other services were not able to meet (e.g., home health services). In the short term this was both desirable and undesirable. On the one hand, the provision of such services is certainly a good thing on its face. On the other hand, the services put a strain on budgets. Thus a conflict was set up between mission goals and goals of organizational maintenance. The long-term value (in cost–benefit terms) will depend on whether the early intervention characteristics of the new services have a salutary effect on the intergenerational problems that are common in refugee communities. If they do, the short-term negative consequences will probably have been worthwhile. If they don't, the risk to the program hardly seems worth it.

APPLYING THE CASES TO UNINTENDED PROGRAM OUTCOMES

In Case 2, the unexpected behavior involved an interaction between the act of evaluation and program activity. Not only were evaluation results used, but organizations' experience with evaluation changed their behavior with respect to how evaluation should be used in the future. In this case, "evaluation use" seems to be manifest in some combination of the application of findings, evaluative thinking, and organizational change to support evaluation. Case 2 is a wonderful example of how "evaluation use" can transcend the mere applications of findings in decision-making processes. If more cases like it are discovered, the collection would provide empirical guidance to those who research evaluation utilization. However, while Case 2 is emotionally satisfying for someone in my business, it does not teach us about how evaluation methodology relates to unexpected program behavior. Cases 16, 17, and 18 do.

In Cases 16, 17, and 18, the programs behaved in unexpected ways, and in each of the cases the evaluation was able to detect and explain the changes. Why? Because in all three, the unexpected changes were of a nature that made them amenable to evaluation with the existing methodology. The evaluations were able to succeed because their logic of drawing meaning from data did not require reaching outside the organizational or temporal boundaries of the program being evaluated. These evaluations could produce credible findings without control groups, without preinnovation historical data, and without long-term follow-up past the formal ending of the program.

To highlight how these kinds of designs are robust in the face of unexpected program activity, contrast them to a synthetic example that

I have stitched together from my work evaluating regulatory agencies and safety programs. While hypothetical, each element of the example has a grounding in reality, and the example as a whole rings true in terms of how an evaluation might play out. In this example an intervention is designed to improve safety by bringing together cross-functional teams for the purpose of analyzing precursor events and root causes that lead to accidents. The primary topics of interest in the evaluation are how well the cross-functional teams work and whether their activity leads to improvements in safety. The methodology is straightforward.

1. Measure along the logic of program action: team behavior, output of problem-solving deliberations, implementation of recommendations, and changes in measures of safety.

2. Use comparison groups from other parts of the company to track safety improvements that were implemented for reasons not related to the program being evaluated, and look at safety data in all groups.

Imagine that halfway through the program, evaluators began to hear murmurings that in addition to team behavior and safety, the program was also having a salutary effect on organizational culture with respect to trust in management, communications, and attitudes toward safety. (This is not much of a stretch. The real evaluations did build in culture measures. But let's pretend that they did not.) What might the evaluators do? The challenge is serious, because measuring culture change entails a lot more than simply tacking on another measure to an existing design. It would involve overlaying an entirely new design on the existing evaluation plan. A new design would be necessary because the original evaluation plan could get all the data it needed, from anywhere in the company, through perusal of archival data. Measuring organizational culture requires collecting data from people. Thus, unlike the original design, in the add-on design the timing of data collection with respect to the program timetable becomes critical.

Depending on their methodological proclivities, the evaluators may choose to conduct focus groups and interviews to assess organizational culture, or they may decide to use some of the well-validated scales that are available. But these tactics are weak because the critical question is whether the innovative safety program caused those changes. To know that, some kind of comparison data are needed. The focus group approach has some advantage over the survey approach because at least the evaluators could ask the old-timers if things were different back then. But memory dims and attitudes are distorted by the fervor of the moment. It is not a very strong design.

Had the evaluators thought of it, they would have collected baseline data, either by means of focus groups or surveys. But that opportunity is gone. They still have the possibility of implementing a cross-sectional design. If they could find other parts of the company that are similar, they could run their focus groups or deploy their surveys there. But there are still problems. One is tactical—managers in those other organizational units were not involved in the evaluation because nobody ever considered them stakeholders. Why should they contribute time and effort now, when it is not clear what is in it for them and when sensitive questions are being asked? The second problem is methodological. We would have a posttest-only, nonequivalent group design, which is better than a posttest-only design with no control group, but still weak. What we really need is historical data (preferably from multiple control and experimental groups) combined with posttest data from those same groups. That data might come from focus groups or surveys, but whether qualitative or quantitative, the logic of comparison is the same.

COMPARING THE CASES

The safety culture example differs from Cases 16, 17, and 18 because in those cases, their methodologies were capable of coping with the unexpected changes that arose. In my safety example, the original design is incapable of coping with the unexpected change. I have no idea what percentage of evaluations are like Cases 16, 17, and 18, versus my example. My hope is that, over time, the evaluation community will assess enough cases to determine the correct ratio. More important, I would like to see information collected that could tell us something about the circumstances under which each kind of evaluation is designed.

As the diversity of change due to program action increases, it seems increasingly unlikely that evaluations designed for narrow purposes will be effective. How can evaluation be set up to provide maximum agility under these conditions while still retaining their capacity to generate powerful conclusions about stated program goals? To answer this question, it is useful to think about three areas of action: methodology, problem formulation, and the definition of stakeholders.

Methodology

One important element of methodology is application of the monitoring approaches I advocated in Chapter 5 that are useful for providing as much lead time as possible for reacting to unforeseen change. A second aspect of methodology is to include a "flexibility" criterion in the list of issues considered when making choices about data. I think it makes sense for evaluators to ask themselves whether the choice of a particular data source supports or inhibits post hoc changes in the evaluation design. For instance, reliance on routinely collected data in an organization's IT system can be drawn on to make pre–post control group comparisons that might not have been contemplated when the evaluation was first designed. If questionnaires or interviews were used, baseline data would not be available. Moreover, trying to implement questionnaires in groups not previously involved in the evaluation might entail time, cost, and a high risk of failure. To illustrate, imagine a decision about whether to use clinical records on patients' diagnoses and outcomes in a health setting or structured interviews with patients to assess their health status. It is not hard to imagine that the interviews would provide far richer information than the clinical records, but it is also true that reliance on interviews would make it difficult to include another comparison group in the middle of the study. Difficulty in adding a comparison group when using interviews does not mean that using records is preferable, but the inherent flexibility of records use is an issue that should be considered when data choices are made.

Problem Formulation

It may be that agility is a matter of shifting the problem definition to fit the available data. One way to look at definition shifting is to think of any given evaluation question as a sample from a larger population of related evaluation questions. No single member of the population is exactly the same, but there may be enough similarity to serve the purpose. To draw again on the "safety" example presented above, it may be impossible to implement a defensible design if the need were defined in terms of the impact of the program on organizational culture. But in the setting being evaluated, organizational culture might be closely related to the concept of labor–management relations. Why? Because in this setting, organizational culture is largely defined by pervasive mistrust and hostility between labor and management. Cast in these terms, one might be able to find indicators of labor relations that can be compared back in time and across parts of the company. The number of disciplinary actions, or the outcomes of those actions, might work. Records of hearings may provide fodder for content analysis. None of these indicators is exactly "organizational culture," but in this context, given the nature of the culture that is changing, disciplinary data may suffice. Note the use of the terms "in this context," and "nature of the culture that is changing." There is nothing obvious or automatic about making these kinds of decisions. Local expertise is needed.

Definition of Stakeholders

Imagine that as the need to assess the impact of the safety program on organizational culture developed, I decided that good measures of culture across the company, even absent baseline data, would be worthwhile. Would I be able to get the control group data? Remember that in my example other parts of the company do not know about the evaluation, so providing data does not avail them much, and the questions may be seen as asking for sensitive information. No matter how much lead time monitoring gave me, I may not be able to conclude the necessary negotiations in time.

The situation might be different had I taken an expanded view of who my stakeholders were. For instance, in my original identification of stakeholders, I would not have included vice presidents of operating divisions that were not implementing the novel program. Why should I? Doing so would involve extra work, longer implementation time, and more complicated negotiations with the stakeholders who were actually funding the innovation. Furthermore, given the original evaluation design, there was no need for control groups and thus no incentive to go beyond the division where the evaluation was taking place.

The simple advice (to myself) might be: Next time, include those other vice presidents. This is fine advice, except for the fact that that advice is not just simple—it is simplistic. Implementing this plan would take more time, which in turn might delay other parts of the work plan. Approaching those other stakeholders may require asking my sponsor to establish some difficult relationships. There is the risk that the higher the profile of the program, the greater the likelihood of pushback from the rest of the company. Is the extra insurance worth that risk? In any case, who are the right groups to include? In my example it is obvious that the divisional vice presidents are the right people. But if some other unexpected outcome developed, other groups may be more important. Furthermore, a good relationship with the vice presidents may not be good enough. I might discover too late that I should also have been working with local union chairmen in those other operating divisions. Thus, as with all the other tactics I advocate in this book, implementing any one corrective action carries risk, and implementing several compounds the risk. There is no formula for making choices, but there are two useful principles that can be applied.

The first principle is that the strength of evaluators' relationships with stakeholders should vary. By applying this principle, it is possible to take an expansive view of who the stakeholders are and then to pursue strong and weak relationships as needed. To continue the safety example, I know enough about the organizational structure of the companies I am working with to understand that divisional vice presidents are key to any evaluation activity that might transcend the boundaries of the original evaluation plan. I may not know when or how I might need to transcend those boundaries, but I should be smart enough to know that something might pop up that would require my doing so. Thus I may want to establish a mechanism that keeps them informed and asks for advice, but which does not require their assent to any actions I take.

The second principle is that it is not necessary to include all stakeholders at the same time. I would not be able to do the evaluation without cooperation from labor and management in the division where the program was taking place. But I could wait until after the program and evaluation start before trying to establish relationships with the other groups. In fact, waiting may have some distinct advantages. First, from the perspective of organizational change, it may be a good idea to establish the program and the evaluation as a fait accompli before making its presence too visible in the company. Second, once the program had been established, its champions may feel more comfortable brokering the necessary conversations.

The explanation above brings us back to the matter of agile evaluation. If we are going to measure unintended outcomes, agility is necessary. Cases 16, 17, and 18 were agile with respect to the changes in evaluation that were required, while my safety example was not. Our problem is that analysis of agility in Cases 16, 17, and 18 provides hindsight about only a few evaluation situations. It would be nice to be able to abstract lessons from these cases, and from the principles articulated earlier in this book, in order to know in advance how much agility should be designed into an evaluation.

PREDICTING THE NEED FOR AGILE EVALUATION

Predicting the need for agile evaluation is impossible. It is impossible because we operate in an uncertain environment where the degree of uncertainty is hard to estimate and where we can never be sure if the dynamics of complex systems are at play. But as with so many other things in life, a great deal of useful insight can be had by acting as if an estimate of the impossible can be made.

As a prelude to the discussion, it is worth taking the time to appreciate just how easy it is to design an agile evaluation. Whether qualitative or quantitative, all that is needed is to have a design that does not depend on either historical data, or long-term follow-up data, or control group comparisons, or rigid data collection instruments. Unfortunately powerful evaluation often requires using one or more of these four techniques, and the more we have to rely on them, the greater the likelihood of producing a brittle evaluation. The key phrase in the previous sentence is "often requires." "Often" is not always. Can we manage with an evaluation that does not depend on historical data, long-term follow-up data, control group comparisons, or rigid data collection instruments? When we can, our designs will be inherently agile and we will not need to go to any special effort to make them more so.

Can we manage with inherently agile designs? To address this question it is necessary to answer three subsidiary questions.

1. What priority do stakeholders place on establishing causal relationships between their program and its impact?
2. How sure are we that real-time observation of unfolding events can establish change due to program operations?
3. How sure are we that comparison data will be available over a broad range of program outcomes?

If causality is important, and if real-time observation alone won't do the trick, and if comparison data won't be available, then we better take steps to build agility into our evaluation.

How difficult will it be to achieve the needed amount (and type of) agility? The answer depends on considerations of methodology, context of the program's operation, and the nature of the program being evaluated.

Methodology

Sometimes an evaluation must depend on rigid data instruments (e.g., a psychometrically validated scale), time-sensitive data collection (e.g., organizational culture at a specific stage in a program's development), or comparisons with activity under nontreatment conditions. Instrument rigidity, time sensitivity, and reliance on nontreatment comparisons all make for brittle evaluation designs. The more we rely on them, the greater the need to design agility into the evaluation plan.

Context

As the discussion about social/organizational context has shown (Figure 9.1), a program's environment is a major driver of change that may affect evaluation. To that discussion we must add the fact that some program environments change more rapidly or more unexpectedly than others. Rapid change can be a problem when the critical evaluation question requires consistent program operation over time. Unexpected change, however, is the real problem because if the pace of change were known, it would figure as just one more consideration to factor into planning. By its essence (i.e., that it is unexpected), specifics about what will happen cannot be included in evaluation planning. But in large measure, the only thing that matters is the likelihood of change, not its particulars. Certainly knowing the details would be helpful, but the nature of "agility" is that the details do not have to be known. If sudden change of any kind is likely, evaluators are well advised to invest more time, resources, and intellectual capital into building an agile design. Important elements of a program's environment include the stability of demand for its services, its regulatory and legislative environment, its stakeholders and champions, and the attitudinal and cultural milieu in which it operates.

None of these can be measured in a precise way, but use of a diverse group of experts (as advocated in Chapter 7) can provide a sense of whether a program's environment will remain stable. Of course, that environment can change in many ways that will have no bearing at all on the evaluation. In fact, most such changes will have no bearing on the evaluation. But some proportion of change will affect the evaluation, so the greater the likelihood of any kind of change, the more important it is for evaluators to invest in agility.

Two elements in the discussion above portend how this argument will develop. First, there was only a small amount of space devoted to the discussion of context, and even less to methodology, while a quick glance below shows much more space devoted to program characteristics. Second, the term "program" seeped into the discussion of methodology and context. As we shall see, not only is the program being evaluated a critical determinant of the need for agility, but methodology, context, and program also must be considered jointly.

Program

With respect to the difficulty of achieving an adequately agile evaluation, the key issue is the degree to which it is possible to specify program outcomes in advance. To illustrate variation in ability to specify outcomes, compare two programs whose primary purpose was to improve an educational outcome. The first educational intervention is Case 5 (p. 214), which sought to evaluate the School Success Profile Intervention Package (SSP-IP), a structured, whole-school intervention designed to improve schools' ability to help students achieve their full academic potential. The outcomes are reasonably predictable and straightforward—achievement, dropout rates, and the like. The second educational intervention is the Kalamazoo Promise, "a pledge by a group of anonymous donors to pay up to 100 percent of tuition at any of Michigan's state colleges or universities for graduates of Kalamazoo's public high schools" (*en.wikipedia.org/wiki/Kalamazoo_Promise*). The Kalamazoo Promise has a simple goal and a simple mission: "*Vision*: The greater Kalamazoo Community will become a world leader in education, investing in youth to elevate the quality of life for each resident. *Mission*: The Kalamazoo Promise transforms the community and stimulates the economy through a new generation of learners" (*www.kalamazoopromise.com*).

Although both Case 5 and the Kalamazoo Promise have well-defined objectives, they differ in an important way. The SSP-IP as an intervention is confined to a school system. The Kalamazoo Promise is contiguous with a political entity called the City of Kalamazoo Michigan, complete with its rich network of civil society organizations, businesses, interest groups, city departments, and social services. Each of those entities is able to take independent action, to see different opportunity in the Promise, and to react to it differently. Furthermore, their reactions may interact and evolve over time. For instance, it is not much of a stretch to think that the Kalamazoo Rotary Club would institute a tutoring program, which over time would identify troubled youth, and which would, in turn, begin to coordinate with the mental health system. What outcomes might be attributable to the *joint* tutoring and the mental health services? How might that innovative coordination affect other civic organizations and activities? More important, how could an evaluator plan to assess those outcomes, considering that those outcomes arose as self-organized behavior and without any reliable way to guess that they would appear? Now, add this one development path to all the others that might arise, and then contemplate the possible interactions among them. It is not hard to see why an evaluation would gravitate toward inherently flexible designs that could extract meaning from data by observing events as they unfolded.

Overall Determination of the Need for Agility

There is no such thing as an "agile methodology." There is only agile evaluation—a system in which methodology, context, and program combine to give the evaluation more (or less) potential to assess program outcomes that were not envisioned at the beginning of the evaluation exercise.

To illustrate why method, program, and context must be considered jointly, consider a methodology that exhibited three characteristics. First, outcome measurement depended on validated scales for populations with particular characteristics. Second, data had to be collected at well-specified times. Third, a control group was chosen specifically because it was similar to the experimental group with respect to the kinds of changes that were expected. Is this an agile methodology? No. Is lack of agility a problem? It depends. Imagine if this design were dropped into two scenarios. In the first, the innovation being evaluated was carefully designed to consistently provide a well-defined service over an extended period of time. In the second, the innovation was a process whose purpose was to allow an organization to adapt its activities over time. As for context, let's say that in the first scenario the innovation is insulated from its organizational and social context, while in the second the innovation has strong connections to many aspects of its context. The methodology is equally rigid in both scenarios. But the methodology's low potential for agility is much more problematic in the second scenario than in the first. Looking at the design alone will not tell us whether we should invest in increasing the agility of our design.

The neat tripartite framework described above avoids two big problems. First, there is no way to quantitatively measure where an evaluation sits on any of the three dimensions—methodology, context, and program. Second, the framework implies a linear system without interactions among the dimensions. In fact, it seems quite plausible that a great deal of nonlinearity and interactive behavior is likely. So, for instance, because of nonlinearity and interaction effects, an evaluation that was low on two dimensions and moderately high on a third might require more effort at building agile capacity than an evaluation that was moderately high on all three dimensions. The determination is exquisitely sensitive to the details of local circumstance.

These limitations notwithstanding, it is useful to think about agility as if methodology, context, and program were separate. By doing so, expert judgment can be used to get a general sense of rankings on each dimension. And it does seem plausible that the higher an evaluation is on more dimensions, the greater the likelihood that an agile design will be needed. Finally, we know we can never arrive either at a trustworthy estimate of the need for agility in general or an estimate of the need for agility with respect to particular program changes. After all, we are dealing with surprise that is by definition unpredictable. We are back to the cat-herding metaphor that I used in Chapter 2. We have only a general idea of where those cats are. All we can do is our best to herd as many of them as possible in a general direction.

IN SUM

This chapter focused on the few cases that showed surprising outcomes due to program activity. While these are few, there are two reasons to care about designing evaluation that can detect these surprises. One reason is that unexpected outcomes do arise, and we are paid to detect changes that are wrought by the programs we evaluate. The second reason is that, as citizens and taxpayers, we have an obligation to look beyond the narrow confines of predetermined outcomes.

It is easy to design an evaluation that is inherently agile. All one has to do is to *not* depend on historical data, *avoid* a focus on long-term impact, *reject* control groups, and *eschew* rigid data collection instruments. Formulating evaluation in this way, however, precludes many powerful evaluation methods and severely limits the kinds of program effects that can be evaluated. Can we make do with inherently agile designs? The answer depends on the priority stakeholders place on establishing causal relationships between their program and its impact, our beliefs as to whether real-time observation of unfolding events can establish causal relationships, and our estimates of whether comparison data will be available over a broad range of program outcomes.

If we do need to design for agility, how difficult will it be to do so? Making that determination requires joint consideration of methodology, the context in which the program is operating, and the nature of the program that is being evaluated. Interactions among these three elements render it impossible to arrive at a precise assessment of how much or what kind of agility is needed. Despite these limitations, treating methodology, context, and program as if they were independent can produce evaluation designs that are more usefully agile than could otherwise be contrived.

Chapter 13

Concluding Thoughts

Writing this book led me to explore a multitude of practical and theoretical topics and to consider relationships among many different aspects of the evaluation craft. The experience left me with heightened appreciations that I did not have when I started.

I came to appreciate the role that stability plays in making decisions about how to perform evaluation. Stability can vary with respect to the program theory of the innovation being evaluated, the operations of the program being evaluated, the information available to the evaluator, and the logical structure of the evaluation design. I saw how stability affected evaluation when I placed cases on the evaluation and program life cycles. I saw how stability affected evaluation when placed in a social/organizational framework. I saw how stability affected evaluation when I placed cases on the continuum from unforeseen to unforeseeable surprise. I came to realize that change is ever present, but that not all change is the same. It's not that I was ignorant of this fact when I began. Of course I knew it. But my knowledge in the beginning was blunt. Change is change, and either there is a lot of it or a little. If I thought about it at all, that is how I must have thought about it. (As if I can remember, after so much time has passed and all the intellectual effort I have put into the subject.) I now realize how differentiated change can be and how important it is to understand those differences in order to do successful evaluation. I see this now as I look back over the methods I suggested, at the cases that were so generously contributed, and at the various frameworks I proposed.

I came to appreciate just how much evaluation is a craft—an endeavor requiring special skills and long practice. For all our use of quantitative methods, systems thinking, resort to social science research, invocation of program theory, qualitative analysis, and all the other tools that fill our evaluation armamentarium, our work still comes down to judgment about the application of specific tools to specific circumstances. We have guidelines for which tools to pick and how to apply them. It is easy enough to know what probably will or will not work. But there is always more than one way to succeed, and anything we do will have strengths and weaknesses to balance. The need for judgment showed when I thought about what is gained and lost from implementing tactics to deal with surprise. The need for judgment showed when I tried to place cases in various frameworks and when I made suggestions about what evaluators might have done to avoid the surprises they encountered.

I came to appreciate the unity of diverse social constructs—of how both programs and evaluations are interventions in a social context, and why they operate according to the same rules. There is an economy to this similarity because it means that the same intellectual tools apply equally to both planning and evaluation. The similarity also aids communication and collaboration between evaluators and planners because, in some sense, both groups have the same problems and use the same methods to solve those problems. I don't mean that conflict of interest never exists, or that familiarity does not breed contempt. But I do believe that by appreciating how programs and evaluations are the same in a deep way it is possible to do evaluation that is more methodologically sound and more powerful in its ability to support those who have the responsibility to allocate scarce resources in ways that affect people's lives.

Finally, I came to appreciate my hunch that it is possible to move evaluation's response to surprise from firefighting to systematic action. I don't know how much any specific suggestion I have made or idea that I have advanced will steer this movement. But after reading the sum total of what I have written and considering all the conversations I have had with colleagues and reviewers, I am confident that if more people joined the conversation, evaluation could be made more useful to decision makers, even under high levels of uncertainty and surprise.

CASES

Grasping at Straws and Discovering a Different Program Theory

AN EXERCISE IN REENGINEERING ANALYSIS LOGIC IN A CHILD CARE EVALUATION SETTING

Dennis P. Affholter

DESCRIPTION OF THE CASE

From 1974 through 1978, Abt Associates Inc. studied the cost of child care and the effect on children's development in day care centers (Ruopp et al., 1979). The main element of the National Day Care Study (NDCS) included data collection on children cared for in 67 day care centers in Atlanta, Detroit, and Seattle. Additional data were collected from the staff and on various aspects of programming and services in these centers. The Administration for Children, Youth, and Families (ACYF, in the then Department of Health, Education, and Welfare) funded the study. The primary independent variable was staff:child ratio, the major element of the Federal Interagency Day Care Regulations (FIDCR). Generally, the more favorable the ratio, better assessments of child development would be expected within the regulated range of from 1:5 to 1:10.

UNEXPECTED EVENTS

The regulated range of the primary independent variable restricted the range of possible observations. In retrospect, this might have been a red flag that strong effects would not be observed. The statisticians involved in the study, which included statisticians and educational researchers from Harvard University, discussed the potential effect of this restricted range in the independent variable in limiting the range of outcomes observed. However, for a variety of political, bureaucratic, and theoretical reasons, the project stakeholders concluded that important effects would be observed even under the restricted range of the key independent variable. Essentially, the idea was that a higher staff:child ratio permitted more individualized attention to and more one-on-one time with children during a critical time of their cognitive and social–emotional development.

The study design was a strong one, using Lee Cronbach's generalizability theory to conduct measurement studies that in turn provided reliable, quantitative estimates as well as data collection design elements for the many important measures to be used for analyses of costs and of children's developmental outcomes.

As data came in and analysis began on a great many dependent variables, it became clear that expected effects would not be found. The best that could be said was that a few effects ran in the expected direction, even if they were not statistically significant. Because the FIDCR were scheduled for review and potential revision, ACYF was extremely interested in whatever could be gleaned from the NDCS. Because of the cost implications for day care centers of regulating staff:child ratios, findings of no effect on children's development of that regulatory tool—if those results held up—would not be very helpful.

RESPONSES TO THE UNEXPECTED EVENTS

As the situation emerged, a reanalysis was begun that started by observing bivariate scatter plots between staff:child ratio and various dependent measures. Observation of these graphs revealed that the few positive results that were found were attributable to three outliers, all of which came from day care centers operated in a single city by the same corporate entity. Discounting these outliers brought the conclusions back to square one; that is, expected changes were not observed.

Once the nonrelationship between the key independent variable and the dependent variables was firmly established, the researchers began to rethink just what might be at work in day care centers that also might be relevant to children's positive development. The staff:child ratio is, in fact, a composite of two measures—number of caregiving staff and number of children. What would happen if this measure were disaggregated; that is, if the effects of number of teachers and the effects of number of students were considered separately? This inquiry led to an unanticipated and extremely important finding. Regardless of the number of staff, smaller groups of children had better outcomes. In other words, within a limited range of staff:child ratios, the number of staff did not matter. Only the number of children did. Smaller groups did better.

More sophisticated analyses followed, all taking a finer and more powerful lens to the question of child group size. Specialized factor analyses were done to estimate the reliability of independent and dependent variables measured. Regression models of developmental value added were adapted from educational research. Specially written regression programs were used to adjust for outlying influences in the data (bisquared iterative weighting, which was not then available as a part of standard statistical analysis packages) and to account for less-than-perfect reliability in the measurements taken. As these analyses proceeded, it became clear that child group size was an important and powerful predictor of outcome. This finding went on to play an important part in subsequent child care regulations.

From the Executive Summary, Children at the Center:

> The NDCS found that higher quality care is associated with two low-cost ingredients (smaller groups of children and caregivers with child-specific education/training). The number of classroom staff per group (caregiver/ child ratio) was not an important contributor to quality within the policy-relevant range of 1:5 to 1:10. Ratio was strongly related to differences in cost.... The ... revision of current federal day care regulations could allow the government to buy better care at slightly lower cost. More children could be better served within current budgets.

REFERENCES

Ruopp, R. R., et al. (1979). *Children at the center.* Cambridge, MA: Abt Associates.

> ## Case 2

Shifting Sands
in a Training Evaluation Context

James W. Altschuld and Phyllis M. Thomas

DESCRIPTION OF THE CASE

An associate dean in a large college of education wanted to open a market for training and evaluation services in the business sector. His university reputation was partially dependent on achieving success in that arena. Part of a contract from a nearby Fortune 500 company called for assistance with evaluation. A faculty member and a graduate research assistant were asked to do the work. The funds were small, the task was vague, the environment was politically charged, and the time line was short. Much was riding on the effort. What could be done that would be positive for both the company and the college?

We met with company trainers to determine evaluation needs. Relations were cordial but uneasy. The trainers wanted to know why the contract had been signed and what it was supposed to do. Were we there to evaluate their work? Could jobs be threatened? A good system was in place, so why fix what wasn't broken? What could this "ivory tower" university team do for them? Gaps in communication were apparent everywhere.

Based on our discussions we developed an overall evaluation framework including assessing needs, examining product conceptualization, monitoring development, and looking at refined use of training products and programs. Given the budget and time line, one current training package was selected for testing a follow-up evaluation strategy. This evaluation involved assessment of a training program to enable field engineers to provide service for a new and major computer system developed by the corporation and sold throughout the world. As this was being proposed an unexpected obstacle emerged.

UNEXPECTED EVENTS

After several meetings about what to evaluate, it became clear to us that the evaluation portion of the contract was more of an afterthought than anything meaningful to the company. Key administrators and staff simply did not support it. "Just get out of our hair" was the message, and it was loud and clear:

> We don't want the evaluation to rock the boat. All we want is a one-page scaled questionnaire to be sent to a sample of those trained to service this new product. Just ask: Did the training meet its goals? Are they using what they were taught? Is there something in the training that should be revised? That's all we need to know.

This reaction caught us off guard, especially as it came from a powerful, high-level administrator. Fortunately, we were able to quickly develop another approach based on what we learned from the trainers after we had broken the ice and they were willing to share their concerns about the evaluation of training in the company (see Table 1).

In the past, unless the tasks were performed exactly as demonstrated in training, trainees risked being fired. This was common to the belief system and thus it was no surprise that all prior surveys produced results that were 100% positive about the impact of training and did not yield useful information. With this knowledge, the alternative was put forth at a public forum with all the key players in attendance. Bringing it up this way worked well.

> We [evaluators] can do the survey for you, but we would be taking your money on false pretenses. It will likely lead to 100% agreement and will not be of much value.
>
> Will you allow us to do something different? The questions will be worded so that respondents can tell us what they were actually doing when servicing the product. We also propose using both sides of the one-page form plus a separate page for several open-ended questions. Finally, if the evaluation surveys are sent to us rather than the company, respondents may respond more frankly. Again, we can do the survey the way you have done previously, if you wish. How should we proceed?

TABLE 1. Characteristics of the Shifting Sands in the Evaluation

Characteristic	Comments
Unclear expectations	The purpose of the contract and what the evaluation could/should accomplish were vague for both company trainers and external evaluators.
Fear of evaluation	Dread of evaluators, evaluation, and potential results was heightened.
Gaps in communication	Communication channels were lacking within the company, within the university, and between the two groups.
Unexpected shifts in viewpoints	Preliminary work by the evaluators was almost discarded when a new demand caused a major shift in the evaluation's direction.
Positive interactions	Information and insights gained from initial meetings were essential for the evaluators' dealing with the unexpected.
Unanticipated outcomes	The positive outcomes were never dreamed of by the evaluators and the company at the onset of the process.

After a moment of silence, a reply came: "You seem to have learned a lot about our organization, and your way of doing the evaluation makes more sense. Go with it."

RESPONSE TO THE UNEXPECTED EVENTS

Now we had the support to move in a meaningful direction, and the evaluation worked better than anticipated (see Table 2). New item wording helped to identify many tasks that were performed differently in the real world than in the pristine training center. In addition, because the product was reliable and seldom broke down, sometimes service personnel needed to make repairs 3 to 4 years after they completed training. In open-ended comments they reported that when performing service they often relied more on practical advice from informal networks of colleagues than on their training. These evaluation results were a revelation to the company.

The constraints imposed on the evaluation led to a most successful effort. A tense situation was leveraged to produce unforeseen and valuable outcomes, although they were not in view at the beginning of the project. Four key outcomes were:

TABLE 2. New Features in Evaluation Strategy to Address Corporate Culture

Feature	Description
Reword items for social acceptance.	Items worded so that it would be socially acceptable for respondents to indicate what they actually did instead of what was expected of them. New wording stated that "some aspects of training may be more important than others" and "you may have to do some things differently in the field than the way in which you were trained; if so, please respond accordingly."
Maximize use of space.	Multiple short scales with each item increased the number of questions. Using both sides of a one-page machine-readable form allowed for scoring 73 items in a single pass.
Add open-ended items.	Two open-ended questions were added on a separate sheet for comments.
Maintain confidentiality.	Surveys were sent directly to the external evaluators, thus maintaining confidentiality and encouraging respondents to answer more honestly.

1. *Expansion of training.* The corporation added one day to the on-site training at the center. This was very expensive, given that there were 12,000 trainees worldwide, half from outside of the United States. Nearly all needed travel expenses, and there would be lost revenue from pulling trainees off the service line.

2. *Widespread use of new evaluation form.* The evaluation form was so well received that the company printed thousands of blank forms with its general structure. Administrators wanted to employ the format for other types of training.

3. *Creation of a new evaluation position.* The company hired a full-time evaluator. Undoubtedly, the evaluation contributed to this happening.

4. *Increased receptivity to and support for evaluation.* There seemed to be a subtle shift in corporate culture. The evaluation report framed findings as to how they might be used to improve what the training center might do in the future. That the company incurred a huge expense to expand training suggests enhanced acceptance of the value of evaluation for later endeavors.

In summary, a low-budget evaluation led to a large return on investment. If this had been anticipated, the budget would have been many times more than it was.

Case 3

Evaluating Programs Aimed at Promoting Child Well-Being

THE CASE OF LOCAL SOCIAL WELFARE AGENCIES IN JERUSALEM

Anat Zeira

DESCRIPTION OF THE CASE

The Israeli local Departments of Social Services (DSS), backed by the Ministry of Welfare and Social Services,[1] are responsible for providing a broad package of social services to populations in distress. During the past decade the Ministry of Labor and Social Affairs has allocated a significant amount of money to promote community-based services for at-risk children and their families. As a result, numerous intervention programs for this population were set up. Some were developed in Israel while others were brought in from other countries and adapted to the Israeli population and needs.

This project took place in Jerusalem, Israel, where the Jerusalem DSS offers a variety of community-based interventions aimed at improving children's well-being in families where neglect of children is found or suspected. The ultimate goal of the programs is to enhance the child's well-being by focusing on parenting skills, usually in an attempt to prevent out-of-home placement. These intervention programs vary in scope, nature, and philosophy and provide social workers with a wide range of options to treat at-risk children and their families.

Because many of the intervention programs appear to use the same strategies and methods, yet sometimes they are called by different names and require different budgets, a great dilemma for administrators is how to select which programs to develop and disseminate. A further source of confusion is that it is not always clear whether the programs really serve the intended target population and if program goals are being achieved. It is also not always clear what considerations the social workers have in mind when referring specific clients to specific programs. In addition, workers who operate such programs in the local social welfare agencies in Jerusalem were asked to provide empirical evidence on the success of the intervention programs in order to maintain their operation.

To help administrators clarify the issues mentioned above and to help social workers obtain empirical evidence on the success of the programs they operate, a university researcher (the author) was asked to design a year-long program evaluation project. The purpose of the project was two-fold: first, to examine whether the programs achieve their ultimate goals of enhancing child well-being; second, to investigate whether there is a differential success—that is, do some programs work better with certain clients?

Participants were a university researcher and a group of third- (and last-) year bachelor of social work students taking a research seminar, "Monitoring Intervention Outcomes with Children and Families in Deep Distress"; 20 front-line social workers running the intervention programs; and five administrators at various levels in the Jerusalem DSS and local welfare agencies. A steering committee for the project consisted of a team of municipal administrators and university researchers, and representatives of the funding organizations provided advisory and observed the various stages of the project.

UNEXPECTED EVENTS

To facilitate the evaluation, social workers who implemented the programs were asked to identify the program goals. Every professional act has a goal; without a clear and specific goal there is no rationale for implementing an intervention. A common definition of goal formulation pertains to a specific client situation that is to be changed or maintained during a feasible time frame. A goal also must be realistic in the sense that it should be something within the worker's resources and the service mission statement. In developing goals, the social worker must take the client's expectations and ability into account. The goals also must be compatible with the client's strengths and abilities. The assumption was that workers would be able to provide sensible goals to the intervention programs they ran.

At a very early stage we realized that workers faced severe difficulties in identifying the programs' goals in a clear and measurable way. For example, workers' stated aims were "to improve the mother's self-image," "to increase parenting," or "to increase mother's confidence." These goals are insufficient because no reason or context for improving self-image or parenting is given (such as improving parenting to increase a child's safety); there was no background parameter against which to evaluate any change in the parents. Moreover, it is very difficult to measure their success.

Because the final aim of clarifying goals is that social workers evaluate their own practice, an apt first measure of success can be derived from the indicators used to refer a client to the program. For example, a social worker referred a mother to a program because she suspected that she was neglecting her young children. Neglect was defined as not using community health service (e.g., not giving the children immunizations in time), sending children to day care centers inadequately dressed for the weather, and/or suspected malnutrition. We found that the social workers tend to formulate their goals around the mothers, rather than considering the major goal of increasing the safety of the children; in this case, the social workers' goal was to increase the mothers' use of community health services. However, because a reason for this was not explicitly formulated as a goal, the mothers' visits to the services were not monitored, nor was it clear, for example, whether the children had received the immunizations. The unintended difficulties involved formulating the program goals resulted in a significant delay of conducting the evaluation program as intended.

The design of the evaluation included a strong component of partnership between the workers and the research team. This strategy was chosen mainly in order to increase response rates on behalf of the social workers. We let the social workers decide on the variables to be assessed and had the final word on determining what tools would be used. This strategy led to a second unintended consequence. That is, workers did not come up with any measure for child well-being; thus, at the end of the project, even if a child was not removed from home, they could not tell whether their programs benefited the children. They could only infer success by the state of the parents.

At the same time, a third undesired result was a relatively low response rate. Despite all efforts and the dear price the project paid for allowing the workers the final word on measures, not all workers completed the evaluation forms. Thus it was very hard and sometimes impossible to draw conclusions about the programs.

RESPONSES TO THE UNEXPECTED EVENTS

The unintended events described above had led us after a few months to reconstruction of the various phases of the evaluation project. At this point it was clear that 1 year is not enough to complete the evaluation process. The result was an extension of the project to a second year, followed by a search for further funding for this extension. The steering committee agreed on two new goals for the project: (1) to train social workers in developing clear and precise treatment goals, and (2) to construct measures for assessing the outcomes of the programs under investigation.

Hence, instead of evaluating the program, we began training the workers how to identify and articulate program goals. In a series of workshops, the social workers practiced formulating goals and matching them with appropriate outcome measures. While this consequence (i.e., outcome) was not planned, it proved to be a very important one for the DSS management, as it had a wider effect on the organizational level of Jerusalem DSS. In order for a program to be included in the DSS annual budget, workers now must include program goals and some measure for their attainment.

Toward the end of the second year of the project, it had become clear that the defined programs' goals and the selected outcome measures were not sufficient to capture the ultimate goal of enhancing child well-being. Because most of the goals were still focused on the mothers, there was a clear need to include a specific measure for child well-being. In accordance with the project's concept of strong practitioner–researcher partnership, we began looking for such a measurement tool.

An agreement could not be achieved on one single measure that would depict the various aspects of what was meant by child well-being and that also would be suitable for the age range of the children. Therefore the steering committee has supported the extension of the original evaluation project to a third year. The goal is to develop and measure children's well-being. Of course, this extension has required yet another increase in the funding for the project.

After several discussions on the best means of data collection and after reviewing several standardized measures, we decided to design our own scale of child well-being. We knew that a newly designed measure might suffer from an unknown reliability and validity, but we were determined to create a measure that may be useful to monitor the well-being of the children at different points during the intervention process and that could be routinely used by social workers who run any program for at-risk children.

When designing a new measure, there are many points to consider. First are feasibility issues. For example, a paper-and-pencil instrument and a complex level of the language must be considered with illiterate populations. Simple language is required to increase the use of self-report measures by a disadvantaged population. There are also problems in reading the questions aloud to illiterate clients, especially when a measure deals with sensitive issues such as sexual relationships. Furthermore, a lengthy scale may not be adequate for very young respondents because they may become tired or upset if it takes too long to complete the questionnaire. Another consideration pertains to the degree of ease in processing the data required. For example, is processing straightforward, or does it require a sophisticated statistical procedure? Does the scale score truly meet the social worker's needs? For example, a statistically significant cutoff point may not be clinically significant, leading the social worker to deceptive conclusions. The concepts "clinical significance" and "statistical significance" should be considered, and a critical examination of the measure's score and its reflection of the client's state should be conducted. These issues were discussed and agreed upon during the process of creating the new child well-being measure.

With regard to the third unintended event of low response rates despite all efforts to involve the social workers in the design of the measurement tools, and especially that of child well-being, no reasonable solution could be found. The results of the evaluation project are based on about half of the participants and thus not representative of the total program clientele and have a limited validity. In order to enhance response rates in the future, it is suggested to involve the highest levels of the local agencies' directors and to appoint them responsible for data collection.

The summary report of the project made a significant, yet another unintended contribution. It included a precise presentation of the goals of each program that were used to evaluate its outcomes; it provided a review of empirical and theoretical literature related to the intervention programs; it described the methods used for assessing the attainment of the outcomes (e.g., sampling, measures); and it presented the results for every program (i.e., to what degree goals were achieved) and their significance specifically for the social workers in the project and for the social work profession in general. Copies of the report were distributed to all participants and to the university's library. Discussions of this report concluded this project. It seems that, most of all, the project increased awareness of the problems of evaluation. The social workers have reflected on the report in terms of missing information, expectations that were not met (e.g., inconclusive results due to low response rates), and specific suggestions for improving the measures and procedures. The discussions around the feasibility of evaluation measures resulted in very specific requests for changes in the instruments, usually to construct a shorter, simpler version. We hope all these lessons will be implemented in future projects.

ACKNOWLEDGMENT

The project was supported by an Ashalim–JDC grant. Special thanks to Yossi Tamir, Rina La'or, Dorit Biran, and the staff of the Department of Social Services in the Municipality of Jerusalem, without whose help the project would not have been possible.

NOTE

1. Due to political constellations the name of this Ministry tends to change from time to time.

Assessing the Impact of Providing Laptop Computers to Students

J. Dan Strahl, Deborah L. Lowther,
and Steven M. Ross

Data collection plans have much in common with engineering projects. Objectives are well defined, and critical contingencies considered. However, once shovel is put to earth, what lies below (rock, sand, or soil) might be quite different than expected, thereby necessitating adaptability, creativity, and change. Such was the case in the authors' evaluation of the statewide Freedom to Learn (FTL) program in Michigan (Lowther, Strahl, Inan, & Bates, 2007).

DESCRIPTION OF THE CASE

FTL was a competitive grant program designed to place laptop computers in the hands of students and provide teacher professional development in technology integration. During 2004–2005 FTL grants were awarded to 199 Michigan schools. Schools represented public and private districts from rural and major metropolitan areas. The initial FTL implementation primarily occurred at the sixth-grade level and each school was to have at least one trained Lead Teacher. The program also provided highly trained Super Coaches, who were assigned to a number of schools and Lead Teachers in their immediate area and were to provide mentoring and professional development.

Education Innovations, Inc. (EI), collaborating with the Center for Research in Educational Policy (CREP) at the University of Memphis, was chosen as the third-party independent evaluator of the FTL program. The evaluation was based on a 2-year plan that incorporated a mixed-method design (Johnson & Onwuegbuzie, 2004). Specifically, the evaluation involved the use of validated observation measures to conduct whole-grade observations of randomly selected classrooms and prearranged observations of targeted classrooms. It also involved administering validated surveys to FTL students, teachers, Lead Teachers, and Super Coaches. Additional data sources included professional development evaluations and Michigan Department of Education grant audit reports. Student-level Michigan Educational Assessment Program scores were to be analyzed as data became available.

The original evaluation plan required Lead Teachers and Super Coaches to participate in data collection by completing EI/CREP–provided observation training, conducting classroom observations, and administering surveys. Trainees were to conduct a combination of targeted and whole-grade observations.

UNEXPECTED EVENTS

In the first year of the program data collection obstacles were immediately encountered. Delayed implementation occurred in many schools due to late fund distribution. This inhibited the appointment of Lead Teachers. A domino effect of the late funding was also evidenced in the procurement of equipment. After purchase, myriad logistical decisions had to be made, including infrastructure, software, maintenance, and student guideline issues. Because Lead Teachers were appointed late in the year, many were unable to participate in observation training. The reality was that many schools were not up and running until very late in the spring of the first program year. The end result was inability to collect observation data for many of these schools.

Another factor was a lack of initial meaningful communication between participating schools and program administrators. Thus it was difficult to effectively communicate observer training details to the participants. In many cases Lead Teachers were unaware of their responsibility for conducting classroom observations. This greatly contributed to a lack of buy-in. This combination of factors, plus Lead Teachers' lack of time, resulted in insufficient numbers of observations. Although the FTL grant indicated that all schools were to participate in the evaluation, only 48% (95 of 199) of the FTL schools actually participated in one or more aspects.

Compliance was further exacerbated by labor issues in the state. The FTL sponsors had little contractual control over program implementation and no mechanism for ensuring compliance with evaluation requirements. One large urban district erected roadblocks to any evaluation activities in their jurisdiction. This blockage occurred even though evaluation participation was a requirement for receiving the laptop grants. As the evaluation team satisfied each restriction imposed, the district erected additional ones. Although the evaluation team persisted, it ultimately became clear that lack of cooperation and time constraints made it impossible to collect data in that district.

Yet another obstacle involved the Super Coaches. Their participation in conducting observations was important to ensure adequate data collection in schools having only one or very few FTL teachers. Once again a lack of communication, buy-in, and a clear definition of roles led to problems. Many Super Coaches did not know the schools to which they were assigned. Conversely, many Lead Teachers did not know the identity of their Super Coach/mentor. Among Super Coaches asked to conduct observations, many were unable or unwilling to allocate the time, especially since they were not receiving additional compensation. So yet another source of data collection was diminished.

In summary, ineffective communication resulting in misconceptions and confusion among school, district personnel, and program leaders combined to create unanticipated and unnecessary barriers manifested in ill-defined roles, decreased program buy-in and bureaucratic obstacles. Although many participating teachers were highly motivated, the initial year's data collection fell far short of what was anticipated or desired.

RESPONSES TO THE UNEXPECTED EVENTS

After the initial year's work, steps were taken to improve and augment the data collection. First, external observers were used to fill the gap created by limited participation of the Super Coaches and Lead Teachers. External observers were recruited, hired, trained, managed, and paid by EI/CREP. These individuals were almost exclusively retired educators. This strategy enabled EI/CREP to assign independent observers to schools statewide. The observers were paid upon completion of their work and only if the work was performed correctly. Costs were passed on to the program. Lead

Teachers were once again asked to conduct observations in their own schools and generally did so successfully and in far greater numbers.

In conjunction with the program sponsor, the evaluator began an aggressive communication program to remind all participants of their roles and responsibilities. Teachers were apprised of training schedules and strongly encouraged to attend. Training was held at locations across the state in order to reach as many teachers as possible. Communication was in the form of e-mails, online newsletters, and phone calls.

These communication efforts continued during the data collection to keep observers abreast of deadlines and requirements. Feedback and information concerning issues and problems were also solicited from all participants. Efforts were made to maintain constant communication with all program stakeholders. This process included district and state personnel, FTL staff, and remaining Super Coaches.

In addition, the evaluator provided each Lead Teacher with a customized "turnkey" packet with specific instructions for observations, surveys, and data submission. Everything needed for successful completion of evaluation activities was included. Similar packets were provided to the external observers.

The major outreach effort yielded significant results. Due to increased contact with stakeholders at all levels, participation in the evaluation was greatly increased. It yielded greater participant buy-in and created an environment in which Lead Teachers were anxious to participate. The evaluation staff found itself fielding early requests for materials from many participants eager to begin. Although the evaluators determined that it would be impossible to collect data in the one major urban area noted earlier, every other part of the state did participate.

As a result of the additional efforts, the second year's data collection was highly successful. Incomplete or poor data from observers was minimal. The second year evaluation also was much richer and more meaningful. The evaluation yielded valuable formative feedback not just on the program intervention, but also the program implementation.

REFERENCES

Johnson, R. B., & Onwuegbuzie, A. J. (2004). Mixed-methods research: A research paradigm whose time has come. *Educational Researcher, 33*(7), 14–26.

Lowther, D. L., Strahl, J. D., Inan, F. A., & Bates, J. (2007). *Freedom to learn program*. Memphis, TN: Center for Research in Educational Policy, University of Memphis.

```
┌──────────────┐
│    Case 5    │
└──────────────┘
```

Quasi-Experimental Strategies When Randomization Fails

PROPENSITY SCORE MATCHING AND SENSITIVITY ANALYSIS IN WHOLE-SCHOOL REFORM

Gary L. Bowen, Roderick A. Rose,
and Shenyang Guo

DESCRIPTION OF THE CASE

Randomized experiments have long been treated as the gold standard in program evaluation. However, evaluators of school-based programs may find it difficult to recruit schools for random assignment into intervention and control conditions. This is greatly complicated by the fact that permission to recruit a school must often be secured from the school district. This leads to two problems: first, there is a costly two-stage recruitment process involving solicitation of the district and then subsequently of the schools; second, randomized experiments are viewed unfavorably by both the district and the schools, with both generally preferring to receive the treatment. The evaluation of the School Success Profile—Intervention Package is an example of an evaluation where problems occurred in the recruitment stage of the evaluation life cycle that made the random assignment of schools to each experimental condition impossible and the assumption of randomness questionable.

The School of Social Work at the University of North Carolina at Chapel Hill received funding from the William T. Grant Foundation (Foundation) for a 3-year project to evaluate the effectiveness and sustainability of a research-based intervention in a sample of middle schools (sixth to eighth grade) in North Carolina: the School Success Profile—Intervention Package (SSP-IP). The SSP-IP is unique among school-based interventions in that the program lays the groundwork for schools to develop their own solutions to challenges that limit the ability of students to achieve their full academic promise. The program is administered in a whole-school fashion, and the parameters of the grant sought from the Foundation dictated that the evaluation be experimental. Together, these required that the counterfactual be based on entire schools not receiving the program. Alternative designs that could accommodate whole-school programs such as a quasi-experimental cohort design were not considered.

However, the proposed evaluation design also included a concession intended to address the costs of recruitment, implementation, and evaluation in the context of the practical constraint that permission for recruitment must come from the district. The districts were to be contacted and solicited for participation, and the sites subsequently recruited from among these pools of districts. To reduce costs, multiple sites from each district were to be included in the experimental sample.

The evaluation proposed a 3-year longitudinal experimental design and the use of school performance data from North Carolina's Department of Public Instruction (DPI) to examine whether the intervention package could improve the academic trajectories of individual students. Consulting with the Foundation, our power analysis showed that we needed 11 treatment schools, with 33 control schools.

UNEXPECTED EVENTS

The sample selection for this study began with setting criteria for a sampling frame, which was described in the proposal and modified slightly in the follow-ups as a two-stage sampling design. We indicated that we would first select from clusters (districts) around the state with high concentrations of the "No Recognition" schools. ("No Recognition" means that from 60 to 100% of the students in the school were meeting grade-level standards, but the school failed to achieve expected student grade-to-grade growth.) These clusters would have a sufficient number of schools in the sampling frame, in total, to randomly assign 11 of them to treatment and 33 to control. Performance data from these control schools would be monitored from DPI administrative files, and no further contact would be made with these schools.

When we began the recruitment process in January 2004, we immediately encountered obstacles to our sampling design that required adjustments. We experienced problems in the process of refining the sampling frame and subsequently in the recruitment phase of evaluation. We were caught off guard by both the difficulty and the significant amount of time and effort required to recruit districts for participation. Two of five school districts initially contacted for participation declined to participate because of other districtwide program initiatives. One of the five school districts agreed to participate only when we agreed to allow the district to choose which qualifying schools would participate in the experimental sample, which effectively rendered the sample and assignment nonrandom. In the end, only two of the five districts from the original pool of eligible districts agreed to participate. The most significant complication arose when the latest school performance data were made available when recruitment was to begin. Fewer schools within these districts met the criteria for "No Recognition" schools, which resulted in a smaller number of schools per cluster. The number of districts needed to sample 44 schools and assign them randomly to treatment was simply too high to be feasible for implementation. The sample size determined by our power analysis could not be achieved within our proposed design parameters and thus compromised our ability to detect intervention effects and examine contextual variation in the nature of these effects.

The resulting decisions had unfortunate consequences for the randomized design that we had proposed, which resulted in a potential violation of the stable unit treatment value assumption (SUTVA; Rubin, 1978) that, conditional on covariates X, treatment and nontreatment outcomes are unrelated to treatment assignment. Analyzing SSP-IP preintervention data, we found that the 11 intervention schools systematically differed from all remaining schools on several variables.

RESPONSES TO THE UNEXPECTED EVENTS

We considered quasi-experimental strategies, primarily propensity score matching (PSM), as a means to address the violation of SUTVA. PSM, developed by Rosenbaum and Rubin (1985), is a powerful strategy to address this evaluation challenge. Our objective was to choose 33 comparison schools that best matched the 11 intervention schools. We used a logistic regression, modeling treatment assignment on a set of variables suspected of being related to treatment assignment. Several different models were tested. We then used the propensity scores—the predicted values of the logistic regression—to choose 33 controls. This process uses observed data to approximate group randomization and make the resultant intervention and comparison groups more balanced on observables.

Limitations of PSM have been acknowledged in the literature. One of the major limitations of PSM is that it cannot control for selection bias due to unobservables. To address this limitation, we conducted several sensitivity analyses to gauge the robustness of our approach. Beyond this, PSM has its detractors and its proponents. The detractors believe that PSM cannot realistically emulate the internal validity of a randomized design when assumptions about selection bias are violated. Proponents of the method note that procedure performs equally well as a randomized design when selection bias is not a plausible threat to the validity of a treatment effect. We felt that the low power of the design, a facet of statistical conclusion validity, was a far more difficult problem to surmount than selection bias. The issue for the present evaluation was not actually assignment—we know how the schools were assigned—but of characteristics artifactually related to that assignment process that may have induced bias in the treatment effect estimates.

The question that our PSM analysis intended to answer was whether we could predict membership in the treatment groups on the basis of these characteristics. Subsequently, if that answer was yes, then we could use these characteristics to control for selection when estimating the treatment effect. Although the sample was very small, the results of the logistic regression demonstrated that both geography and other factors were related to treatment assignment. The two groups of schools were no longer different on observed covariates after matching, and the data met the requirement of SUTVA. Results of the sensitivity analysis for the preintervention period also confirmed our hypotheses.

Despite these results, our consultations with the sponsor of the evaluation led us to redefine the project from an impact evaluation to a basic research study. The seed for this was planted in the proposal. We noted our intention to make use of economics inherent in recruiting at the district level and implementing the intervention in clusters of schools determined by common district or geography. This intent was carried through to its logical conclusion when faced with a quickly approaching start date and in the context of a power analysis, which greatly underestimated the number of schools required. Our experience has important implications for the political aspects of program evaluation.

In conclusion, when randomization fails, evaluators should consider using special treatments in data analysis, but should be cautious about assuming that funders will support these types of treatments. PSM at the school level is one such robust method that is particularly useful in the evaluation of school-based interventions. A rigorous evaluation must employ multiple evaluation methods and sensitivity analysis.

REFERENCES

Rosenbaum, P. R., & Rubin, D. B. (1985). Constructing a control group using multivariate matched sampling methods that incorporate the propensity score. *The American Statistician, 39*, 33–38.

Rubin, D. B. (1978). Bayesian inference for causal effects. *Annals of Statistics, 6*, 34–58.

Case 6

Unexpected Changes
in Program Delivery

THE PERILS OF OVERLOOKING
PROCESS DATA WHEN
EVALUATING HIV PREVENTION

Bryce D. Smith
Danny Sprouse
Kevin L. DeWeaver

DESCRIPTION OF THE CASE

HIV/AIDS is a significant threat to public health and as such is one of the focus areas for Healthy People 2010, a comprehensive list of objectives to improve the public health of Americans (U.S. Department of Health and Human Services, 2000). To prevent the acquisition and transmission of HIV/AIDS, effective behavioral interventions are needed (Coleman & Ford, 1996; Robinson, Bockting, Rosser, Miner, & Coleman, 2002). The southern region of the United States had a higher rate of HIV/AIDS than all other regions in the country together from 2001 to 2005 (Morbidity and Mortality Weekly Report, 2007). To respond to this crisis, a community-based organization (CBO) in metro Atlanta, Georgia, provides interventions to members of the worst-hit populations, including men who have sex with men (MSM; Smith & Bride, 2004). This case reports on the evaluation of the Relationships, Intimacy, and Sex workshop, an HIV prevention intervention delivered by this CBO to caucasian MSM. The study evaluated outcomes of a three-session small-group intervention that totaled 9 hours of delivery time in comparison to a no-treatment comparison group. The outcomes that were being assessed include the number of sex partners, number of unprotected sex events, and knowledge of HIV transmission risks.

The Relationships, Intimacy, and Sex workshop had a sex-positive emphasis as applied to issues of healthy relationships and sexual communication for MSM. These messages were provided via affirming rather than shaming messages to decrease HIV risk behaviors such as unprotected sex. The workshop was conceptualized as three sessions, one per week over 3 weeks, with each session expected to be 3 hours long. Broadly speaking, the first session focused on creating, developing, and nurturing relationships between men and examining the barriers to these relationships. The second session addressed issues of intimacy, including sexual negotiation and sexual activity. The third session was designed to increase knowledge about HIV/AIDS/STDs and transmission risk while exploring ways to reduce HIV risk in sexual activity. The intervention sessions consisted of activities such as mini-lectures, full-group discussions, break-out group discussions and role-plays, handouts, and slides that ensured fidelity to the overall content of the intervention.

HIV prevention efforts have advanced considerably in the United States. Substantial federal, state, and local funding are directed toward the provision of interventions that have shown evidence of effectiveness in rigorous evaluation studies. In order for effective behavioral interventions to be diffused for use by local HIV prevention providers and maintain their effectiveness they must be conducted with as much fidelity to the original intervention as is reasonably possible.

UNEXPECTED EVENTS

The workshop was initially provided once a month as a three-session intervention meeting once per week over 3 weeks (for a total of 9 hours), and the group was conducted in this way three times over a period of 5 months. Recruitment was a significant challenge, such that only 25 men completed the workshops, and a workshop was not conducted for 2 months because not enough men could be recruited to start one. Much qualitative feedback was provided by the participants to the program coordinator at the agency about ways to improve the group, and the most frequent suggestion was to have fewer sessions. The program coordinator modified the activities so that they were all conducted with the entire group and no longer done in dyads or small groups. No changes were made to the content or length of the slides. This was intended to decrease the length of the workshop through the change in delivery method without appreciably changing the content. Starting with the fourth cycle, the intervention was provided in two ways: (1) in two sessions that were each 4 hours long for a total of 8 hours, and (2) in one session that was 6 hours long. Ultimately, 24 men completed the two-session workshop and 24 men completed the single-session workshop, for a total treatment group sample of 73.

This unanticipated change in delivery method caused two primary adjustments to the evaluation. The first adjustment was in the data analysis and interpretation. It could be argued that instead of a single treatment arm, as was originally designed, we now had three treatment arms that employed different delivery methods. Because it was expected that the intervention would be delivered in the same way every time, no systematic or standardized data were collected on the activities or the delivery method used during the actual sessions. This created a gap in knowledge regarding what was actually conducted and how it was delivered. We do not know precisely which activities were changed, and we do not know the amount of change that had to occur to decrease the original 9-hour intervention to 8 hours or to the considerably shorter 6 hours. Subsequently, we did not have the data we would need to control and account for the differences between the treatment groups.

The second adjustment was in the conclusions, as the ability to attribute changes in outcomes to the intervention was limited by the intervention being delivered in three different ways. Having not collected any data on how many dyadic and small-group breakouts were eliminated in the two shorter treatment versions, we had no way of quantifying the differences between the treatment subgroups, so we were limited in what we could conclude about the effectiveness of the activities provided.

As a mental health clinician I was concerned that we may have lost some of the richness that the dyadic activities and subsequent report-backs from those activities may have provided. During the planning and development of the intervention, we believed that one of the strengths of the intervention was the one-on-one role plays and the report-backs that the participants shared with the larger group. I was concerned that reducing the number of these dyadic activities might have reduced the potential effectiveness of the intervention. But since we were not documenting the number of these activities, there was no way to compare the groups based on that factor.

RESPONSES TO THE UNEXPECTED EVENTS

We were fortunate to have the outcome data from each of the subgroups, and as a result of the unexpected delivery method change, multiple unplanned assessments of potential differences between the samples participating in the three delivery methods had to be conducted and any differences controlled for in hypothesis testing. While there were no differences between the treatment subgroups for the outcome variables at baseline or posttest, three demographic variables were found to have differences of statistical significance: age, race, and HIV serostatus. Post hoc tests revealed that for age, the one-session group was significantly older than the two-session group by a mean difference of 8.6 years. The difference in race was clearly due to the presence of six African American men in the three-session group, while there are no African Americans in the other two groups. Last, there were considerably more HIV-positive men in the three-session group (56%) than either the two-session group (12.5%) or the one-session group (4.3%). These variables then had to be controlled in analyses of the treatment group data. While this was a reasonable solution to the problem, it did not change the fact that we were not documenting the dyadic activities in any way and would not be able to control for that factor in our analysis nor discuss them suitably.

The unexpected change in delivery method would have been a manageable challenge if the evaluation had been collecting data specifically about the delivery method. Since we never expected the delivery method to change we were not collecting those data, and our evaluation was not comprehensive enough to be able to adapt to this kind of change. We would still be able to calculate the findings for the outcome variables, but without these key process data we would not be able to fully place these findings in the context of the services provided, limiting their utility.

Because we do not know exactly how the content was delivered, this would also limit how the intervention could be diffused to other providers. The oversight of not collecting the session data means that the intervention, if it were found to be effective, would require additional evaluation to make sure that providers knew what would be the most effective delivery method. If the evaluation had found tremendous change in the outcome variables of interest, then another evaluation that included process data (including delivery method) would have been required prior to its replication and diffusion.

Although the evaluation still produced beneficial results for the stakeholders, these results were limited by the unexpected changes in program activity and the evaluation design that was not comprehensive enough to respond to those changes. The primary stakeholders include the agency, dissertation committee, and myself. The agency was understandably comfortable with the changes in delivery method and felt that any limitations in the evaluation were justifiable given the desire to meet the needs of the target population. They learned that they were going to have to explore new ways to recruit their target audiences and retain them through multi-session workshops and interventions. The agency concluded that the intervention was worth continuing and expanded how it would be provided in the future.

My dissertation committee was most interested in the possibility of three different treatment arms in the evaluation. There was discussion of being able to compare the treatment subgroups, but the overall evaluation was not powered for those analyses and there were no statistically significant findings. However, the committee found the evaluation study strong enough for a successful dissertation defense.

In conclusion, the unexpected change did not cause anything that could be considered a fatal flaw for the evaluation. I learned to always collect process data regardless of how sure I may be about the program and regardless of what I am expecting to happen. There were several limitations that may have negatively affected the dissemination of the findings, and we hope that future evaluations of this workshop will be more comprehensive and have broader utility.

REFERENCES

Coleman, L. M., & Ford, N. J. (1996). An extensive literature review of the evaluation of HIV prevention programmes. *Health Education and Research, 11,* 327–328.

Morbidity and Mortality Weekly Report. (2007). *Update to racial/ethnic disparities in diagnoses of HIV/AIDS—33 states, 2001–2005.* March 9, 56(09), 189–193.

Robinson, B. E., Bockting, W. O., Rosser, B. R. S., Miner, M., & Coleman, E. (2002). The sexual health model: Application of a sexological approach to HIV prevention. *Health Education and Research, 17,* 43–57.

Smith, B. D., & Bride, B. (2004). Positive impact: A community-based mental health center for persons affected by HIV. *Health and Social Work, 29,* 145–148.

U.S. Department of Health and Human Services. (2000). *Healthy People 2010: Understanding and improving health* (2nd ed.). Washington, DC: U.S. Government Printing Office.

Case 7

Evaluating Costs and Benefits of Consumer-Operated Services

Unexpected Resistance, Unanticipated Insights, and Déjà Vu All Over Again

Brian T. Yates

DESCRIPTION OF THE CASE

This was the first multisite evaluation of the effectiveness, costs, benefits, cost-effectiveness, and cost–benefit of adding consumer-operated services (COS) to traditional mental health services (TMHS). At eight sites throughout the United States, 1,827 consumers diagnosed as mentally ill were assigned randomly either to continue receiving TMHS or to participate in a COS program while continuing to receive TMHS. Prior to this, evaluations of COS outcomes had involved small samples and often conceptualized COS as an alternative to TMHS rather than as a possibly useful addition (cf. Emerick, 1990; Segal, Silverman, & Tempkin, 1995). Only one study had reported potential cost savings for consumers (Dumont & Jones, 2002); it was quasi-experimental and used a small sample.

In the cost-focused part of the evaluation, the original questions were:

1. How much does adding COS cost?
2. Is any improvement in psychological, social, or economic outcomes worth the cost?

3. Which of three COS models provide the lowest cost and were the most cost-effective and cost-beneficial?

I ended up answering (1) in much less detail than I had hoped. I found that (2) was the wrong question entirely, as explained later in this report. Finally, I eventually realized that (3) was the wrong question; it should have been:

3′. Which site(s) had the least expensive ways of *delivering* COS?

Over the eight sites, 1,827 consumers participated in 2- to 4-hour interviews at the beginning of participation, and 4, 8, and usually 12 months afterward, providing data on costs, amount of participation in specific TMHS and COS activities, and psychological as well as service utilization outcomes.

In TMHS, individual and group therapy as well as occasional pharmacotherapy were common. COS added peer counseling, education about services one could receive, training in advocacy for self and others, assistance with housing and basic needs, legal counseling, case management, and printed communications about mental health topics. These and similar services were delivered by fellow consumers, never by mental health professionals, in either drop-in centers, noncredit course formats, or peer counseling settings. Directors of COSs were consumers; COS boards were consumer controlled.

Individual COSs responded to the Guide For Applicants (GFA) to obtain funding for inclusion in the multisite study as a study site, as did a variety of sites that wished to serve as the coordinating center for the sites and study. Individual COSs could and did apply, as did statewide networks of COSs. University researchers often were included in the COS application to facilitate data collection; to interact with the researchers, project officers, and coordinating center; and sometimes to provide guidance. Only established sites could apply—both the COS and paired TMHS were required to have been in operation for at least 2 years prior to application.

UNEXPECTED EVENTS

Four unintended consequences occurred in the portion of the evaluation concerned with costs.

1. *Confusion of "costs" and "benefits."* A major unanticipated difficulty was the extent to which researchers, administrators, and consumers con-

fused "cost" with "benefit." *Costs* (resources such as staff time and space that were consumed by the program so it could operate) were confused with *benefits* (monetary *outcomes* of a program that result from the processing of resources in program activities, such as increased consumer income and decreased consumer use of health and criminal justice services; cf. Brent, 2003; Levin & McEwan, 2001). Although the federal program announcement specified that "direct and indirect costs" of COS programs would be measured, asking those programs to report costs was translated into measurement not of the value of resources *used* by the programs, but only of programs' monetary *outcomes* (i.e., benefits). Most COSs expressed surprise that costs *of* their programs were going to be measured at all! The traditional focus of researchers affiliated with COSs on outcomes rather than on costs of interventions (Yates, 1994), as well as some programs' concern that reporting their expenditures could reveal accounting irregularities, may have fostered this misunderstanding.

2. *Resistance to measuring program costs of program components.* Programs' resistance to measuring costs prevented program expenditures from being measured at a level of specificity that could link use of specific resources to performance of specific program activities—part of the planned, formative analysis of cost-effectiveness and cost–benefit for individual sites and for COSs as a whole (Yates, 1996). Plans detailed in the funded proposal for measuring the amount and value of each major resource used in each component of treatment were rejected by most program directors and consumers. Many of the eight sites only were willing to report their total annual budget—not even actual expenditures. A primary reason for this opposition may have been that most consumers, program operators, and researchers thought measuring costs of providing specific services would consume research resources that could have been spent measuring more outcomes more accurately. My retrospective insight was that these interest groups may have wished to focus on effectiveness to the exclusion of costs and monetary outcomes, so COS could be listed as an evidence-based practice by federal agencies to increase and stabilize funding for COS programs.

3. *Resistance to monetizing volunteered and donated resources.* Even more surprisingly, evaluating the *non*monetary resources used by COS, including volunteered time and donated space, equipment, supplies, food, and other materials, was contentious. My experience in other settings had been that the more volunteered time, space, and other resources a program uses, the prouder that program is of letting potential funders know what a "deal" they are getting when they provide monetary funding for the

program (Yates, Haven, & Thoresen, 1979). COS programs seemed to use large amounts of donated resources, so they had been considered especially amenable to measurement of these variables. COS programs resisted measurement of these nonmonetary costs, however, expressing fear that reporting the monetary value of these donated resources along with the actual money received by programs would make COS programs appear more expensive than they were.

4. *Unused program capacity and unrepresentatively high cost.* One site had extremely high costs per consumer. Findings from a site visit and consideration of elementary economic theory provided me with another insight. The combination of (1) a decision by one COS site to only serve participants in the study and no other consumers, (2) a small planned sample size for that site, and (3) delays at other sites in recruiting study participants led the COS site to recruit fewer consumers than it could have. Because this site had largely fixed "overhead" costs, including commitments to pay fixed consumer staff good salaries as well as long-term space leases, that site could not readily reduce expenditures despite fewer consumers needing services. This caused costs per consumer to be higher than would otherwise have been the case, resulting in unrepresentative cost per consumer, and potentially poor cost-effectiveness and cost–benefit for that site.

RESPONSES TO THE UNEXPECTED EVENTS

1. and 2. *Responses to confusion of "costs" and "benefits," and to measuring costs of program components.* The funder mollified resistance to measuring program costs, exhibited primarily in the form of denial that costs were called for in the GFA. Using a strategy suggested by the funder, programs could elect to report costs in "standard" or "enhanced" formats. The enhanced format preserved the original plan to measure the amount of each type of resource used in each major component of the COS program. The standard format allowed programs to report each quarter a single cost figure for expenditures, or even just their budget "bottom line." The enhanced format was soon compromised by several programs when they reduced the number of components in their program from several they initially identified to just one. Ultimately, only one of eight COS sites provided sufficiently detailed data on resource expenditures for program components, despite intense technical assistance (including many long phone calls, site visits, detailed manuals, and development of computer spreadsheets tailored to each site for ease of collecting and reporting cost data).

Attempting to collect data on benefits as well as costs, I did succeed in including potential income as well as possible cost savings in the common protocol that all consumer participants completed at baseline and every 3 months thereafter for a year. Consumers reported use of specific health, criminal justice, and other services for the 4 months preceding each interview using structured recall. Consumers reported how much income they received from a variety of sources as well in the same 4-month recall at each interview. These data are being analyzed and may allow a cost–benefit analysis of adding COS to TMHS. Unfortunately, validation of these self-reports with data from funding sources for health services was prevented by the complexities of varying time frames between states for Medicaid reporting and programs' reticence, despite several site visits that we made to facilitate Medicaid data reporting by COSs.

3. *Responses to resistance to monetizing volunteered and donated resources.* Resistance to monetizing donated resources was moderated to levels that produced compliance with data requests by reducing the perceived threat while also noting a potential benefit to programs of quantifying volunteered and donated resources. This was one area of real success. I repeatedly and publicly promised COS programs I would never report COS costs as a lump sum of expenditures and volunteered resources, but would always provide a breakdown of those two types of resources. In addition, I compared the value of volunteered to purchased resources, framing volunteered resources as value returned on expenditure of monetary resources.[1] Programs that generated large amounts of volunteered resources appreciated being able to show that quantitatively to funders. For some COSs, volunteered and donated resources exceeded their funded budgets (cf. Yates et al., 2010).

4. *Responses to unused program capacity and unrepresentatively high cost.* Finally, costs for the site that had few or no consumers during some periods of program operation were adjusted by excluding costs for periods when no consumers were served. This program still had artificially inflated costs, arguably, because fewer consumers were served than was possible during the periods when they were operating. Understanding this led me to the additional insight that costs of COS programs were not so much a function of one of the three service models followed by the COSs, but of the degree to which program overhead costs were *fixed* as opposed to *variable*. More specifically, comparison of how different COS programs adapted to varying demand for their services suggested that programs which could readily increase or decrease staff, office space, and other resources in response to changes in consumer demand were more likely to have lower cost per con-

sumer (as detailed in Yates et al., 2010). Given findings for psychological and other outcomes (cf. Campbell, 2004), these least-expensive COSs also appeared to be the most cost-effective and cost-beneficial. This unexpected finding was déjà vu all over again: Yates (1978) had found that flexibility of the delivery system for obesity treatment was a stronger determinant of cost-effectiveness than the type of obesity treatment offered.

ACKNOWLEDGMENTS

Thank you, consumers of mental health services everywhere, for asserting your rights to the best programs for the most people within the context of all-too-limited funding, and for participating in research designed to foster those rights while justifying better funding. Thank you, researchers and policymakers, for conducting and supporting research that attempts to answer questions about the effectiveness, benefits, costs, cost-effectiveness, and cost-benefit of specific human service procedures. Thank you especially, Jean Campbell, Danyelle Manning, and Matthew Johnsen, for your emotional support throughout this process. The multisite study referred to in this publication was made possible by Grant Number SM-52328 awarded to the Missouri Institute of Mental Health Coordinating Center from the U.S. Department of Health and Human Services (DHHS), Substance Abuse and Mental Health Services Administration (SAMHSA), Center for Mental Health Services (CMHS); and by a sabbatical appointment for the author as Visiting Professor at the Center for Mental Health Services Research in the Department of Psychiatry at the Medical School at the University of Massachusetts, Worcester, Massachusetts. The opinions and hypotheses expressed in this publication regarding costs of consumer-operated services and the nature and reasons for the unintended consequences described herein are the author's, however, and neither those of the institutions listed above nor of coauthors on other publications cited herein.

REFERENCES

Brent, R. J. (2003). *Cost–benefit and health care evaluations.* New York: Elgar.

Campbell, J. (2004, May 7). *Consumer-Operated Services Program (COSP) Multisite Research Initiative: Overview and preliminary findings.* St. Louis: Missouri Institute of Mental Health.

Dumont, J., & Jones, K. (2002, Spring). Findings from a consumer/survivor defined alternative to psychiatric hospitalization. *Outlook, 4–6.*

Emerick, R. (1990). Self-help groups for former patients: Relations with mental health professionals. *Hospital and Community Psychiatry, 41,* 401–407.

Levin, H. M., & McEwan, P. J. (2001). *Cost-effectiveness analysis* (2nd ed.). Thousand Oaks, CA: Sage.

Segal, S., Silverman, C., & Tempkin, T. (1995). Characteristics and service use of long-term members of self-help agencies for mental health clients. *Psychiatric Services, 46,* 269–274.

Yates, B. T. (1978). Improving the cost-effectiveness of obesity programs: Reducing the cost per pound. *International Journal of Obesity, 2,* 249–266.

Yates, B. T. (1994). Toward the incorporation of costs, cost-effectiveness analysis, and cost–benefit analysis into clinical research. *Journal of Consulting and Clinical Psychology, 62,* 729–736.

Yates, B. T. (1996). *Analyzing costs, procedures, processes, and outcomes in human services: An introduction.* Thousand Oaks, CA: Sage.

Yates, B. T., Haven, W. G., & Thoresen, C. E. (1979). Cost-effectiveness analysis at Learning House: How much change for how much money? In J. S. Stumphauzer (Ed.), *Progress in behavior therapy with delinquents* (pp. 186–222). Springfield, IL: Thomas.

Yates, B. T., Mannix, D., Freed, M. C., Campbell, J., Johnsen, M., Jones, K., et al. (2010). *Costs of consumer-operated services: Research findings for three models implemented at eight sites for 1,827 consumers.* Manuscript in preparation, American University, Washington, DC.

NOTE

1. This was the excellent idea of Michael Freed, a graduate student at the time on the research team.

Case 8

Keep Up with the Program!

ADAPTING THE EVALUATION FOCUS TO ALIGN WITH A COLLEGE ACCESS PROGRAM'S CHANGING GOALS

Kristine L. Chadwick and Jennifer Conner Blatz

DESCRIPTION OF THE CASE

The first statewide college access network in the nation, the Ohio College Access Network (OCAN) was founded in 1999 as a public–private partnership among KnowledgeWorks Foundation (KWF), the Ohio Board of Regents (OBR), the Ohio Department of Education (ODE), and preexisting college access programs in communities across the state. Within the overall goal of increasing the number of Ohioans who matriculate to and graduate from college, the original objectives for OCAN included stimulating the creation of new college access programs where none currently existed, providing resources for existing college access programs to gain experiential knowledge of specific college access initiatives throughout the state, and serving as a resource in the field of college access and retention and other higher education-related subjects.

In the second quarter of 2003, the KWF took two major steps to help OCAN move to the next level of organizational maturity: it worked with OCAN to implement a strategic planning process and issued a request for proposals (RFP) for a 3-year evaluation of OCAN. The goals of the evaluation, as described in the RFP, were threefold. The first goal was to focus on examining the effectiveness and influence of OCAN as a statewide college access organization. The second goal centered on OCAN member programs, the services they provide to their respective communities, and participant outcomes and successes. The final goal focused on the partnership among KWF, OCAN, OBR, and other collaborating agencies. In addition, KWF desired an emphasis on qualitative design and methodology due to the need to explore and describe this innovative initiative.

Edvantia, Inc.[1] was the successful bidder on the evaluation contract. The proposed evaluation was aligned to the three goals identified in the RFP, which had organized the goals by level of the system: intermediate organization (goal 1), member programs (goal 2), and statewide partnerships (goal 3). To align with these goals, the evaluation included data collection on member program involvement in OCAN services through items in a member program survey, attendance data from OCAN workshops, and interviews with OCAN staff and key stakeholders (goal 1); case studies of a purposive selection of five diverse member programs to gain a deeper understanding of the programs served by the statewide organization, surveys of member program services, and tracking of students receiving services from all member programs (goal 2); and interviews and reviews of legislation and policies to understand the partnerships involved in OCAN and their contributions to furthering the goals of college access (goal 3). In the fall of 2003 the scope and schedule of the evaluation project plan were finalized.

UNEXPECTED EVENTS

While the evaluation project plan was being finalized, the strategic planning process was producing a draft strategic plan for 2005 through 2007. In January 2004, the OCAN executive director met with each board member to go over the draft strategic plan, solicit feedback, and ensure inclusiveness. In February 2004, a strategic planning retreat was held; in June 2004, the strategic plan was approved. The strategic plan included three overarching goals involving program development, advocacy, and sustainability.

The program development goal focused on providing valued services to member organizations to ensure college access and success using strategies such as the development and use of guidelines for member organization service delivery and experimentation with innovative models of college access programming. The strategic plan outlined three strategies for achieving OCAN's advocacy goal of becoming the recognized leader of college access in Ohio by aligning resources to promote the work and success of OCAN and its members, such as developing a comprehensive marketing program. OCAN's third strategic goal involved establishing a sustainability plan for OCAN and its member organizations through use of various strategies, such as establishing and maintaining a prominent and diverse board of directors.

In early February 2004, as evaluation instrumentation was being finalized and data collection was about to begin, a phone call between the evaluator and KWF program officer occurred that altered the evaluation focus. While discussing the draft strategic plan and an unrelated topic of challenges in developing a database for college access programs to track student service recipients from high school through the postsecondary system, it became clear to the program officer and evaluator that OCAN member college access programs did not have a consistent way to track participant outcomes, and thereby it would be a challenge to address the second goal of the evaluation, which centered around outcomes for OCAN member programs. In thinking about how to proceed with the evaluation, it was determined that what would be most helpful to OCAN and KWF would be to focus less on quantifiable outcomes and more on progress this still-developing statewide program was making toward its three strategic goals of program development, advocacy, and sustainability. This demonstrates how the risk of working with a young organization, still in formation, required significant flexibility when considering evaluation.

RESPONSES TO THE UNEXPECTED EVENTS

With the three strategic goals to frame the evaluation, the evaluation team was faced with a challenge: KWF did not want to significantly alter the evaluation design, yet wanted the evaluation focus to be on the strategic goals. The evaluation team reviewed the overall plan and all instruments to determine how best to meet the changing needs of the program and the design and methodological preferences of KWF. During February 2004, several suggested revisions to the evaluation design and instrumentation were circulated by the evaluation team to both OCAN staff and the KWF program officer. The revised evaluation plan and data collection instruments now aligned with the strategic goals, yet still included most of the originally approved approaches, including a member program survey, five case studies, and a review of statewide college access policy changes. However, now all revised data collection protocols related to one or more of the strategic goals, and the major evaluation questions were grouped according to the strategic goals. Given the innovative nature of this first-of-its-kind program, risks were relatively high that long-term sustainability would be difficult for OCAN to achieve without a strong commitment to continuous improvement, development of outcome measures (and outcome data!), and a coherent, focused agenda. Organizing the evaluation design and reporting around the same focused agenda the program was following served to further KWF's goal of OCAN becoming self-sustainable and helped OCAN make key improvements in its operations toward strategic goals. For instance, first-year evaluation results suggested that OCAN could better provide program development services by offering regional workshops; by the final year of the evaluation, these regional workshops were in place. The continuing struggle to roll out a functional student tracking system that would allow OCAN and its member programs to capture outcome data was a continuous theme in the evaluation results around program development. Member programs had mixed opinions of OCAN's marketing efforts, and these findings in the evaluation reports helped OCAN to revise and tailor its marketing and advocacy efforts in ways that achieved strategic goals and maintained boundaries between local member programs' missions and OCAN's mission.

The alignment of the evaluation with OCAN's strategic plan also helped OCAN to clarify its role with its member college access programs. Through analysis of stakeholder input it became clear that OCAN's role with its membership is that of an intermediary organization that, in accordance with its strategic goals, provides program development, advocacy, and sustainability support to members, but that does not necessarily govern and cannot easily track the direct services delivered to students. This was an "unintended, but very positive" consequence of evaluation that resulted in a clearer focus for OCAN and a way to more appropriately measure the impact and influence of its work going forward.

In the case of the OCAN evaluation, even though KWF set the evaluation's initial focus, that focus soon turned out to be less than optimally relevant in the changing dynamics of this growing and developing statewide college access network. Aligning the evaluation with the new strategic goals that set the path for OCAN's activities permitted the evaluators to be highly responsive and tailor the evaluation to the evolving questions that OCAN and its funder, KWF, most needed answered at that stage of OCAN's development.

NOTE

1. Until September 1, 2005, Edvantia, Inc., was the Appalachia Educational Laboratory (AEL). For ease of reading, Edvantia will be referenced.

Assumptions about School Staff's Competencies and Likely Program Impacts

Laura Hassler Lang, Christine E. Johnson,
and Shana Goldwyn

DESCRIPTION OF THE CASE

The Applied Data Analysis for Principals and Teachers (ADAPT) was a randomized controlled trial implemented in the fall of 2004 by the Florida State University Learning Systems Institute. The purpose of the trial was to examine the impact of classroom- and school-level data-driven decision making on middle school reading outcomes. Specifically, the purposes of the study were to determine: (1) educators' baseline knowledge, skills, and attitudes related to using student performance data in reading to guide curricular and instructional decision making; (2) the effectiveness of an online course in addressing identified gaps in knowledge, skills, and/or attitudes required to use data for decision making; and (3) the impact of data-driven decision making on student performance in reading as measured by the Florida Comprehensive Assessment Test (FCAT), the state's norm-referenced and criterion-referenced achievement test administered in grades 3–10.

The sample included 125 principals, assistant principals, reading coaches, and reading/language arts teachers from 25 middle schools in Florida, and was examined in three phases. During Phase I, each of the participants was given the Test of Assessment Skills and Knowledge (TASK) as a pretest. Baseline knowledge of each practitioner subgroup was examined and compared.

The schools were randomly assigned to treatment (n = 12) and control groups (n = 13). Participants in the treatment group (n = 57) completed a 16-week, 3-credit online course designed to provide a foundation in assessment, analysis of student performance data, and the instructional components of reading. Participants in the control group (n = 68) did not take the online course. The online course was developed following a regional pilot study in which face-to-face training sessions on the same topic were not successful. Lack of success was primarily due to logistical and fidelity issues (e.g., convening all participants at the same time/location and inconsistencies in emphasis/content across trainers), issues that could be more easily addressed in an online format.

The online course, instructed via the Blackboard Academic Suite™ course management system at Florida State University, consisted of nine instructional units sequenced according to the following four components of the reading assessment framework: screening assessment, progress monitoring, diagnostic assessment, and outcome assessment. Each unit contained between two and five lessons. Unit tests and activities at the end of each lesson provided opportunities for practical application and feedback relative to concepts studied. The Blackboard discussion board, e-mail, and World Wide Web functions also were integrated into the course content. External links provided access to online resources such as the National Reading Panel's recommendations for teaching vocabulary and a list of valid and reliable reading assessments compiled by the Florida Center for Reading Research (FCRR). Each student completed a final action research project to demonstrate the application of assessment and reading skills. Successful completion of the course fulfilled one of six competencies required for the state's teacher certification in reading.

The course was taught by three faculty members (the primary authors of the course) and five trained mentors: four teachers certified in middle school language arts by the National Board for Professional Teaching Standards and one graduate student, a former English teacher who served on the instructional design team. Treatment group participants were assigned to one of six class sections, each containing an average of 11 students and taught by an instructor–mentor team. All of the treatment group principals and assistant principals were purposefully assigned to the same section. Teachers and reading coaches were randomly assigned to one of the remaining five sections.

Both treatment and control group participants were pre- and post-tested on knowledge/skills, self-assessed reading competencies, and attitudes toward reading assessment at the beginning and end of the course. This phase also examined treatment and control group differences on pre–post gains on the TASK.

Phase II focused on understanding the application of skills and beliefs to data analysis in practice. In this phase, the two groups were given a Web survey conducted near the end of the 2004–2005 school year to determine the extent to which principals, reading coaches, and teachers used data to inform instructional and curricular decisions. The treatment and control groups' responses were compared to examine differences.

Phase III focused on the relationship between the gains in knowledge and skills and student performance in schools. Using hierarchical linear modeling, Phase III examined treatment–control group differences in student performance on FCAT reading and mathematics during the intervention year (2004–2005) and following year (2005–2006) to determine whether use of data to inform instruction made a difference in student achievement.

UNEXPECTED EVENTS

The study yielded two unexpected outcomes: (1) the low baseline level of knowledge and skill among principals, reading coaches, and teachers using data to drive instruction (Phase I), and (2) results of first-year impacts on student performance in mathematics, but not in reading, which was the focus of the course content and subject population (e.g., reading coaches and language arts teachers) (Phase III).

Phase I

Although the study's primary research question was whether the use of student performance data to inform instruction has an impact on student achievement, we first designed and delivered professional development to ensure that study participants had the prerequisite skills and knowledge to do so. We predicted that many participants at the outset would have some but not all of the knowledge and skills required, particularly teachers, whom we expected would have less access to this type of training than principals or reading coaches. Florida's middle school reading coaches, funded for the first time in 2004–2005, had received face-to-face training from the Florida Department of Education at the start of our study. Principals and assistant principals in Florida are required to have master's degrees, increasing the likelihood that they have been taught testing and measurement concepts, such as validity, reliability, and interpretation of test results. In addition since 2001, some principals in Florida have received training in the use of data to drive instruction, including face-to-face workshops conducted throughout Florida by the principal investigator and one of our online instructors.

What surprised us was the extent of the deficit among all three subgroups of participants (principals and assistant principals, reading coaches, and teachers) on the skills and knowledge pretest, a 99-item multiple-choice test consisting primarily of questions from the course textbook, *Developing and Using Classroom Assessments* (3rd ed.) by Albert Oosterhof (2003). For the treatment group, the mean number of items correct (out of 99) was 53 (53.54%) for principals and assistant principals, 56 (56.57%) for reading coaches, and 52 (52.53%) for teachers. The control group showed similar pretest results by subgroups, which were not significantly different from those of the treatment group.

Sixty-nine of the 99 items met our criterion for low performance (fewer than 70% of participants answering the item correctly). Although participants seemed to understand test formats and reading components, fewer than 70% understood how assessment scores and results are interpreted and applied to instructional decision making. The areas of greatest weakness were:

- Level of cognitive ability a test item measures.
- How to use and interpret standardized test scores.
- How to identify appropriate types of validity or establish evidence of validity.
- The extent to which results are consistent or generalizable (reliability).

Phase III

To date, we have analyzed results of the Florida Comprehensive Assessment Test administered in March 2005 and March 2006, the year of the intervention and the subsequent year. In March 2005, the treatment–control group difference in student gains was not statistically significant in reading. However, it was statistically significant in mathematics on both the norm-referenced (FCAT-NRT) and criterion-referenced (FCAT-CRT) tests. A possible explanation of this result may be the indirect influence of the principal on use of data to inform instruction schoolwide and the relative ease of analyzing and using student performance data by mathematics teachers, compared to that of reading teachers. Ironically, we initially planned to examine FCAT reading results only. Had we not added FCAT mathematics to the analysis, we would have overlooked this outcome entirely.

Also surprising was that these results did not hold true for the second year. For the FCAT tests administered in March 2006, there were no treatment effects in math. However, we did find treatment effects for the criterion-referenced state test in reading when analyzed at the school level.

RESPONSES TO THE UNEXPECTED EVENTS

Phase I

Because of the low baseline knowledge of practitioners and lack of difference between groups, the online course was developed to target specific areas of weakness.

Overall, results indicate that the online course was effective in increasing the skills and knowledge required to use reading assessment data to inform instructional and curricular decisions. The mean pre–post gain was higher for the participants who completed the course (treatment group) than those who did not take the course (control group), and this difference was statistically significant ($t = 16.99$, $df = 123$, $p < .01$).

Moreover, the course was effective for all three subgroups: principals and assistant principals, reading coaches, and teachers. For each subgroup, the mean gain score was significantly higher ($p < .01$) for the treatment group than for the control group: principals and assistant principals ($t = 8.01$, $df = 20$, $p < .01$), reading coaches ($t = 7.09$, $df = 18$, p < .01), and teachers ($t = 13.02$, $df = 81$, $p < .01$). For the treatment group, the mean number of items correct (out of 99) on the posttest was 76 for principals and assistant principals, 80 for reading coaches, and 75 for teachers—substantially higher than pretest levels.

Phase III

Because the 2005 FCAT was administered so soon after course completion, we did not expect changes in practices to be fully infused in treatment group classrooms or schools. Any differences resulting from the intervention were likely to be greater when principals, reading coaches, and teachers began the following year (2005–2006) equipped with the necessary knowledge and skills to use student performance data to drive school and classroom decision making. As suspected, when the following year of data was analyzed (2005–2006), there were treatment effects in the criterion referenced test in reading, and no significant treatment effects in math. The response to unexpected results manifested itself as a question to ponder in future research: What specific knowledge and skills do practitioners need in order to target specific content areas?

ACKNOWLEDGMENTS

Portions of this research were funded by Grant No. R305B04074 from the National Center for Education Research.

REFERENCE

Oosterhof, A. (2003). *Developing and using classroom assessments* (3rd ed.). Upper Saddle River, NJ: Prentice Hall.

Mixed Method Evaluation of a Support Project for Nonprofit Organizations

Riki Savaya and Mark Waysman

DESCRIPTION OF THE CASE

While nonprofit organizations are playing an increasing role in many areas of society, they face a number of unique difficulties. As with all complex, multipurpose organizations, they, too, require clarity of mission; solid managerial practices; long-range planning capacity; a healthy organizational culture; and many specific skills to ensure long-term functioning, growth, and development. Yet they are often founded and administered by well-meaning individuals who have no formal training or experience in management, fundraising, lobbying, public relations, and so forth, and thus often lack crucial skills needed to ensure their organizations' growth and effectiveness. As a result, they may not be able to negotiate the rapidly changing social policy environment over time; they may lose out in competition for scarce resources, and they may not be able to muster adequate organizational energy to focus on their goals of social change and community support. It is not surprising that research has shown that underinvestment in organizational development may cause organizations to fail.

SHATIL was founded by the New Israel Fund, a foundation that supports NGOs, to provide capacity building to its grantees in order to enhance their effectiveness. Since its founding SHATIL has provided direct assistance to hundreds of community-based nonprofit organizations in five main areas: organizational consultation, fundraising and finances, advocacy, media/public relations, and volunteer recruitment and management. In an effort to learn from the accumulated experience of more than a decade of its work and to enhance its accountability to both its clients and its funders, SHATIL contracted with the authors to conduct an evaluation of its activities.

The following aims were stipulated by SHATIL in advance:

1. To map the characteristics of organizations that apply to SHATIL.
2. To map the services provided to these organizations.
3. To assess the perceived contribution of SHATIL to the stability and goal attainment of these organizations.
4. To evaluate the satisfaction of these organizations with the services provided by SHATIL.

To achieve these aims, the evaluation was carried out using a sequential three-phase mixed method design.

- *Phase 1.* The first phase consisted of (1) personal interviews with SHATIL staff and (2) a series of four focus groups with representatives of a variety of consultee organizations. Data from this phase were intended to help identify and clarify issues of greatest concern to client organizations that should be addressed in Phase 2.

- *Phase 2.* Structured questionnaires were constructed and mailed to all (several hundred) organizations who received services in the 2 years prior to the study. Data from this phase were to provide a representative picture of the features of the consultee organizations, the services they received, their satisfaction with and other issues pertaining to the services they received from SHATIL, and the perceived impact of these services on their organizational development.

- *Phase 3.* A second round of focus groups, this time with representatives of the most and least satisfied organizations, who were identified in the analysis of responses to the previous phase.

The design was implemented as planned.

UNEXPECTED EVENTS

In the first round of focus groups, information on an unintended consequence of the program emerged: Some of the participants expressed strong feelings that they had been patronized by SHATIL staff, who, they said, at times conveyed the message that "we know better than you what is good for you." This unexpected finding influenced our subsequent data collection and analysis.

RESPONSES TO THE UNEXPECTED EVENTS

In planning the second phase of the study, we therefore decided to add to the questionnaire items that directly examined the sense of patronage. The findings from the large sample of consultee organizations revealed that only a small minority (15%) actually felt that they had been patronized. If we had not queried this issue in the questionnaire, we might have overestimated the prevalence of the problem.

The finding that not all the organizations felt patronized raised yet another question that was not part of the original evaluation design: Can we characterize those organizations who felt they had been patronized? Further analyses of the dataset revealed that the problem was raised primarily by ethnic minority organizations. We were thus able to identify an important issue impacting the potential effectiveness of SHATIL's work with a small but significant proportion of its clients. In addition, we were able to identify the types of clients for whom this issue may be of greatest concern. In response to this finding, SHATIL sought ways to increase the cultural sensitivity of their service delivery.

The above situation illustrates the advantage of sequential, multiphase designs for addressing unforeseen issues and the advisability of leaving room for changes in the design and implementation of the evaluation.

Case 11

Evaluating the Health Impacts of Central Heating

Jeremy Walker, Richard Mitchell,
Stephen Platt, and Mark Petticrew

DESCRIPTION OF THE CASE

The study described here was commissioned to evaluate the impacts on health of a publicly funded program of thermal improvements to domestic residences in Scotland. The main component of the program was the provision (free of charge to program clients) of modern central heating systems, but other thermal enhancements (e.g., insulation of lofts and cavity walls) were also offered where appropriate. At its inception, eligibility for admission to the program was restricted to (1) households in public sector housing whose homes lacked central heating, and (2) households in the private sector in which the householder or her/his partner was aged 60 or over, and whose home either lacked central heating or had a central heating system that was broken beyond economical repair. The eligibility criteria for the program were widened in May 2004 and again in January 2007 to admit additional groups of elderly clients. Detailed reviews of the operation of the program are available (Scottish Executive, 2006, 2007).

The objectives of the program, as defined by the funders (the Scottish Government), have been published (Scottish Executive, 2000). The program's main goals were to improve health; reduce pressure on the National Health Service; lower the cost of home heating (and thus the prevalence

244

of fuel poverty); and reduce CO_2 emissions. The evaluation described here was commissioned to assess the health impacts of the program. A separate evaluation covering the effects of the program on fuel poverty has also been conducted (Sheldrick & Hepburn, 2007), but is not referred to further in the present account. A description of the strategy and methods used by the health impact evaluation is available (Walker, Mitchell, Platt, Petticrew, & Hopton, 2006). In summary, the evaluation collected longitudinal data relating to heating usage and health from a sample of program clients. Data were captured via interviews in clients' homes. An initial interview was conducted shortly before the planned application of the intervention, while a final interview was obtained 2 years after the initial contact. Changes in health status across these two sampling points (i.e., pre–postintervention) were compared to those observed over the same time frame in similar data obtained from a sample of comparison households not recruited into the program. Via this comparison, any health changes attributable to the program could be identified. Results from the evaluation are publicly available (Platt et al., 2007), but are not considered here. Rather, the focus in the present discussion is on challenges encountered by the evaluation that may have wider application to comparable evaluations in other contexts.

UNEXPECTED EVENTS

Two classes of unexpected event were encountered during the evaluation. First, it became apparent at a very early stage (indeed, during planning) that it would be impossible to recruit a comparison group consisting entirely of households that (1) did not possess central heating and (2) were not involved in the program. The reasons for this were twofold. First, the baseline prevalence of central heating in the population was fairly high, meaning that the number of homes without central heating available as potential comparators was limited. Second, the attractive nature of the program intervention (i.e., the provision of modern heating apparatus and associated thermal enhancements at no cost to the recipient) meant that a high proportion of eligible households without such heating would be expected to take advantage of the program and would thus not be available as potential control households. Recognizing these factors, it was accepted that the comparison group could not feasibly be constituted as a genuine "control" group in the strict experimental sense (i.e., a group similar in important respects to the intervention group but not receiving the "treatment"). Rather, it was accepted that the comparison group would unavoidably include a proportion of homes that already possessed central heating.

Second, it was found that both the intervention group (i.e., program clients) and the comparison group were subject to "contamination" over the period of the study. Some intended clients in the evaluation sample did not in the event receive the intervention, while a further proportion of the comparison group acquired central heating outside the program. These instances of "misclassification" effectively diluted the distinction between intervention (program) and comparison groups, making estimation of the health impacts less precise than would have been the case had the integrity of the groups been preserved. There were a number of reasons why subjects may have ended up misclassified (or, more correctly, assigned a status in the evaluation that did not correctly reflect their eventual experience). First, some intended recipients of the heating intervention did not eventually receive it for practical reasons (e.g., there was found to be no main gas supply in the street/block), or because they underwent a change of heart. With regard to the latter, a number of actual instances were reported of recipients (especially older people) ultimately deciding that they did not wish to endure the disruption of a full central heating installation. Second, some recipients may have inadvertently misreported their heating status at the baseline point by indicating that they had a preexisting central heating system. This could arise because the terms of the initiative permitted a new heating system to be provided (for private-sector households) where existing central heating was broken beyond economical repair. Third, a proportion of control households would, naturally, be expected to acquire central heating over the duration of the study as a normal home improvement measure.

RESPONSES TO THE UNEXPECTED EVENTS

The first class of unexpected event—the impossibility of isolating a true control group—was accepted as a largely unavoidable limitation of "real-world" interventions: unlike in a controlled experiment, it is clearly not possible in free societies to randomize individuals to live in heated or unheated homes. The experience of this evaluation illustrated the general difficulties inherent in collecting evidence from what may be termed "natural experiments" where the researcher does not have full control over delivery of the intervention. However, it must be stressed that while this challenge is common in evaluations, it is not insurmountable. Howden-Chapman et al. (2005) have demonstrated how the impacts on health and the internal environment of a free-to-client package of housing improvements can successfully be assessed via a genuinely randomized design. In the present evaluation, the response to the challenge of being unable to obtain a true control group (in the experimental sense) was to regard the comparison group as a subset of households whose heating arrangements would be expected to remain broadly static over the period of the evaluation. Contrasting their health experiences over time (in what was expected to be a largely unchanging domestic thermal environment) would thus still provide useful insight into the health experiences of the intervention group, whose heating arrangements were expected to change en masse from unheated to centrally heated.

The response to the second class of unexpected event—contamination of the groups—was to analyze the data on the basis of the original subject-to-group allocations. Thus where a household in the intervention group did not ultimately receive the intervention, data from that household were still included in the analysis of intervention group results. Similarly, comparison group households that acquired central heating during the course of the evaluation were retained for analysis in the comparison group, even though their heating status had changed. This approach may initially seem questionable, but it in fact mirrors the principle of "intention to treat" (Newell, 1992), which is commonplace in clinical trials. An intention-to-treat analysis has been defined as "a procedure in which all patients allocated randomly to a treatment in a clinical trial are analyzed together as representing that treatment, regardless of whether they completed the trial or even received the treatment after randomization" (Everitt, 2006, p. 122). In the evaluation described here, this analytical paradigm was justified on the grounds that findings would be conservative (i.e., would incline toward understatement of the [unknown] "true" effects of the intervention) and any risk of spurious positive results would be minimized. An informal estimate of the effects of misclassification may be obtained by undertaking a separate analysis based on subjects' *actual* allocation status (i.e., whether they received the intervention). This was performed for the study discussed here, and the findings were not materially different from those obtained under the intention-to-treat approach.

The challenges described above—that is, the difficulties of constituting a control group and of maintaining the integrity of intervention and comparison groups—are likely to be faced by many evaluations, both of public health interventions and of initiatives in other fields. Evaluation practitioners should consider, at an early stage of planning, measures to minimize the threats posed by these challenges to the reliability of evaluation findings.

REFERENCES

Everitt, B. (2006). *Medical statistics from A to Z: A guide for clinicians and medical students*. Cambridge, UK: Cambridge University Press.

Howden-Chapman, P., Crane, J., Matheson, A., Viggers, H., Cunningham, M., Blakely, T., et al. (2005). Retrofitting houses with insulation to reduce health inequalities: Aims and methods of a clustered, randomised community-based trial. *Social Science and Medicine, 61*, 2600–2610.

Newell, D. (1992). Intention-to-treat analysis: implications for quantitative and qualitative research. *International Journal of Epidemiology, 21*, 837–841.

Platt, S., Mitchell, R., Petticrew, M., Walker, J., Hopton, J., Martin, C., et al. (2007). *The Scottish executive central heating programme: Assessing impacts on health* (Research Findings No. 239/2007). Edinburgh: Scottish Executive. Retrieved August 29, 2008, from *www.scotland.gov.uk/Resource/Doc/166020/0045175.pdf*.

Scottish Executive, The. (2000). *Free central heating for pensioners and families* (Scottish Executive Press Release SE2497/2000). Edinburgh: Author. Retrieved August 26, 2008, from *www.scotland.gov.uk/News/Releases/2000/09/7f6012fec4f8-4275-9068-675f04cf2419*.

Scottish Executive, The. (2006). *Central heating programme and warm deal annual report 2004–2005*. Edinburgh: Communities Scotland. Retrieved August 29, 2008, from *www.communitiesscotland.gov.uk/stellent/groups/public/documents/webpages/otcs_015222.pdf*.

Scottish Executive, The. (2007). *Central heating programme and warm deal annual report 2005–2006*. Edinburgh: Communities Scotland. Retrieved August 29, 2008, from *www.communitiesscotland.gov.uk/stellent/groups/public/documents/webpages/otcs_018132.pdf*.

Sheldrick, B., & Hepburn, D. (2007). *Assessing the impact of the central heating programme on tackling fuel poverty: The first three years of the programme 2001–2004*. Edinburgh: Scottish Executive. Retrieved August 29, 2008, from *www.scotland.gov.uk/Resource/Doc/172144/0048163.pdf*.

Walker, J., Mitchell, R., Platt, S., Petticrew, M., & Hopton, J. (2006). Does usage of domestic heating influence internal environmental conditions and health? *European Journal of Public Health, 16*, 463–469.

Recruiting Target Audience

WHEN ALL ELSE FAILS, USE THE INDIRECT APPROACH FOR EVALUATING SUBSTANCE ABUSE PREVENTION

Molly Engle

DESCRIPTION OF THE CASE

Substance abuse prevention in pregnant women was and continues to be a serious problem in women of childbearing age. Recreational drugs, alcohol, and tobacco use and abuse can and does compromise the fetus and the mother. The National Institute of Drug Abuse (NIDA) estimates about 15% of women of childbearing age currently use or abuse substances that will be detrimental to their health or the health of the fetus. Health care providers tend to focus on current health status and often ignore the past behavior, yet past behavior is the best predictor of future behavior, and health care providers need to be mindful of the mother's previous behavior as well.

In the mid-1990s, we saw an opportunity to influence the health care provided by primary care providers in women who used and/or abused substances during pregnancy. NIDA awarded to the Behavioral Medicine Unit, Division of Preventive Medicine, Department of Medicine, University of Alabama School of Medicine, a 4-year grant to develop and implement an obstetric intervention targeted at health care providers in obstetric practices in Birmingham, Alabama. The proposed target audience consisted of all health care providers in obstetric practices who had direct contact with pregnant women who might be using or abusing legal or illegal substances, including and not limited to tobacco, alcohol, and other drugs (cocaine, marijuana, heroin, methamphetamines, etc.).

We assessed the perceptions of community obstetrician–gynecologists (OB/GYNs) of substance use prevalence among their caseload (Hoegerman, Schumacher, Phelan, Engle, & Raczynski, 1993). This assessment provided us with information on the need for specific training in identification, management, and referral practices for women who use or abuse substances. We also determined the provider's interest in participating in an intervention training program that addressed substance use assessment and management. Of the 50 randomly selected OB/GYNs, 65% expressed interest in participating in such training. Given that there were 27 single- and multiprovider private practices identified in and around Birmingham, we anticipated a sufficient population from which to draw a sample for a full-scale intervention. This was not to be the case.

For the full-scale intervention, we planned a controlled, delayed-treatment design. Recruited practices were to be randomly assigned to one of two treatment groups. We were randomly assigning practices, not providers, to avoid contamination within practice. We anticipated recruiting 18 practices, nine in each group. We planned to assess both groups at baseline, administer the intervention to group 1, assess again at 6 months postintervention; administer the intervention to group 2, and assess again 6 months postintervention. We assessed providers on knowledge of substance use and abuse; self-efficacy to assess, manage, and refer women who used or abused substances during pregnancy; and on practice patterns. Knowledge and self-efficacy (Schumacher et al., 2000) were to be assessed using a self-report paper-and-pencil test. Practice patterns were to be assessed through blind chart review by two certified health information managers (Houser et al., 2000).

UNEXPECTED EVENTS

We identified 27 single- and multiprovider obstetric practices in and around Birmingham. We selected private (i.e., not government funded) and community-based (i.e., not part of a medical training program or public health department) practices. All providers and staff in the practice were eligible to participate in the study. This included physicians, registered nurses, licensed practical nurses, medical assistants, and office personnel. The original plan was for the project obstetric physician to recruit the study participants by contacting the practice physicians. This contact was multifaceted and included letters, telephone calls, and office visits. This approach failed to provide us with the anticipated number of practices. Given that the evaluation plan as well as the intervention relied on recruiting and enrolling providers, we could not proceed with the project without participants. Nothing in the preliminary work prepared us for this. The project was stalled until we identified a viable recruiting strategy.

The other unintended outcome was with the response rate for the postintervention assessments. Providers agreed to completing three assessments: baseline, 6 months postassessment, and 6 months after that. We were able to collect the baseline assessment without difficulty, as that assessment was completed with project staff present. The postintervention assessment provided us with about a 53% response rate for both groups compared with an 81% at baseline. When we attempted to collect the second postintervention assessment 12 months after baseline, we found that participants did not return the assessment packet. We realized that for the evaluation to be useful, we needed to have at least a 51% response rate. Once again, we needed a different strategy.

RESPONSES TO UNEXPECTED EVENTS

We convened a focus group of nurse managers from primary care practices who had worked with members of the investigator team on other projects (Engle et al., 1996). In the course of the focus group, we discovered that physician–physician contact was not the best way to recruit practices. Physicians typically give over the running of the practice to practice managers. Those practice managers can either be nurse managers, business managers, or some other classification. The focus group consensus was that physicians will agree to whatever the managers commit them and their practice. So if the manager says that the physician will participate in the intervention, the physician will participate. If the manager says that the practice/physician is not able to participate, the provider will not.

We changed our focus for recruiting as a result of this information. The project obstetric physician still coordinated the recruiting, targeting the practice manager. The multifaceted approach of phone calls, letters, and personal contacts were all used. Using this method, we were able to recruit practices into the project.

We realized that to increase our response rate, we would need to give the providers incentives. We secured permission from the funding agency to shift some funds into incentives. We provided a $10.00 incentive attached to the evaluation materials when they were sent to the providers.

This proved effective and resulted in an overall response rate of 69% on the final assessment.

ACKNOWLEDGMENTS

This case description was made possible with support from Grant No. DA08441 from the National Institute on Drug Abuse. This project would not have been successful without the considerable contributions of Joseph E. Schumacher, Shannon H. S. Houser, Connie L. Kohler, Sharon T. Phelan, James M. Raczynski, Ellen Caldwell, and Kim D. Reynolds, investigators on this project, and Barbara Yarber, health information manager.

REFERENCES

Engle, M., Phelan, S. T., Kohler, C. L., Schumacher, J. E., Raczynski, J. M., & Reynolds, K. (1996, December). *Recruiting provider practices in participating in office-based health care promotion research.* Presented at the 8th Annual International Institute for the Clinical Application of Behavioral Medicine Conference, Hilton Head, SC.

Hoegerman, G. S., Schumacher, J. E., Phelan, S. T., Engle, M., & Raczynski, J. M. (1993). Perceptions of substance use by community obstetricians. *AMERSA Substance Abuse, 14*(2), 89–96.

Houser, S. H. S., Engle, M., Schumacher, J. E., Caldwell, E., Kohler, C. L., Phelan, S. T., et al. (2000). Resolving confidentiality barriers in research data collection. *Journal of AHIMA, 71*(3), 62–64.

Schumacher, J. E., Engle, M., Reynolds, K. D., Houser, S. H. S., Mukherjee, S., Caldwell, E., et al. (2000). Measuring self-efficacy in substance abuse intervention in obstetric practices. *Southern Medical Journal, 93*(4), 406–414.

Unintended Consequences of Changing Funder Requirements Midproject on Outcome Evaluation Design and Results in HIV Outreach Services

Lena Lundgren, Therese Fitzgerald,
and Deborah Chassler

DESCRIPTION OF THE CASE

This chapter presents the case of an evaluation of HIV outreach services to 700 Latino adult injection drug users. A community-based health care services agency, in collaboration with a university school of social work, was awarded a 5-year service and evaluation grant to provide outreach and case management services to a high-risk population. The target population was adult Latino injection drug users and their sexual partners.

Program objectives to be examined through the outcome evaluation included reduction in needle sharing; increase in condom use; increase in testing rates for HIV, STIs, HAV, HBV, and HCV; increase in entry into substance abuse treatment; and increase in job training and GED preparation participation. In addition to HIV education and prevention services, the program also provided basic services such as free showers, laundry and food, and referrals to a number of external services such as substance abuse treatment, mental health treatment, and employment training. The funding source required that each individual be interviewed at intake, 6 months following intake, and initially, 12 months after intake.

UNEXPECTED EVENT 1: CHANGE IN FEDERAL REGULATIONS

Since its inception the project, as well as all federally funded projects under this program, had been required to provide ongoing Government Performance and Results Act (GPRA) data. Each organization was required to collect in-person interview data at intake as well as at 6-month and 12-month follow-up interviews. Therefore the outcome evaluation, designed with these reporting requirements in mind, examined changes in HIV risk behaviors from intake to 12 months after intake.

However, in the second year of the funded project, new Substance Abuse and Mental Health Services Administration (SAMHSA) regulations were implemented that affected project data reporting requirements. The new changes in project reporting requirements eliminated the mandated requirement for 12-month follow-up interviews and made this a voluntary option for each federally funded program. No longer mandating 12-month follow-up data collection, SAMHSA instead shifted its focus to: (1) making certain that projects adhered to the contractual agreement of an 80% six-month follow-up rate; and (2) requiring the collection of additional data at discharge, which had not been part of the original data collection plan. As a result of these changes, the project staff felt they no longer had the capacity to conduct 12-month interviews.

From an outcome evaluation point of view this created a significant problem in that measuring change in drug use, needle-sharing, and sexual risk behaviors in a population of chronic heroin users over less than a 1-year time period is not ideal. Changes in addictive behaviors often take place over longer time periods (Leshner, 1997; Prochaska, DiClemente, & Norcross, 1992). Now, due to these new federal regulations, behavior change had to be examined over a 6-month time period. Hence, evaluators were concerned that the existing evaluation design would not accurately measure client behavior change associated with program participation.

RESPONSE TO CHANGE IN FEDERAL REGULATIONS

The university evaluation team had participated in all program development and planning phases since the inception of the project. As a result, an alternative outcome evaluation strategy was built into the project. Specifically, project and evaluation staff had agreed that the evaluators would consult and aid in the development of a client-level management information system (MIS), which included data from each service encounter for each client. They also had an agreement that the evaluation team would conduct ongoing data analyses of the service encounter database.

Through the use of this encounter database, the evaluation team was able to examine client change for a number of outcomes associated both with a client's length of stay in the program and their level of program service use. Merging encounter database information with the GPRA data, client outcomes could be compared for those who had been receiving services based both on the length of time involved with program services and the number of service encounters. Hence, one of the key findings of the evaluation study was that, controlling for age, gender, education, income, level of drug use, mental health status, and criminal justice status, the number of service encounters were significantly associated with a lower likelihood of needle sharing at 6 months after program intake (Lundgren et al., 2007). Evaluators also found that length of time involved in the outreach effort was associated with increased likelihood of entry into more complex substance abuse treatment services (Lundgren & Fitzgerald, 2007).

UNEXPECTED EVENT 2: CHANGE IN STATE REGULATIONS

Similar to most community-based HIV outreach services, the project management of the project evaluated had hired outreach staff who were seen as sensitive to the needs and issues of the participants they were serving. Specifically, most of the outreach staff hired at the inception of the project were individuals in recovery. Nationally, substance abuse treatment agencies often hire employees who are in recovery (Taxman & Bouffard, 2003).

However, many substance abusers who are in recovery also have criminal records. New policy guidelines from the Massachusetts state government's Executive Office for Health and Human Services went into effect in June 2002, requiring the program to begin performing criminal background checks on all new and existing employees who may have unsupervised access to clients. After June 2002 the project had to obtain and review all existing and potential employees' criminal records and determine whether any of the criminal activities listed prohibited keeping or hiring an employee. Individuals who had a criminal record related to drug use or sales were prohibited from working with clients without a special waiver from the state. In order to hire or maintain employees who had been banned from employment because of their criminal history, the project had to, under new state regulations, petition the state on behalf of each of these banned new hires. The petition process would need to include verification from a criminal justice system official that the employee no longer poses an "unacceptable risk of harm to a person served by the program." However, many criminal justice officials are reluctant to provide this information. Instead, the project must then obtain the services of a qualified mental health provider to assess the employee and certify that he or she does not pose a risk to persons served by the program (Massachusetts Law Reform Institute, 2006).

Not only are these assessments by mental health providers difficult and expensive to obtain, they do not release the agency from legal responsibility. Therefore, in addition to the project's time and financial investments made on behalf of the new or existing employee, the program must take legal responsibility for an employee with no proven track record.

Understandably, the project was only willing to petition the state for a waiver for previously hired, experienced staff, limiting the program's willingness to hire new staff with similar qualifications. The new legislation resulted in the hiring of new staff who were often inexperienced at working with people in recovery, in this case the adult injection drug users the project was funded to serve. These new hires were often reluctant to conduct the street outreach necessary for finding this transient target population, resulting in less capacity to both recruit the new clients and conduct the necessary follow-up interviews at 6 months after intake.

RESPONSE TO CHANGE IN STATE REGULATIONS

Several methods were used by the evaluation team to respond to this challenge and still conduct a credible evaluation. First, new interviewer/outreach trainings were developed. Specifically, in the interviewer training sessions the more experienced outreach workers served as mentors. These mentors discussed such topics as safety, understanding the daily patterns of drug use by heroin users, and assessing the best time to conduct interviews. These mentors also participated in the street outreach with the new workers. Furthermore, the evaluation team refocused their part of the training of new outreach/interviewing staff not solely to discuss the data collection instruments but also on ways to conduct interviews with adult drug users in a professional and safe manner. The co-principal investigator, an experienced clinician, conducted training on motivational interviewing techniques as well.

Second, throughout the project, the evaluators had monitored the data quality of each interviewer and provided immediate feedback to the specific interviewer if there was a quality problem with any questionnaire.

If the questionnaire indicated that the interviewer/outreach worker had problems with either technical problems such as skip patterns or with asking sensitive questions such as questions about injecting drugs, the evaluation team provided immediate phone retraining within a week of the problem interview. If the interviewer had serious problems with data collection, the evaluation team requested that the interviewer not conduct more interviews prior to retraining. Finally, if the interviewer continued to have problems the outreach mentor and evaluation trainer provided ongoing in-person interviewer training.

REFERENCES

Leshner, A. (1997). Addiction is a brain disease, and it matters. *Science, 278*(5335), 45–47.

Lundgren, L., & Fitzgerald, T. (2007). *Patterns of HIV prevention service use among Latino injection drug users.* Unpublished report, Center for Addictions Research and Services, Boston University.

Lundgren, L., Fitzgerald, T., Desphande, A., Purington, T., Kuilan, N., Oettinger, C., et al. (2007). *Frequency of HIV prevention service use and HIV risky behaviors among Latino injection drug users: Program findings from project La Voz.* Paper presented at the 2007 SAMHSA Grantees Meeting, Washington, DC/ Atlanta.

Massachusetts Law Reform Institute. (2006). *The CORI Reader* (Ernest Winsor, Ed.). Retrieved August 28, 2007, from *www.masslegalservices.org/docs/3d_ Ed-2d_Rev.pdf.*

Prochaska, J .O., DiClemente, C. C., & Norcross, J .C. (1992). In search of how people change: Application to addictive behaviors. *American Psychologist, 7*(9), 1102–1114.

Taxman, F. S., & Bouffard, J. A. (2003). Substance abuse counselors' treatment philosophy and the content of treatment services provided to offenders in drug court programs. *Journal of Substance Abuse Treatment, 25*(2), 75–84.

Generating and Using Evaluation Feedback for Providing Countywide Family Support Services

Deborah L. Wasserman

DESCRIPTION OF THE CASE

This formative evaluation project was designed to help county-level service coordination agencies build capacity for collecting and using evaluation data to enhance outcomes for families of children with mental health needs.

The project was an extension of an initial statewide evaluation of a small state-level funding stream meant to supply non-Medicaid reimbursable services for families of children and adolescents with mental health needs. That initial evaluation reported on 88 county-level service coordination councils responsible for using these funds to supplement Medicaid reimbursable services with nonreimbursable services (e.g., transportation, art or animal therapy, safety renovations, parental respite). In addition to disbursing these funds, a very small part of their work and budget, these councils were responsible for coordinating the various services (e.g., mental health, children's protection, alcohol and other drugs [AOD] and mental, school-based) available to families with mental health needs, helping recipient families navigate among complicated service systems and avoid duplication of services. In addition to any records they were maintaining about their larger service coordination efforts, for this funding-stream evaluation council coordinators were asked to institute more detailed and complete record keeping and reporting including per-family (rather than aggregate) registration and termination data. Although the evaluators' primary role was to supply aggregate data to the state (i.e., the funder) regarding numbers of families receiving these auxiliary services and their possible effect on family empowerment or mental health outcomes, the evaluators were also concerned about county compliance, which would affect the reliability of the results. In order to enhance compliance, the evaluators provided county boards with monthly reports of initiation (registration and pretest data) and termination (posttest) data received. In other words, counties received aggregated information about paperwork submitted on each participating family. Where available, these data were matched with baseline and outcome data (functioning, problem severity, hopefulness, and satisfaction) held in a statewide database and required by state funders to be collected by service providers (not coordinators) every 6 months. For many of these counties, these reports served as a valuable source for documented headcount of services provided, new cases enrolled, terminated cases, and so on. Over the 2-year evaluation period, the state funders along with some county councils came to see the evaluative process as a potential quality improvement asset.

As a result of the apparent utility of the data, state funders initiated a second evaluation project, one that would involve 10 highly motivated counties selected from the pool of all the counties in the state. These pilot counties would volunteer to participate in an "enhanced" data collection, reporting, and evaluation process—the setting for the case study described here. In this second evaluation, the overall question of interest was whether counties could use the additional information to promote common procedures and integrated action across multiple agencies and organizations to better respond to the needs of these multiple-need children and families.

For this enhanced evaluation effort, the ten selected counties participated in a voluntary test of information generation and use. Participating counties were selected for their enthusiasm for collecting data to answer new questions, their compliance record to date, and their location in the state relative to other participating counties. In addition to receiving compliance reports and statewide outcome reports, the 10 pilot counties would also receive county-level descriptive data and outcome reports. These county-level reports would provide answers to specific evaluation questions identified at the county level as being germane to local coordinators and service providers. Each county service coordinator worked with the evaluator to generate data collection and management tools for answering their local questions. These tools became part of a pool of tools available to the other counties. Reports to the pilot counties would coincide with the outcome reports for the larger evaluation.

UNEXPECTED EVENTS

From the time of the evaluation design through the selection of participating counties to the time when the first more detailed outcomes report was to be delivered, the purpose of the pilot project had morphed. At its inception, the pilot project followed the initial evaluation and involved feedback of data collected solely to evaluate the funding stream for non-Medicaid reimbursable services. Because of the first evaluation, counties had more thorough records on these families receiving non-Medicaid reimbursable funds than they had of the majority of their families not involved with this funding stream. But county-level evaluation questions quickly began to extend to all service coordination efforts and beyond the small portion of effort limited to families receiving non-Medicaid reimbursable services. Meanwhile, at the state funding level, because the initial funding-stream evaluation was coming to a close and also because of the success of the data collection process, state administrators expanded the focus and funding for the pilot project to more generally include comprehensive (Medicaid and non-Medicaid) service coordination. Thus the enhanced pilot evaluation changed focus from involving only the families involved in the limited array of non-Medicaid-reimbursable services to including all families receiving any portion of the full universe of coordinated services.

This change, which emerged naturally and logically from the processes the counties and state were experiencing, presented an unforeseen practical problem: the time lag between new focus, data collection, and reporting. As promised by the evaluation contract for the pilot project, the evaluators released county-specific outcome data from the final outcomes report generated by the original limited-scope evaluation. But the reports looked different from what the counties had expected. In many, it appeared that required baseline data collection had been incomplete. Scaling up to include all service coordination had required changes in rules for how data points would be constructed. For instance, in an attempt to make reporting more consistent across counties, state funders had created stricter guidelines for the window of time that could elapse between registration and outcome data collection in order for data to be considered baseline. Use of non-Medicaid funding was a minor portion of most families' activities and, at registration for the non-Medicaid funding stream, many had already provided baseline data at an earlier date when they had received other services. In the first evaluation, these earlier dates were considered baseline. But with the tighter guidelines, for some families it appeared that no baseline data were collected. Also, the new expanded population would now include families receiving AOD services in addition to those receiving mental health services. Due to the agreement regarding the initial evaluation, the evaluators had access to outcome data held in the mental health service database, but did not have access to this information for families receiving AOD services. Identifying the challenges and then establishing systems for locating and reporting outcome data across the different services would occur over time, but not in time for the first outcome report. On a statewide level, the missing data points made little statistical difference. However, on a local level, for some counties, it appeared that compliance had been very poor.

Evaluators recognized they were caught between two commitments. They had promised that an outcome report would be presented at a meeting of all 10 counties with state administrators. But due to the timing, for some counties this report would be missing information where baseline data were collected but not yet retrieved, or where the gap between baseline data collection and registration date (based for many families on registration for use of services funded by the supplementary funding stream) was wider than the one allowed by the new guidelines. The circumstances differed for each county, and the explanations for what appeared to be missing data were complicated. In one-on-one meetings with county coordinators, evaluators presented these results couched in language that helped each understand how to read the county-level reports within the context of the data collection circumstances they were experiencing—ones that were in the process of changing. However, many of the county coordinators feared that these reports had too much potential to be misinterpreted and resisted their release. They were concerned that, despite the pilot nature of their county's participation, state-level funders would be reviewing the reports for accountability purposes and overlook the extenuating circumstances. In the face of soaring evaluation anxiety and resistance, the evaluators recognized that publicly delivering these outcome reports would undermine the confidence the evaluators were seeking to build as an essential component of the pilot evaluation: pilot counties needed to be enthusiastic about collecting, analyzing, and using their data.

RESPONSES TO THE UNEXPECTED EVENTS

As the evaluators recognized the responsive nature of good evaluation design, they decided to scrap the county-level outcome report, despite the contractual commitment to presenting it. Outcome reports would be suspended entirely until systems for entering and retrieving data could be worked out. Of higher priority than producing an outcome report was to reduce the anxiety and get the disgruntled counties back on board. Without them, there would be no pilot evaluation at all.

Based on this decision the evaluators informed the funder that an outcome report would be counterproductive at this point in the project, renegotiated the deliverable, and e-mailed a letter to participating service coordinators to prepare them for the upcoming meeting where they expected to receive the now-dreaded outcome reports. This letter served three purposes: first, it allayed service coordinators' anxiety by acknowledging it as understandable; second, it reinforced the project objective of empowerment through data use; and third, it acknowledged the usefulness of formative data for purposes of both reporting and quality improvement.

As a result of this letter, anxiety was reduced and the meeting became highly productive, with plans for bringing additional pilot counties into the program for the following year. The evaluators also initiated policy changes that would lead to including wording in initial contracts with the new counties that would acknowledge the challenges of retrieving outcome data from across systems and provide a range of options for doing so. Over the next year, new systems were established, reports were generated that responded to specific county questions, and enthusiasm for using the data began to build. In time, as counties developed their abilities to use data collection systems for all service coordination families, funders had access not only to more complete outcome data, but also to additional information about outcomes as they related to types and amounts of services received and the family conditions of the young people who received them. With the changes, the evaluators' role changed from policing compliance and mechanically producing county-level reports to becoming coaches for counties as they worked to identify evaluation questions, generate pertinent data collection systems, and use reports for both accountability and quality improvement.

Trauma and Posttraumatic Stress Disorder among Female Clients in Methadone Maintenance Treatment in Israel

FROM SIMPLE ASSESSMENT TO COMPLEX INTERVENTION

Miriam Schiff and Shabtay Levit

DESCRIPTION OF THE CASE

The present study was designed to provide information to guide program planning and evaluation of substance abuse programs in Israel. Specifically, the intent was to examine (for the first time in Israel) the prevalence of posttraumatic stress symptoms (PTS) and posttraumatic stress disorder (PTSD) and depressive symptoms among female clients with a history of drug abuse who are treated in methadone clinics in Israel. We also intended to explore the associations between PTS and (1) the severity of their trauma history and (2) their mental health state and relapse to drug abuse 1 year later. Attention to trauma has proved useful for substance abuse treatment in the United States. Specifically, victimization to childhood physical or sexual abuse has been associated with later substance use and abuse among women (see Logan, Walker, Cole, & Leukefeld, 2002, for a review). For example, women with substance use problems are more likely to have a history of being sexually and physically assaulted than

263

women without such problems (Covington, 1997). PTSD is a significant problem for women in substance abuse treatment (Dansky, Byrne, & Brady, 1999; Schiff, El-Bassel, Engstrom, & Gilbert, 2002). While the existence of PTS and disorder is severe as is, it is also comorbid with several other mental health problems such as depression, suicidal tendencies, and anxiety (Hein, Nunes, Levin, & Fraser, 2000; Kendler et al., 2000), and also serve as a risk factor for relapse to drug use (Swendsen & Merikangas, 2000). Several validated interventions for PTSD have been developed and tested for their efficacy in the United States (Foa et al., 1999; Najavits, 2003), but not in Israel. The current study was an effort to establish the ground for PTSD treatment among female clients in methadone maintenance clinics in Israel. As a first step, we intended to examine the prevalence of trauma history, PTSD, depression, and general psychological distress among those women who are treated in four (of 11) methadone clinics. Structured interviews were administrated based on well-validated research tools such as Foa, Cashman, Jaycox, and Perry's (1997) Posttraumatic Diagnostic Scale (PDS) and the Brief Symptoms Interview (BSI; Derogatis & Melisaratos, 1983; Derogatis & Savitz, 1999).

UNEXPECTED EVENTS

We piloted the study in two methadone clinics in which the social workers who work at these clinics also served as interviewers. Unexpectedly, the proposed effort to address trauma raised several concerns among those social workers. First, they assumed that all their women clients went through several traumatic experiences and thus all suffered from PTSD. Holding this assumption, they did not see any point in formal evaluation of such well-known and homogeneous phenomena. The worldwide statistics that having trauma does not mean one suffers from PTSD (e.g., Alim et al., 2006; Keane, Marshall, & Taft, 2006) were not so persuasive for them. Second, the social workers felt that asking the questions revived those women's traumatic experiences (causing them reexperience symptoms) and therefore were somewhat unethical. Third, the interviewers felt very overwhelmed by the topic and expressed feelings similar to secondary traumatic stress (Baird & Kracen, 2006; Bride, 2007).

RESPONSES TO THE UNEXPECTED EVENTS

We took the social workers' concerns seriously for two reasons. First, we respect local knowledge and the wisdom of people closest to a problem.

Second, the reason for the study was to plan clinical interventions. Without the support of the social workers in planning and implementation, those interventions would likely fail. We therefore addressed the social workers' concerns in several ways. First, going over the protocols of the interviews revealed that the most difficult part in the questionnaire was when the participants were asked to detail their traumatic experiences. Given the facts that those women experienced several kinds of trauma including severe and prolonged sexual abuse (see also Dansky et al., 1999; Gilbert, El-Bassel, Schilling, & Friedman, 1997; Kilpatrick, Resnick, Saunders, & Best, 1998), getting into those details made the participants as well as the interviewers become very emotionally overwhelmed. Following expert advice in the field of trauma among substance users (Hein, personal communication, 2006), we decided to ask the women about the nature of the traumatic event without elaborating on it. We guided the interviewers to intentionally stop the participant if she gets into details and to commence the closed-ended part of the scale immediately upon completion of this question, thus removing any opportunity for respondents to elaborate on their traumatic experiences.

Second, we removed the BSI questionnaire and added two scales that do not examine psychological distress and pathology: (1) the Short Working Alliance Inventory (Hovath & Greenberg, 1989; Tracey & Kokotovic, 1989) and (2) the HOPE scale that measures the concept of "hope" (Snyder et al., 1996). While this information is useful in its own right for program planning, it also served the purpose of balancing the interview to address less emotional topics. The HOPE scale also enabled us to complete the interviews on an optimistic note.

Third, we hired interviewers as part of the research team, all experienced clinicians in the field of social work, so that the burden of the interviews would not fall entirely on the regular staff members. We also limited the number of weekly interviews conducted by the same person to three for the methadone regular staff and five for the hired staff. In addition, we established a support system for the interviewers. The first author met the interviewers biweekly to create space for sharing feelings, thoughts, and concerns. She also made her personal cell phone number available for the interviewers and encouraged them to call whenever they would like to share with her any thoughts or feelings related to the study. Indeed, the interviewers both from the methadone clinics and the research staff used this opportunity throughout the data collection phase. All these procedures made the data collection process slower and more expensive.

Fourth, we decided to postpone the planned 1-year interview follow-up aimed at revealing potential changes in the women's mental health. We made do with computerized data gathered on a regular basis at the methadone clinics that were made available for us. These data summarized for each woman results of her observed urine tests screening positive for heroin and cocaine.

Fifth, we taught the topic of trauma and PTSD and its consequences among drug users during the routine staff meetings in order to raise staff awareness to the importance of paying full attention to this topic and lowering their resistance to this study.

Sixth, following the completion of the data collection we arranged for a retreat event open to each participant in the study. Following the staff advice, each methadone clinic arranged its own retreat (e.g., brunch in a coffee shop near the beach or a "women's day" with lectures and pleasure activities). We were invited to two of those retreats where we were able to run a brief booster session on the purpose of the study, present major results, and discuss the women's feeling following the interview. None of the women complained or indicated any long-term effects of the interviews. On the contrary, they showed great appreciation for us paying attention to their suffering and sorrows and for the retreat.

Finally, we made efforts by writing grants to raising funds to train the staff in specific evidence-based interventions designed to decrease PTS.

These changes made the process more acceptable and served the purpose of program planning. We have managed to collect data from 144 female clients on their trauma history, PTS and PTSD, and the associations between therapeutic alliance and PTS and hope. However, they also changed the nature of the data received and, therefore, the insights that guided program development. First, as we removed the BSI scale, we did not have data on the women's depressive symptoms and general psychological distress. Thus we could not get a whole picture of the women's mental health problems. Second, we found that those women have high levels of hope, indicating that they did not give up on their efforts to rehabilitate themselves. Thus, despite their symptoms, they do have strengths, a fact that encouraged us to continue our efforts toward improving our services and interventions for this population. We also found that although the therapeutic alliance with their social worker (clients' report) was high, it was not associated with their levels of PTS, thus supporting the literature in two different ways: (1) that although strong therapeutic alliance is an essential condition for treatment, PTS does not disappear only through good relationships with the therapist but by using specific interventions targeting PTSD directly (Foa, Rothbaum, Riggs, & Murdock, 1991; Hembree, Rauch, & Foa, 2003); and (2) that similar to recent efforts in the United States (Wiechelt, Lutz, Smyth, & Syms, 2005), practitioners in the field of substance abuse should be trained to assess and treat clients with

PTSD. As Hembree et al. (2003) indicate, for trauma survivors, feeling trusted, validated, and supported is an essential component in treatment. If such an alliance is already established in the methadone clinics, it seems to be the right setting for the conduction of the intervention. Consequently, we shifted our efforts toward providing the methadone clinic staff with training and supervision on special intervention designed to reduce PTS— the prolonged exposure therapy for PTSD, a well-known efficacious and efficient treatment in the United States (Foa et al., 1999; Foa, Hembree, Cahill, Rauch, & Riggs, 2005) and also well known in Israel. We neglected for now the original plan to monitor the female clients' mental health by following their symptoms and illicit drug use on routine bases over time.

ACKNOWLEDGMENTS

This study was funded by the Warburg Foundation of the American Jewish Joint Distribution Committee and the Rosenbaum Foundation, Hebrew University.

REFERENCES

Alim, T. N., Graves, E., Mellman, T. A., Aigbogun, N., Gray, E., Lawson, W., et al. (2006). Trauma exposure, posttraumatic stress disorder, and depression in an African American primary care population. *Journal of the National Medical Association, 98*(10), 1630–1636.

Baird, K., & Kracen, A. C. (2006). Vicarious traumatization and secondary traumatic stress: A research synthesis. *Counselling Psychology Quarterly, 19*(2), 181–188.

Bride, B. E. (2007). Prevalence of secondary traumatic stress among social workers. *Social Work, 52*(1), 63–70.

Covington, S. (1997). Women, addiction, and sexuality. In L. Straussner & E. Zelvin (Eds.), *Gender and addictions: Men and women in treatment* (pp. 79–95). Northvale, NJ: Aronson.

Dansky, B. S., Byrne, C. A., & Brady, K. T. (1999). Intimate violence and posttraumatic stress disorder among individuals with cocaine dependence. *American Journal of Drug and Alcohol Abuse, 25*(2), 257–268.

Derogatis, L. R., & Melisaratos, N. (1983). The Brief Symptom Inventory—An introductory report. *Psychological Medicine, 13*(3), 595–605.

Derogatis, L. R., & Savitz, K. L. (1999). The SCL-90, Brief Symptom Inventory, and matching clinical rating scales. In M. Maruish (Ed.), *The use of psychological testing for treatment planning and outcome assessment* (2nd ed., pp. 679–724). Mahwah, NJ: Erlbaum.

Foa, E., Cashman, L., Jaycox, L., & Perry, K. (1997). The validation of a self-report measure of PTSD: The Posttraumatic Diagnosis Scale. *Psychological Assessment, 9*, 445–451.

Foa, E., Dancu, C. V., Hembree, E. A., Jaycox, L., Meadows, E. A., & Street, G. P. (1999). A comparison of exposure therapy, stress inoculation training, and their combination for reducing posttraumatic stress disorder in female assault victims. *Journal of Consulting and Clinical Psychology, 67,* 194–200.

Foa, E. B., Hembree, E. A., Cahill, S. P., Rauch, S. A. M., & Riggs, D. S. (2005). Randomized trial of prolonged exposure for posttraumatic stress disorder with and without cognitive restructuring: Outcome at academic and community clinics. *Journal of Consulting and Clinical Psychology, 73*(5), 953–964.

Foa, E. B., Rothbaum, B. O., Riggs, D. S., & Murdock, T. B. (1991). Treatment of posttraumatic stress disorder in rape victims: A comparison between cognitive-behavioral procedures and counseling. *Journal of Consulting and Clinical Psychology, 59,* 715–723.

Gilbert, L., El-Bassel, N., Schilling, R. F., & Friedman, E. (1997). Childhood abuse as a risk for partner abuse among women in methadone maintenance. *American Journal of Drug and Alcohol Abuse, 23*(4), 581–595.

Hembree, E. A., Rauch, S. A. M., & Foa, E. B. (2003). Beyond the manual: The insider's guide to prolonged exposure therapy for PTSD. *Cognitive and Behavioral Practice, 10,* 22–30.

Hien, D. A., Nunes, E., Levin, F. R., & Fraser, D. (2000). Posttraumatic stress disorder and short-term outcome in early methadone. *Journal of Substance Abuse Treatment, 19*(1), 31–37.

Horvath, A. O., & Greenberg, L. S. (1989). Development and validation of the Work Alliance Inventory. *Journal of Counseling Psychology, 36*(2), 223–233.

Keane, T. M., Marshall, A. D., & Taft, C. T. (2006). Posttraumatic stress disorder: Etiology, epidemiology, and treatment outcome. *Annual Review of Clinical Psychology, 2,* 161–197.

Kendler, K., Bulik, C., Siberg, J., Hettema, J., Myers, J., & Prescott, C. (2000). Childhood sexual abuse and adult psychiatric and substance use disorders in women. *Archives of General Psychiatry, 57,* 953–959.

Kilpatrick, D. G., Resnick, H. S., Saunders, B. E., & Best, C. (1998). Victimization, posttraumatic stress disorder, and substance use and abuse among women. In C. Wetherington & A. Roman (Eds.), *Drug addiction research and the health of women* (pp. 285–307). Rockville, MD: National Institute on Drug Abuse.

Logan, T. K., Walker, R., Cole, J., & Leukefeld, C. (2002). Victimization and substance abuse among women: Contributing factors, interventions, and implications. *Review of General Psychology, 6*(4), 325–397.

Najavits, L. M. (2003). Seeking safety: A new psychotherapy for posttraumatic stress disorder and substance use disorder. In P. Quimette & P. J. Brown (Eds.), *Trauma and substance abuse: Causes, consequences, and treatment of comorbid disorders* (pp. 147–169). Washington, DC: American Psychological Association.

Schiff, M., El-Bassel, N., Engstrom, M., & Gilbert, L. (2002). Psychological distress and intimate physical and sexual abuse among women in methadone maintenance treatment programs. *Social Service Review, 76*(2), 302–320.

Snyder, C. R., Sympson, S. C., Ybasco, F. C., Borders, T. F., Babyak, M. A., & Higgins, R. L. (1996). Development and validation of the State Hope Scale. *Journal of Personality and Social Psychology, 2,* 321–335.

Swendsen, J., & Merikangas, K. (2000). The comorbidity of depression and substance use disorders. *Clinical Psychology Review, 20,* 173–189.

Tracey, T. J., & Kokotovic, A. M. (1989). Factor structure of the Working Alliance Inventory. *Psychological Assessment: A Journal of Consulting and Clinical Psychology, 1,* 207–210.

Wiechelt, S. A., Lutz, W., Smyth, N. J., & Syms, C. (2005). Integrating research and practice: A collaborative model for addressing trauma and addiction. *Stress, Trauma, and Crisis, 8,* 179–193.

From Unintended to Undesirable Effects of Health Intervention

THE CASE OF USER FEES ABOLITION IN NIGER, WEST AFRICA

Valéry Ridde and Aissa Diarra

This case study of an evaluation carried out in Niger describes a situation in which the evaluators uncovered effects that the client had not anticipated in the evaluation design, but which helped the client improve the intervention. The methodology employed was qualitative, with data analyzed from an anthropological perspective. All data collection took place while the innovative program was in operation. Sources of data included the NGO staff, service providers, service recipients, decision makers, and local authorities.

DESCRIPTION OF THE CASE

In many countries in Africa, access to heath care is very much constrained because patients must pay for services (Ridde, 2008), whereas the abolition of user fees has the potential to save around 230,000 children under age 5 each year in 20 African countries (James, Morris, Keith,

& Taylor, 2005). This case study was carried out in Niger, where only 4% of mothers in the poorest quintile used skilled care at delivery and 63% in the richest quintile. In 2006 an international NGO decided to start an intervention in two districts. Each of these districts has approximately 500,000 inhabitants, a district hospital, and slightly more than 20 health centers (CSI) where women (rarely) come to consult and to give birth. The health centers are managed by a nurse and overseen by a community-based management committee. The intervention consisted of abolishing user fees for deliveries and prenatal consultations in order to increase the financial accessibility to health care. Before the intervention was inaugurated, a community awareness and information campaign was undertaken in the villages with the help of administrative and traditional authorities and local leaders. All required drugs and medical supplies were provided by the NGO. To compensate for financial losses to the cost recovery system related to the abolition of user fees, operating grants were given to all health centers in the two districts. The nurses received a monthly bonus in addition to their salary to cover any extra clinical and administrative workloads. Refresher courses were provided to them on site.

Early in 2007 the director of the NGO contacted us to find out whether we were interested in carrying out this evaluation. In line with our usual approach to evaluation (Ridde & Shakir, 2005; Ridde, 2006, 2007), and after several conversations to understand how the NGO intended to use the results, we set up a multidisciplinary team of three evaluators (one researcher in public health from Canada and two physician–anthropologists from Niger) to respond to the call for tenders. Our proposal was selected and the evaluation took place in April 2007 over 22 workdays, of which 14 were in the field. Ten evaluation questions were retained, having to do with the attainment of the intervention's targets and the implementation processes. Data sources were the registers of the 43 health centers, eight focus group discussions, 85 in-depth interviews, participant observation in 12 health centers, and self-administered structured questionnaires (n = 57, health staff).

UNEXPECTED EVENTS

The introduction of an innovation such as abolishing user fees in Niger's health system provoked some unexpected reactions from health care workers and the population. Analysis of these unanticipated effects was not envisioned in the evaluation design requested by the client.

From the Population's Perspective: Medicines Associated with the Distribution of Food Aid

Two years before this health intervention, the NGO had begun its action in Niger by distributing food supplies during the food crisis in 2005. Thus the abolition of user fees, and the abundance of new consultants and drugs to cope with it, was sometimes interpreted by the population as a distribution of medicine. As with food aid, where the organizers are very aware of pilferage, "there was lots of wastage" in the first weeks of the intervention, one nurse told us. Thus, not knowing whether this windfall would continue, or to make sure they would have medicine for when their children actually became sick, some patients apparently came to the centers to build up a reserve of medications: "There's a big rush on, because it won't last," said a nurse. Thus, according to the nurses, there was a phenomenon of stockpiling.

From the Perspective of the Health Care Workers: Strategies for Recouping the Shortfall

Health care workers have always organized parallel systems to boost their incomes. These parallel practices were integrated into a system where people paid for everything. Thus the act of abolishing some fees and informing the population of that fact made these strategies more complicated (but not impossible) to carry out. Nevertheless, the health care workers managed to adapt perfectly well to the new situation. All of them insisted that the abolition of fees greatly increased their workload "to the point of irritation" and reduced the time available for each patient—a claim that was not borne out by our observations. These statements are somewhat exaggerated; the most motivated workers managed to better organize the distribution of tasks and the roles of the health personnel. Actually, the strategy behind these statements is to pressure the NGO to recognize that they are "overwhelmed" and consequently to increase the bonuses they receive for working in the free system. Some nurses redirect the free drugs from the NGO into the fee-for-service system that continues for other categories of the population who are not beneficiaries of the project. Creating artificial stock shortages of goods supplied for free by the NGO is another way of getting around the NGO's rules. By forgetting to replenish the stocks of health booklets, nurses will create a shortage that will allow them to purchase the same booklets manufactured in neighboring Nigeria, which they then resell to patients privately at a profit. Others are even more creative. On the pretext that the women do not take proper care of the health booklets, some nurses have "required that the booklets be laminated," said one manager, for the same price at which they used to be sold. Other nurses write their prescriptions on a piece of paper that they staple to the booklet, then charge 25F ($0.05) for the staple. We were thus not surprised to see a nurse open, inadvertently, a drawer filled with coins in his office. The other solution is simply to charge for certain services that are free. One woman told us, "I paid 1,000F ($2) for a delivery a few days ago." Another woman recounted that she paid for her first prenatal consultation; but the health workers had chided her for coming in, because they took advantage of the rural inhabitants' lack of information to charge them when they came into town for services, so they said to her, "Hey, city-dweller, why did you come today? Today is for the peasants, they pay cash, so you'll have to pay, too." Some CSIs continue to charge each patient 50F or 25F to pay, we were told, the salary of a guard. Thus one woman reported having been charged several fees: "I didn't have to pay for the *awo* [prenatal care], but I had to pay for the booklet. So, I paid 100 francs for the booklet, 100 francs to have it plastified, and 25 francs for the guard." When we asked women who were waiting in line in front of a CSI why the services had become free, the response suggested to us that it was not always so: "It's because you are here today." We were also told that the abolition of fees "created problems of misunderstanding between the health workers and the population."

The Provider–Patient Relationship: Lack of Understanding

The abolition of user fees had several impacts on medical practice and particularly on the interaction between provider and patient. Many patients consider that the medicines supplied in the free system are, in effect, owed to them by the NGO and made available through the CSIs, and that health workers are only intermediaries whose role is to distribute them. This lack of understanding about the abolition of user fees has led users to develop strategies for hoarding medicines. Thus the majority of nurses (63%) completely agreed with the statement that abolition required them to deal with patients who were not sick and wanted to abuse the free system. According to the nurses, patients have adapted their strategies for acquiring medicines. Some pretend to be sick, and others, who arrive with a healthy child, listen to the description of the symptoms of the mother ahead of them in line and say the same things that will help them get the medicines they want. Since many nurses do not systematically take vital signs (none that we observed did so) and provide care based only on reported symptoms, the likelihood that mothers will be given medicines is quite strong. Some people go from one CSI to another. The massive arrival of cough syrup was perceived by mothers as a great opportunity because they associate it with vitamins. Thus, as one nurse reported, "We were obligated to give the cough syrups to the mothers." Moreover, health workers say patients have become more demanding and insist on receiving the treatment of their choice. They arrive late at night, even for a mild cold. We did not observe any such behaviors during our observations and can only repeat here what was reported by the nurses.

However, patients are not happy, either, with how they are treated. Complaints about health workers are frequent. They complain that workers ration the medicines: "At first, when they arrived, you would be given a tube of ointment, but now you have to bring your child morning and evening for them to put the medication in his eyes." In addition, they find that the workers are scornful toward them, treating them as though they are pretending to be sick and only come to the CSI to get medicines.

RESPONSE TO UNEXPECTED EVENTS

Xu et al. (2006), evaluating the Uganda experience, stated that abolition can have "unintended consequence." In South Africa, nurses already reported that some patients abused the new system after abolition (Walker & Gilson, 2004). In Niger, an analysis of food distributions during the 2005 crisis (Olivier de Sardan, 2007) revealed that malnourished children in the villages were considered "lucky babies" because they gave mothers the right to multiple forms of aid, and some women therefore "borrowed" such children. Other women tried to "cause diarrhea in children so that they would lose weight," to receive aid. The problems associated with the distribution of a per diem in development projects are also well known to field workers and well documented (Smith, 2003; Ridde, 2008). Thus the term "unexpected" is not the most apt, since the workers had to some extent anticipated the behaviors we have just described. For example, knowing that the nurses were going to lose a part of their income, the NGO had decided to pay them a monthly bonus. The pretext was that the intervention would increase their workload (clinical and administrative), but it was also a way (discreet and unacknowledged) of ensuring their participation in the project. The NGO had also decided to change the color of the health booklets (from blue for the government to yellow for the NGO) to prevent the workers' selling those that were supplied free. In summary, the problems encountered could have been known had the program designers had the inclination to check the literature, knowledge of where and how to access that literature, and the background needed to understand it. This, however, constitutes specialized knowledge and skills that the program designers, who in any case were operating under extreme pressure (a few days to write a $2 million proposal), did not have.

Thus what we uncovered in this evaluation may be effects that were not only unexpected but also undesirable, and which the client had not wanted to have exposed by the evaluators. What was unanticipated was the actors' capacities for coping with the new situation and rules (creating shortages, selling the lamination of booklets, etc.). There is an adage that rules are made to be broken. Social anthropologists say that actors always retain some room to maneuver in a system to ensure the status quo. These phenomena are well documented in the literature on development aid (coping strategies) (Olivier de Sardan, 2005; Ridde, 2008) and on organization theory (margins of maneuver) (Crozier & Friedberg, 1977).

Thus the evaluation uncovered practices that the evaluators had not been asked to explore. However, faced with the ethical issues of ensuring that the action would actually benefit the worst off, it seemed to us essential that these practices should be revealed. Of course, they were not described in order to destroy the project or stigmatize the actors, but rather to make the project more effective. In the present case, these unanticipated effects can largely be explained by a lack of familiarity with the scientific literature, the limited experience of the NGO management in the field of intervention, and too little time invested in the project's planning phase. However, the stakeholders were very open-minded and sincerely wanted to improve their intervention. Thus, on the day when the results were presented and the content of the evaluation report was discussed, the participants mostly talked about these unanticipated effects. Only one person challenged them (for emotional reasons linked to his own investment in the project), but all the others agreed with the diagnosis. The two African members of the evaluation team had anticipated these reactions (being accustomed to these types of challenges) and had kept specific items as evidence of the events we described. The qualitative anthropological approach with tangible proof was another coping strategy on the part of the evaluators! Thus those responsible for the intervention largely accepted the operational recommendations coming out of the evaluation. Reducing illicit practices, for example, requires restoring administrative authority. Because the NGO had organized its project at some distance from the administration, the latter was not in a position to engage fully. Today, the NGO works to support the administration directly, rather than as an alternative to it. This obviously will not resolve all the problems, but there is no magic wand to fix corruption. This being said, these illicit practices, although significant, are nevertheless marginal, and this intervention helped improve access to health care services for the local populations. We hope this will endure.

REFERENCES

Crozier, M., & Friedberg, E. (1977). *L'acteur et le système*. Paris: Éditions du Seuil.

James, C., Morris, S. S., Keith, R., & Taylor, A. (2005). Impact on child mortality of removing user fees: Simulation model. *British Medical Journal, 331*(7519): 747–749.

Olivier de Sardan, J.-P. (2005). *Anthropology and development: Understanding contemporary social change*. London: Zed Books.

Olivier de Sardan, J.-P. (2007). *Analyse rétrospective de la crise alimentaire au Niger en 2005*. Paris: Agence Française de Développement. Département de recherche. Document de travail 45. Août 2007: 50.

Ridde, V. (2006). Introduction to the thematic segment of 11 articles. Programmes communautaires et innovations méthodologiques: Participation, accompagnement et empowerment. *Canadian Journal of Program Evaluation: Special Issue, 21*(3), 133–136.

Ridde, V. (2007). Are program evaluators judges and/or knowledge brokers? *Journal of Epidemiology and Community Health, 61*, 1020.

Ridde, V. (2008). The problem of the worst-off is dealt with after all other issues: The equity and health policy implementation gap in Burkina Faso. *Social Science and Medicine, 66*, 1368–1378.

Ridde, V., & Shakir, S. (2005). Evaluation capacity building and humanitarian organization. *Journal of MultiDisciplinary Evaluation, 3*, 78–112.

Smith, D. J. (2003). Patronage, per diems and the "workshop mentality": The practice of family planning programs in Southeastern Nigeria. *World Development, 31*(4), 703–715.

Walker, L., & Gilson, L. (2004). "We are bitter but we are satisfied": Nurses as street-level bureaucrats in South Africa. *Social Science and Medicine, 59*(6), 1251–1261.

Xu, K., Evans, D. B., Kadama, P., Nabyonga, J., Ogwal, P. O., Nabukhonzo, P., et al. (2006). Understanding the impact of eliminating user fees: Utilization and catastrophic health expenditures in Uganda. *Social Science and Medicine, 62*(4), 866–876.

ACKNOWLEDGMENTS

We wish to thank all the members of the NGO, the health workers, and members of the population who agreed to participate in this evaluation. The involvement of Mahaman Moha was essential to the success of the evaluation.

Unintended Consequences and Adapting Evaluation

KATRINA AID TODAY NATIONAL CASE MANAGEMENT CONSORTIUM

Amanda Janis and Kelly M. Stiefel

DESCRIPTION OF THE CASE

Hurricane Katrina devastated Gulf Coast communities in the United States on August 29, 2005, hitting the coastlines of Louisiana, Mississippi, and Alabama. Katrina's destruction created a mass migration, which scattered affected families across the country. To address these families' needs for long-term recovery assistance and social support, the Federal Emergency Management Agency (FEMA) announced its sponsorship of a nine-partner case management consortium called Katrina Aid Today (KAT) with the United Methodist Committee on Relief (UMCOR) as the lead agency. KAT, with guidance from FEMA, established an unprecedented framework for a national case management program inclusive of standardized forms, training, and education of nationwide staff and the selection of a secure Web-based database for data collection and coordination. This standardized system was adopted by nine national nonprofits through contracts with more than 130 community-based agencies in 34 states selected to participate under the umbrella of Katrina Aid Today.

Funding for KAT was made possible through a stream of foreign donations designated for the federal government's response to Katrina, because FEMA had no authority under the Stafford Act to use federal funds to fund

277

disaster case management programs. Until 2007, federal funding was not made available to nonprofits providing disaster case management; however, in 2007 the Stafford Act was amended to grant FEMA funding authorization for case management as a fundable recovery program. This historic breakthrough put KAT in a position to be a model for future recovery programs. Recognizing the unprecedented nature of the disaster as well as the recovery effort, monitoring and evaluation was part of KAT's original design in order to demonstrate how program objectives were achieved.

In the design of KAT's monitoring and evaluation system, a logic model guided the system in outlining program components such as a program goal and inputs, activities that contribute to the system (e.g., staff, a standardized system of delivery). Usually, the design of a logic model is informed based on precedent, experience, or research. KAT's unprecedented scope and design, however, provided limited information from which to base the program's logic model. Instead, UMCOR based KAT's logic model on calculated assumptions and expectations that centered on providing case management to 100,000 households. Absent in this logic model design were the outputs and outcomes that would measure the impact of the recovery of these households. Due to the absence of other recovery indicators, such as obtaining employment or achieving housing goals, the logic model overemphasized the importance of a goal number of cases to be served. Therefore, until additional indicators were introduced later in the program, each consortium partner's success could only be measured by the number of clients they were serving. To further compound this overemphasis of a goal number, each consortium partner's funding was calculated in part on the number of clients they were targeted to serve.

UNEXPECTED EVENTS

KAT's consortium design was created with the assumption that it would take coordination and collaboration among organizations to adequately serve and meet the needs of the target population. With the logic model's sole focus on a caseload target, competition arose among consortium partners as they sought to fulfill grant agreement targets. In this tension was the issue of "quantity versus quality" as a client's movement toward a recovery goal did not need to be comprised in the push to increase caseload volume.

The "monitoring" of KAT's 130 community-based agencies was primarily enabled through each consortium partner's use of a Web-based database, the Coordinated Assistance Network (CAN). Partners were equipped with training and technical assistance on how to use the system, and in turn, CAN's Web-based case management forms made standardized data entry, tracking, and reporting of the consortium's caseload feasible. For each case served, case management information ranging from basic demographics to needs information to case outcomes were entered into the CAN database. After implementation, the identification of additional indicators that could be used to measure client recovery and agency progress emerged, beyond simply the number of clients being served. While some of these additional client indicators were included in the original logic model, they were only included insomuch as they contributed to the overall goal of serving 100,000 households, not for their value as programmatic indicators in their own right. These "additional client indicators" included: the number of recovery plans that were developed, the value and type of services being provided to clients, closing cases for positive outcomes, meeting client needs, and client self-reports of being satisfied with the case management services they received.

In addition to these "unexpected" client results, KAT also proved an effective model of organizational capacity support and growth. KAT was implemented to serve a disaster-affected group of people with little consideration given to how the model for doing so would affect the participating organizations. Yet in order to implement a standardized program among 130-plus community-based organizations, emphasis had to be given to training and technical support. Thus program indicators, in addition to client indicators, naturally emerged as part of KAT, as capacity for case managers and organizations alike was emphasized. Unexpected program indicators include the number of trainings, site visits, conference calls, the number of trained staff, the sharing of resources and information, and so forth.

RESPONSES TO THE UNEXPECTED EVENTS

In responding to these unintended results of the program, the program relied on standardized reporting mechanisms that were aided by consistent technical assistance. Reporting was twofold to account for these client and program indicators. As lead agency of the consortium, UMCOR was in a position to both communicate reporting expectations as well as provide technical assistance to agencies in fulfilling both client and program reporting requirements. Whereas CAN's structure enabled reports to be created on any field in the database, the information coming out of the system for reporting purposes depended on the quality of information being entered. In addition to CAN, the unexpected program indicators were collected as part of agencies' quarterly reporting process. This process was rolled out with much technical assistance, both written and verbal, as to what information was being sought, with the reports becoming routine as the program's time line progressed.

For CAN reporting of client information, the emphasis on improving reporting was termed among the consortium as "CAN Clean-Up." CAN Clean-Ups were implemented through a variety of technical assistance strategies to communicate the need for thorough entry of client information from those doing the reports to those entering the information. These communiqués were guidelines as to what was expected and needed in order the make the data valid and useful. For example, reports to stakeholders and donors included a breakdown of households by the gender of the head of the household, the number of adults, and the number of dependents within each. Initially, these reports showed upwards of 80% of cases without a reported gender, and even higher rates of error on the number of adults or dependents. What unexpectedly emerged was the need to inform the local agencies that the information they were entering was either lacking or missing. CAN Clean-Ups were used to provide local staff with a specific list of their clients and what data needed to be improved for each, such as gender, the number of adults, and the number of children. As a result, based on a targeted monitoring mechanism, KAT was able to report that 96% of single-head households with at least one dependent were headed by a female. This one example of data can be used now to support the need for targeted programming for vulnerable populations. In addition to monitoring efforts, UMCOR monitoring and evaluation staff distributed program documents, a regular newsletter, and Web- and phone-based seminars ("webinars") to emphasize particular aspects of CAN entry and reporting.

Beyond the monitoring aspects of KAT's structure, midterm and final evaluations planned in the program's original design took into account these additional indicators to both document program activities and make recommendations for future disaster case management programs. These efforts included sources of existing information, like CAN, as well as incorporated strategies for collecting new sources of information through client and case manager surveys, focus groups, and interviews. Once these data were all received, qualitative reviews and intensive quantitative analysis took place. At the midterm the design took into account how the project's implementation could be improved given these unexpected results, and at the final, the summative evaluation sought to set forth the program results for both their accomplishments as well as their implications for future program design.

Evaluation of the Integrated Services Pilot Program from Western Australia

Susanne Therese Bahn, Peter Hancock,
and Trudi Cooper

DESCRIPTION OF THE CASE

This case study presents the findings of a Western Australian evaluation of a pilot project that provided integrated services to humanitarian refugees. The evaluation was completed between late 2007 and early 2008. The Integrated Service Centre Pilot Project (the ISC Project) was located in Perth, the capital city of Western Australia. The purpose of the project was to "co-locate" governmental and nongovernmental organizations (NGOs) likely to be used by newly arrived refugees. A decision was made to locate services on the campuses of two primary schools that already housed Intensive English Centres[1] (IEC). The Office of Multicultural Interests of Western Australia (OMI)[2] funded, initiated, and coordinated the ISC Project after consultation with other relevant agencies and government departments. The initiative was developed as a response to the concerns about the existing delivery model of refugee services to humanitarian entrants in Australia, raised through government and NGO consultations in 2005.

Evaluation of the project took place in two phases between June 2007 and May 2008. Baseline data (Phase 1) was collected October–November 2007 and ex post data (Phase 2) were collected in February 2008 (the end of the pilot project). The purpose of the evaluation was to measure perceptions of effectiveness of the program. The evaluation used a qualitative methodology.

Background

The ISC Project was a partnership between state government agencies, primarily the Office of Multicultural Interests, the Department of Education and Training (DET), and the Department of Health (DoH). The Department of Child Protection (DCP) and the Department of Immigration and Multicultural Affairs (DIMA) were also key stakeholders in the project. The project provided services relating to health, including mental health, education, training and employment, and family and community development for humanitarian entrants. The aims and objectives of the ISC Project were to:

- Improve the current delivery of critical relevant services to humanitarian entrants.
- Relieve pressures on mainstream services.
- Adopt a whole-government approach to improve coordination of settlement delivery by providers of services to humanitarian entrants.
- Provide a holistic service that responds to the most critical and immediate needs of humanitarian entrants.
- Promote partnerships and links between relevant government agencies and NGOs.

Two ISC steering committees (LCCs) formed to oversee the project, one for each site. These committees included representatives from relevant key agencies listed above, as well as the school principals, the IEC deputy principals, NGOs, school psychologists, and IEC teaching staff. A project coordinator employed by OMI oversaw the entire project from a central location by supporting staff at both locations and fulfilled the role of executive officer for the LCCs and steering committee meetings.

The ISC Project was piloted in two locations, one in the northern suburbs (ISC1) and the other in the southern suburbs of Perth (ISC2), both of which also contained IECs. The IEC enrollments in these schools were:

- ISC1 (north metropolitan, 2007: 180 IEC students)
- ISC2 (south metropolitan, 2007: 120 IEC students)

Methodology

The qualitative methodology allowed the evaluators to document changes made to the project as it progressed and evolved, creating a valuable closeness to the data with rich and detailed narratives. The data collection methods included interviews (both face-to-face and telephone), focus groups, case study development, and participant observation. The methodology was constant vis-à-vis the two phases of the study.

The "indicative" baseline data was collected after the project had been in operation for 3 months. In terms of the methodology, this meant that the baseline did not reflect conditions prior to the start of the project, as would be expected in a classic research design. We have found that it is not uncommon for requests for tender (evaluation research) to be advertised after projects have commenced, and by the time evaluators have been selected and ethical clearance has been gained, the project to be evaluated has been operational for several months. Even though tenders ask for researchers to collect baseline data, it is very rare that the timing of the tendering process allows this to happen. In this instance, we negotiated an adaptation of the research design for the evaluation that still permitted a two-stage data collection. Phase 2 of the data collection occurred at the completion of the pilot project (ex post). We were able to observe how issues emerged, which issues were resolved or diminished across the life of the project, and which issues remained despite the intervention.

UNEXPECTED EVENTS

A number of unanticipated events occurred during the planning and implementation stages of the ISC evaluation. These events meant that the approach taken to the evaluation had to be adapted (e.g., terminology was changed in reports, and evaluators became more sensitive to cultural issues and the nuances of a predominantly African client database in their data collection processes, but the methodology remained constant, apart from the baseline data issue; see below). Furthermore, unintended outcomes (negative and positive) were also discovered.

Evaluation Design

The first event became apparent at the first meeting with the funding body OMI (after the tender was commissioned). We became aware that the ISC Project had been operating for many months and thus we could not collect true baseline data. This issue prompted us to reconsider the evaluation design.

Originally, we had intended that the evaluation should simply compare baseline data gathered before the intervention with data gathered at the end of the project to provide a summative assessment of the achievements. Because the project had been operating for some months, this research design was not feasible.

Target Group

The ISC Project was designed to support all "new" refugees to the areas where the ISCs operated. The project developed at the same time that a massive influx of African refugees arrived in Australia, dominating all other refugee groups. An unanticipated finding from the project was that 74% of the participants were of African origin. This was the result of a massive influx of African refugees to Australia as a result of issues on the African continent. The needs of African humanitarian refugees were different in important ways from those of other newly arrived migrants. In-depth qualitative data allowed the researchers to gain insights into the needs of this group of humanitarian migrants and allowed us to record the contextual details of the day-to-day running of the project in response to issues raised.

In terms of the target group being predominantly African, evaluators raised this issue on numerous occasions with OMI as well as with stakeholders because data showed that African clients required greater attention and resources, which placed unexpected strain on staff. We believe the data collected for the project highlighted the specific needs of this group of humanitarian refugees and provided useful insight for the development of future projects.

Unintended Program Outcomes

As the evaluation unfolded, four unintended outcomes were observed, not including the evaluation design or baseline issue and the fact that the majority of the program clientele were of African origin. The first two were unambiguously positive. The value of the third depended on one's point of view. The last was unambiguously undesirable.

1. The innovative service eased pressure on mainstream refugee services in more ways than had first been anticipated and which were not listed in the original program objectives (i.e., the ISC staff were able to identify other needs and address these, thereby further relieving pressures on other service providers).

2. Improvements in the new service's outreach ability resulted in providing services over an extended area (i.e., in a wider-than-expected area).

3. The service was able to meet new needs that other services were not able to meet (e.g., providing health services in the home, assistance with operating commonly used household appliances, using new types of food packaging, and negotiating a modern communications system). In the short term this ability had both positive and negative consequences. On the one hand, the provision of such services is certainly a good thing on its face. On the other hand, these services put a strain on budgets. Thus was set up a conflict between mission goals and goals of internal organizational maintenance. The long-term value (in cost–benefit terms) will depend on whether the early intervention characteristics of the new services have a salutary effect on the intergenerational problems that are common in refugee communities.

4. The project placed an unrealistically high workload on staff, thus further challenging the goals of organizational maintenance. Related to this was the finding that the project was underfunded.

RESPONSES TO THE UNEXPECTED EVENTS

The major focus of the ISC research was to evaluate the "official" project objectives. However, the research also allowed for identification of unintended outcomes (positive and negative). All of the above-mentioned unanticipated events and unintended outcomes formed critical components of the final recommendations made to the funding body and highlight the importance for evaluators to be fully aware and expectant of such occurrences.

In this instance the evaluators recommended that the funding agency address and acknowledge the unintended outcomes in specific ways. For example, the evaluators recommended that the funding agency:

1. Seek to ensure that future tenders for evaluation that require a baseline methodology are adapted to ensure that true baseline data can be collected.

2. Acknowledge and ensure that the project is adapted to ensure it is directed at African refugees and/or any new migrant group that emerges. The evaluators also ensured that the African demographics were fully articulated in the final report.

3. Fully study how the pilot project had gone beyond its official objec-

tives and relieved significant other pressures not listed in the project objectives. The evaluators also ensured that stakeholders were aware of this fact, which helped the project to receive emergency funding in mid-2008.

4. Advise that the funding for the project needed to be increased and expanded to account for unexpected high workloads and that greater resources needed to be provided to employ more project staff.

NOTES

1. Intensive English Centres (IECs) are generally located within government schools and are a program for newly arrived entrants and migrants. They provide school curriculum with a heavy focus on teaching English to those from non-English-speaking backgrounds.

2. OMI is the Western Australian government office with responsibility for multicultural affairs.

References

Adner, R. (2004). A demand-based perspective on technology life cycles. *Advances in Strategic Management, 21,* 25–43.

Altschuld, J. W., Thomas, P. M., & McColskey, W. H. (1984). An evaluation model for the development of technical training programs. *American Journal of Evaluation, 5*(4), 33–37.

Audi, R. (Ed.). (1995). *The Cambridge Dictionary of Philosophy.* Cambridge, UK: Cambridge University Press.

Barach, P., & Small, S. P. (2000). Reporting and preventing medical mishaps: Lessons from non-medical near-miss reporting systems. *British Medical Journal, 320,* 759–763.

Behrens, T. R., & Gray, D. O. (2001). Unintended consequences of cooperative research: Impact of industry sponsorship on climate for academic freedom and other graduate student outcome. *Research Policy, 30*(2), 179–199.

Boehm, B., & Egyed, A. (1999). Optimizing software product integrity through life-cycle process integration. *Computer Standards and Interfaces, 21,* 63–75.

Bowen, G. L., Rose, R. A., & Ware, W. B. (2006). The reliability and validity of the School Success Profile Learning Organization measure. *Evaluation and Program Planning, 29*(1), 97–104.

Cabrera, D., & Colosi, L. (2008). Distinctions, systems, relationships, and perspectives (DSRP): A theory of thinking and of things. *Evaluation and Program Planning, 31*(3), 311–317.

Cabrera, D., Colosi, L., & Lobdell, C. (2008). Systems thinking. *Evaluation and Program Planning, 31*(3), 299–310.

Campbell, D. T. (1969). Reforms as experiments. *American Psychologist, 24,* 409–429.

Chen, H. (1990). *Theory-driven evaluation.* Newbury, CA: Sage.

Chermack, T. J., Lynham, S. A., & van der Merwe, L. (2006). Exploring the relationship between scenario planning and perceptions of learning organization characteristics. *Futures, 38*(7), 767–777.

Christie, C. A., & Alkin, M. C. (2003). The user-oriented evaluator's role in formulating a program theory: Using a theory-driven approach. *American Journal of Evaluation, 24*(3), 373–385.

Courtney, M. E., Needell, B., & Wulczyn, F. (2004). Unintended consequences of the push for accountability: The case of national child welfare performance standards. *Children and Youth Services Review, 26*(12), 1141–1154.

Dannemiller Tyson Associates. (2000). *Whole-scale change: Unleashing the magic in organizations.* San Francisco: Berrett-Koehler.

Datta, L.-E. (2008). Response to paper "Systems Thinking" by D. Cabrera et al.: Systems thinking: An evaluation practitioner's perspective. *Evaluation and Program Planning, 31*(3), 321–322.

Dekker, S. (2002). *Field guide to human error investigations.* Hampshire, UK: Ashgate.

Dekker, S. (2007). *Just culture: Balancing safety and accountability.* Hampshire, UK: Ashgate.

Dewar, J. A. (2002). *Assumption-based planning: A tool for reducing avoidable surprises.* New York: Cambridge University Press.

DiNardo, J., & Lemieux, T. (2001). Alcohol, marijuana, and American youth: The unintended consequences of government regulation. *Journal of Health Economics, 20*(6), 991–1010.

Donaldson, S. I. (2007). *Program theory-driven evaluation science: Strategies and applications.* New York: Erlbaum.

Dorner, D. (1996). *The logic of failure.* New York: Holt.

Drenborg, K. H. (1996). The essence of backcasting. *Futures, 28*(9), 813–828.

Fetterman, D. M. (1994). Empowerment evaluation. *American Journal of Evaluation, 15*(1), 1–15.

Firestone, W. A., Schorr, R. Y., & Monfils, L. F. (2004). *The ambiguity of teaching to the test.* Mahwah, NJ: Erlbaum.

Flamholtz, E., & Hua, W. (2002). Strategic organizational development, growing pains, and corporate financial performance: An empirical test. *European Management Journal, 20*(5), 527–536.

Forrest, J. (2008). A response to paper "Systems Thinking" by D. Cabrera et al.: Additional thoughts on systems thinking. *Evaluation and Program Planning, 31*(3), 333–334.

Frank, R. H. (2007). *The economic naturalist: In search of explanations for everyday enigmas.* New York: Basic Books.

Fry, M., & Polonsky, J. (2004). Examining the unintended consequences of marketing. *Journal of Business Research, 57*(11), 1303–1306.

Gajda, R. (2004). Utilizing collaboration theory to evaluate strategic alliances. *American Journal of Evaluation, 25*(1), 65–77.

Ginsberg, P. E. (1984). The dysfunctional side effects of quantitative indicator production: Illustration from mental health care (a message from Chicken Little). *Evaluation and Program Planning, 7*(1), 1–26.

Glenwick, D. S., Stephens, M. A. P., & Maher, C. A. (1984). On considering the unintended impact of evaluation: Reactive distortions in program goals and activities. *Evaluation and Program Planning, 7*(4), 321–327.

Godet, M. (2000). The art of scenarios and strategic planning: Tools and pitfalls. *Technological Forecasting and Social Change, 65,* 3–22.

Green, R. S. (1999). The application of statistical process control to manage global client outcomes in behavioral health care. *Evaluation and Program Planning, 22*(2), 199–210.

Grella, C. E., Scott, C. K., Foss, M. A., Joshi, V., & Hser, Y. I. (2003). Gender differences in drug treatment outcomes among participants in the Chicago Target Cities Study. *Evaluation and Program Planning, 26*(3), 297–310.

Gupta, Y. P., & Chin, D. C. W. (1993). Strategy making and environment: An organizational life cycle perspective. *Technovation, 13*(1), 27–44.

Henry, G. T., Julnes, G., & Mark, M. M. (1998). *Realist evaluation: An emerging theory in support of practice.* New York: Wiley.

Hoek, J. (2004). Tobacco promotion restrictions: Ironies and unintended consequences. *Journal of Business Research, 57*(11), 1250–1257.

Hummelbrunner, R. (2008). Response to paper "Systems Thinking" by D. Cabrera et al.: A tool for implementing DSRP in programme evaluation. *Evaluation and Program Planning, 31*(3), 331–333.

Hyman, H. H., & Wright, C. R. (1971). Evaluating social action programs. In F. G. Caro (Ed.), *Readings in evaluation research.* New York: Russell Sage Foundation.

IBM. (2007). *Achieving tangible business benefits with social computing* (No. GTW01406-USEN-01).

Jarvie, I. C. (1972). Technology and the structure of knowledge. In C. Mackey & R. Mackey (Eds.), *Philosophy and technology* (pp. 54–61). New York: Free Press.

Kaminski, M. (2001). Unintended consequences: Organizational practices and their impact on workplace safety and productivity. *Journal of Occupational Health Psychology, 6*(2), 127–138.

Kaplan, S. A., & Garrett, K. E. (2005). The use of logic models by community-based initiatives. *Evaluation and Program Planning, 28*(2), 167–172.

Kauffman, S. (1995). *At home in the universe: The search for the laws of self-organization and complexity.* Oxford, UK: Oxford University Press.

Keeney, S., Hasson, F., & McKenna, H. P. (2001). A critical review of the Delphi technique as a research methodology for nursing. *International Journal of Nursing Studies, 38*(2), 195–200.

Kildegaard, A. (2001). Fiscal reform, bank solvency, and the law of unintended consequences: A CGE analysis of Mexico. *The North American Journal of Economics and Finance, 12*(1), 55–77.

Koberg, C. E., Uhlenbruck, N., & Sarason, Y. (1996). Facilitators of organizational innovation: The role of life cycle stage. *Journal of Business Venturing, 11,* 133–149.

Lambe, C. J., & Spekman, R. E. (1997). Alliances, external technology acquisition, and discontinuous technological change. *Journal of Product Innovation Management, 14,* 102–116.

Leeuw, F. L. (2003). Reconstructing program theories: Methods available and problems to be solved. *American Journal of Evaluation, 24*(1), 5–20.

Lukas, B. A., & Menon, A. (2004). New product quality: Intended and unintended consequences of new product development speed. *Journal of Business Research, 57*(11), 1258–1264.

Macpherson, A. (2005). Learning how to grow: Resolving the crisis of knowing. *Technovation, 25*(10), 1129–1140.

Manheim, K. (1967). *Man and society in an age of reconstruction: Studies in modern social structure.* New York: Harcourt, Brace. (Original work published 1935)

Marion, R. (1999). *The edge of organization: Chaos and complexity theories of formal social systems.* Thousand Oaks, CA: Sage.

Mathie, A., & Greene, J. C. (1997). Stakeholder participation in evaluation: How important is diversity? *Evaluation and Program Planning, 20*(3), 279–285.

Meyers, W. R. (1981). *The evaluation enterprise.* San Francisco: Jossey-Bass.

Midgley, G. (2008). Response to paper "Systems Thinking" by D. Cabrera et al.: The unification of systems thinking: Is there gold at the end of the rainbow? *Evaluation and Program Planning, 31*(3), 317–321.

Morell, J. A. (1979). *Program evaluation in social research.* Oxford, UK: Pergamon Press.

Morell, J. A. (2000). Internal evaluation: A synthesis of traditional methods and industrial engineering. *American Journal of Evaluation, 21*(1), 41–52.

Morell, J. A. (2004). Evaluating the impact of electronic business systems: Lessons learned from three cases at the Defense Logistics Agency. *Acquisition Review Quarterly,* (January–April), 3–20.

Morell, J. A. (2005). Why are there unintended consequences of program action, and what are the implications for doing evaluation? *American Journal of Evaluation, 26*(4), 444–463.

Mowbray, C. T., Holter, M. C., Teague, G. B., & Bybee, D. (2003). Fidelity criteria: Development, measurement, and validation. *American Journal of Evaluation, 24*(3), 315–340.

Nowell, B. (2008). Response to paper "Systems Thinking" by D. Cabrera et al.: Conceptualizing systems thinking in evaluation. *Evaluation and Program Planning, 31*(3), 329–331.

O'Brien, F. A. (2003). Scenario planning: Lessons for practice from teaching and learning. *European Journal of Operational Research, 152,* 709–722.

Page, S. E. (2007). *The difference: How the power of diversity creates better groups, firms, schools, and societies.* Princeton, NJ: Princeton University Press.

Patton, M. Q. (2002). *Qualitative research and evaluation methods* (3rd ed.). Thousand Oaks, CA: Sage.

Patton, M. Q. (2008). *Utilization-focused evaluation* (4th ed.). Thousand Oaks, CA: Sage.

Patton, M. Q. (2010). *Developmental evaluation*. New York: Guilford Press.

Pedler, M., Burgoyne, J., & Boydell, T. (1996). *The Learning Company: A strategy for sustainable development*. London: McGraw-Hill.

Perrow, C. (1999). *Normal accidents: Living with high-risk technologies*. Princeton, NJ: Princeton University Press.

Petrosino, A., Boruch, R. F., Soydan, H., Duggan, L., & Sanchez-Meca, J. (2001). Meeting the challenges of evidence-based policy: The Campbell Collaboration. *Annals of the American Academy of Political and Social Sciences, 578*, 14–34.

Phimister, J. R., Oktem, U., Kleindorfer, P. R., & Kunreuther, H. (2003). Near-miss management systems in the chemical process industry. *Risk Analysis, 23*(3), 445–459.

Pillai, A. S., & Joshi, A. R. (2001). Performance measurement of R&D projects in a multiproject, concurrent engineering environment. *International Journal of Project Management, 20*, 165–177.

Posavac, E. J. (1995). Statistical process control in the practice of program evaluation. *American Journal of Evaluation, 16*(June), 121–130.

Prasarnphanich, P., & Wagner, C. (2008, February). *Creating critical mass in collaboration systems: Insights from Wikipedia*. Paper presented at the 2nd IEEE International Conference on Digital Ecosystems and Technologies (IEEE-DEST 2008), Phitsanulok, Thailand.

Pugh, K. J., & Zhao, Y. (2003). Stories of teacher alienation: A look at the unintended consequences of efforts to empower teachers. *Teaching and Teacher Education, 19*(2), 187–201.

Reynolds, M. (2008). Response to paper "Systems Thinking" by D. Cabrera et al.: Systems thinking from a critical systems perspective. *Evaluation and Program Planning, 31*(3), 323–325.

Richard, L., Lehoux, P., Breton, E., Denis, J. L., Labrie, L., & Leonard, C. (2004). Implementing the ecological approach in tobacco control programs: Results of a case study. *Evaluation and Program Planning, 27*(4), 409–421.

Rogers, E. M. (1983). *Diffusion of innovations* (3rd ed.). New York: Free Press.

Rogers, P. J. (2008). Response to paper "Systems Thinking" by D. Cabrera et al.: Is it systems thinking or just good practice in evaluation? *Evaluation and Program Planning, 31*(3), 325–326.

Scheirer, M. A. (2005). Is sustainability possible?: A review and commentary on empirical studies of program sustainability. *American Journal of Evaluation, 26*(3), 320–347.

Scott, M., & Bruce, R. (1987). Five stages of growth in small business. *Long Range Planning, 20*(3), 45–52.

Scriven, M. (1991). Pros and cons about goal-free evaluation. *American Journal of Evaluation, 12*(1), 55–62.

Senge, P. M. (1990). *The fifth discipline*. New York: Doubleday.

Sherman, D. J., & Olsen, E. A. (1996). Stages in the project life cycle in R&D organizations and the differing relationship between organizational climate and performance. *The Journal of High-Technology Management Research, 7*(1), 79–90.

Sherrill, S. (1984). Identifying and measuring unintended outcomes. *Evaluation and Program Planning, 7*(1), 27–34.

Snowden, D. J., & Boone, M. (2007, November). A leader's framework for decision making. *Harvard Business Review*, 69–76.

Stacey, R. D. (1992). *Managing the unknowable.* San Francisco: Jossey-Bass.

Stiles, K. (2002). International support for NGOs in Bangladesh: Some unintended consequences. *World Development, 30*(5), 835–846.

Suresh, G., Horbar, J. D., Plsek, P., Gray, J., Edwards, W. H., Shiono, P. H., et al. (2004). Voluntary anonymous reporting of medical errors for neonatal intensive care. *Pediatrics, 113*(6I), 1609–1618.

Surowiecki, J. (2004). *The wisdom of crowds.* New York: Doubleday.

Tenner, E. (1996). *Why things bite back.* New York: Knopf.

Thomas, D. R. (2006). A general inductive approach for analyzing qualitative evaluation data. *American Journal of Evaluation, 27*(2), 237–246.

Van de Ven, A. H., & Poole, S. M. (1995). Explaining development and change in organizations. *Academy of Management Review, 20*(3), 510–540.

van der Knaap, L. M., Leeuw, F. L., Bogaerts, S., & Nijssen, L. T. J. (2008). Combining Campbell standards and the realist evaluation approach: The best of two worlds? *American Journal of Evaluation, 29*(1), 48–57.

Wasserman, D. L. (2008). A response to paper "Systems Thinking" by D. Cabrera et al.: Next steps, a human service program system exemplar. *Evaluation and Program Planning, 31*(3), 327–329.

Wasserman, D. L. (2010). Using a systems orientation and foundational theory to enhance theory-driven human service program evaluations. *Evaluation and Program Planning, 33*(2), 67–80.

Watkins, K., & Marsick, V. (1992). Building the learning organization: A new role for human resource developers. *Studies in Continuing Education, 14*(2), 115–129.

Weick, K. E., & Sutcliffe, K. M. (2001). *Managing the unexpected.* San Francisco: Jossey-Bass.

Weiss, C. H., Murphy-Graham, E., Petrosino, A., & Gandhi, A. G. (2008). The fairy godmother—and her warts: Making the dream of evidence-based policy come true. *American Journal of Evaluation, 29*(1), 29–47.

Williams, B. (2005). Systems thinking: Using systems concepts. In S. Mathison (Ed.), *Encyclopedia of evaluation* (pp. 406–412). Thousand Oaks, CA: Sage.

Williams, B., & Imam, I. (2007). *Systems concepts in evaluation: An expert anthology.* Point Reyes, CA: Edge Press/American Evaluation Association.

Index

Adaptation, 3, 19, 48, 53, 54, 63, 69, 90, 96, 101, 179, 283. *See also* System(s)

Agile evaluation, 83, 85, 113, 121, 157, 169, 172, 176, 186–192. *See also* Design, designed; Methodology

American Evaluation Association, 2, 6

Analysis/interpretation, 37, 121, 130, 131, 132, 142, 146, 155, 159

Assumption, *See* Incorrect assumption(s)

B

Boundary, 3, 21, 24, 59, 92, 95, 101. *See also* Partition, partitioning

Brittle evaluation, 188

Burden, 39, 84, 85, 86, 92, 99, 100, 102, 107, 162, 265

C

Case management, 42, 277–279

Cat, 22, 191

Cause, causes, causing, 5, 6, 9, 15, 22, 31, 39, 45, 48, 64–66, 68, 82, 86, 89, 91, 94, 106–107, 115, 120–122, 131, 139, 146, 161, 166, 182, 187, 192, 202, 218, 221, 223, 227, 241, 264, 274

Causal chain. *See* Cause, causes, causing

Central heating, 244, 246

Chaos, chaotic, *See* System(s), chaos

Clinical records, 85

Co-evolution. *See* System(s), evolution, evolutionary, co-evolution

Collaboration, 23, 24, 25, 28, 31, 32, 34, 53, 61, 97, 112, 194, 253, 278

Complex adaptive system. *See* System(s)

Complex system. *See* System(s)

Computer system. *See* Information technology

Continuous improvement (CI). *See* Lean Six Sigma

Continuous process improvement. *See* Lean Six Sigma

Cross-link, linkage, 3, 5, 19–20, 25–26, 39, 50, 54–55, 62, 70, 90–91, 97, 99, 102, 104–106, 113, 116, 119, 120, 161, 169, 170, 177–178, 180, 226, 236, 282. *See also* Depend, dependent, dependence, dependency, dependencies

Culture, 25, 29, 31, 64, 88, 89, 92, 106, 178, 182–185, 188, 203, 241

D

Decision making, 3, 32, 98, 102, 139, 171, 172, 181, 235, 238, 239

Depend, dependent, dependence, dependency, dependencies, 89, 111, 164, 168, 190, 200, 279, 280, 284. *See also* Cross-link, linkage

methodology/statistics, 56, 91, 122, 150, 158–159, 190, 197–199

system, 5, 8, 19, 20, 36, 54, 55, 57, 61, 67, 75, 90, 91, 95, 98, 99, 105, 192

About the Author

Jonathan A. Morell is a Senior Policy Analyst at the Vector Research Center, a division of TechTeam Government Solutions, and Editor of *Evaluation and Program Planning*. He is also active in the American Evaluation Association, where he has been instrumental in founding two of its topical interest groups—Systems, and Business and Industry—and is a recipient of the Association's Marcus Ingle Distinguished Service Award. His professional life has integrated his role as an evaluation practitioner with his theoretical interests. As a practitioner, he evaluates organizational change, R&D, and safety programs. He is also deeply involved in organizational change design. His theoretical interests include the nature and use of logic models, the role of Lean Six Sigma methodologies in evaluation, complex system behavior, and the nature of practical action.

Contributors

Dennis P. Affholter, Independent Consultant, Paducah, Kentucky

James W. Altschuld, Professor Emeritus, School of Educational Policy and Leadership, The Ohio State University, Columbus, Ohio

Susanne Therese Bahn, Spellenger Research Centre, School of Law and Justice, Edith Cowan University, Joondalup, Australia

Jennifer Conner Blatz, Knowledge Works Foundation, Cincinnati, Ohio

Gary L. Bowen, School of Social Work, University of North Carolina at Chapel Hill, Chapel Hill, North Carolina

Kristine L. Chadwick, Center for Research and Evaluation Services, Edvantia, Inc., Charleston, West Virginia

Deborah Chassler, Center for Addictions Research and Services, Boston University School of Social Work, Boston, Massachusetts

Trudi Cooper, School of Psychology and Social Science, Edith Cowan University, Joondalup, Australia

Kevin L. DeWeaver, School of Social Work, University of Georgia, Athens, Georgia

Aissa Diarra, Laboratoire d'Etudes et de Recherches sur les Dynamiques Sociales et le Développement Local (LASDEL), Niamey, Niger

Molly Engle, Extension Service and Department of Adult and Higher Education Leadership, Oregon State University, Corvallis, Oregon

Therese Fitzgerald, Massachusetts Medical Society, Waltham, Massachusetts

Shana Goldwyn, School of Education, Educational Leadership Program, University of Cincinnati, Cincinnati, Ohio

Shenyang Guo, School of Social Work, University of North Carolina at Chapel Hill, Chapel Hill, North Carolina

Peter Hancock, School of Psychology and Social Science, Edith Cowan University, Joondalup, Australia

Amanda Janis, Catholic Charities USA, Alexandria, Virginia

Christine E. Johnson, Learning Systems Institute, Florida State University, Tallahassee, Florida

Laura Hassler Lang, Learning Systems Institute, Florida State University, Tallahassee, Florida

Shabtay Levit, Association for Public Health, Methadone Maintenance Treatment Programs in Jerusalem and Ashdod, and Paul Baerwald School of Social Work and Social Welfare, Hebrew University, Jerusalem, Israel

Deborah L. Lowther, College of Education, University of Memphis, Memphis, Tennessee

Lena Lundgren, Center for Addictions Research and Services, Boston University School of Social Work, Boston, Massachusetts

Richard Mitchell, Section of Public Health and Health Policy, Faculty of Medicine, University of Glasgow, Glasgow, United Kingdom

Jonathan A. Morell, Vector Research Center, TechTeam Government Solutions, Ann Arbor, Michigan

Mark Petticrew, Public and Environmental Health Research Unit, London School of Hygiene and Tropical Medicine, London, United Kingdom

Stephen Platt, Centre for Population Health Sciences, School of Clinical Science and Community Health, University of Edinburgh, Edinburgh, United Kingdom

Valéry Ridde, Département de Médecine Sociale et Préventive, Université de Montréal, Montréal, Quebec, Canada

Roderick A. Rose, School of Social Work, University of North Carolina at Chapel Hill, Chapel Hill, North Carolina

Steven M. Ross, Center for Research and Reform in Education, Johns Hopkins University, Baltimore, Maryland

Riki Savaya, Shapell School of Social Work, Tel Aviv University, Tel Aviv, Israel

Miriam Schiff, Paul Baerwald School of Social Work and Social Welfare, Hebrew University, Jerusalem, Israel

Bryce D. Smith, School of Social Work, University of Georgia, Athens, Georgia

Danny Sprouse, Positive Impact, Inc., Atlanta, Georgia

Kelly M. Stiefel, Carr's Human Services Solutions LLC, Tenafly, New Jersey

J. Dan Strahl, Center for Research in Educational Policy, University of Memphis, Memphis, Tennessee

Phyllis M. Thomas, Evaluation Consultant, Louisville, Colorado

Jeremy Walker, Centre for Population Health Sciences, School of Clinical Science and Community Health, University of Edinburgh, Edinburgh, United Kingdom

Deborah L. Wasserman, Center for Family Research at COSI, The Ohio State University, Columbus, Ohio

Mark Waysman, Independent Consultant, Rishon Lezion, Israel

Brian T. Yates, Department of Psychology, American University, Washington, DC

Anat Zeira, School of Social Work and Social Welfare, Hebrew University, Jerusalem, Israel